TOTAL LOSS

REVIEWS OF THE FIRST EDITION

'Besides being gripping reading, there is a wealth of information to be learned about the actions of others in emergencies: what worked and what didn't work . . . invaluable . . .'
  Yachting

'Sure, you can learn from your own mistakes, but wouldn't you rather learn from theirs.'
  Sailing

'Should be required reading for anyone going offshore. It will heighten your appreciation of the many things which can go wrong . . . Skippers who keep their mistakes to a minimum will find they have less need of good luck to stay afloat'
  Classic Boat

'All the stories are a celebration of the human instinct for survival – battling against the elements and the odds.'
  Yachting Monthly

'40 stories of tragedy at sea . . . the tales provide gripping if sometimes unsettling reading and many valuable lessons.'
  Cruising World

'The stories will make the reader a better, or a retired, sailor.'
  WoodenBoat

'I believe the book is simply a top 10 "must read" for a really comprehensive anecdotal understanding of accidents and how they happen.'
  Good Old Boat Magazine

PAUL GELDER

TOTAL LOSS

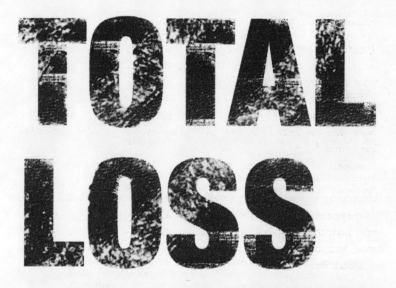

THIRD EDITION

ADLARD COLES NAUTICAL
LONDON

DEDICATED TO ALL SAILORS WHO HAVE SUFFERED THE HEARTBREAKING
LOSS OF THEIR YACHT AFTER A LIFE AND DEATH STRUGGLE. AND LET
US NOT FORGET THE COURAGE AND RESOURCEFULNESS OF THEIR
RESCUERS. THIS BOOK IS A REQUIEM FOR ALL THEIR BRAVE SPIRITS.

Published by Adlard Coles Nautical
an imprint of A & C Black Publishers Ltd
38 Soho Square, London W1D 3HB
www.adlardcoles.com

First published in hardback in Great Britain by Adlard Coles 1985
Reprinted 1986, 1988, 1989
Reprinted by Adlard Coles Nautical 1991
Paperback edition published by Adlard Coles Nautical 1992
Reprinted 1993, 1995, 1996
Second edition published 2001
Third edition published 2008

ISBN 978-0-7136-8783-5

A CIP catalogue record for this book is available from the British Library.

This book is produced using paper that is made from wood grown in managed,
sustainable forests. It is natural, renewable and recyclable. The logging and
manufacturing processes conform to the environmental regulations of the
country of origin.

Typeset in 10.5 on 12.5pt AGaramond

Printed and bound in UK by Cox & Wyman Ltd

CONTENTS

COLLISION

abandon his 32ft catamaran after enduring 70-knot
winds and 20ft seas in the Pacific

FAULTY NAVIGATION

Demarty's yacht put him three-quarters of a mile off course...with disastrous results

FIRE OR EXPLOSION

FAILURE OF GROUND TACKLE
OR MOORING LINES

BEING TOWED

PREFACE

TWO DAYS SPENT ON A SOUTH PACIFIC coral reef in 2006 in the remote Tuamotus, a chain of atolls known as 'the dangerous archipelago' in French Polynesia, gave me a unique insight into emotional drama of shipwreck and the practical considerations of rescue. As a journalist, I was an eyewitness to the work of the salvage team that ultimately saved the famous 53ft wooden ketch *Gipsy Moth IV*. She had been swept on to a reef 200 miles or so north-east of Tahiti after a navigational blunder.

In just 48 hours, thanks to the skills of the team and some extraordinary luck, the scenario went from tragedy to triumph. The crippled ketch had her holes patched and, on a homemade wooden 'sledge' nailed to her starboard side, was towed off the reef by an ocean-going tug. Francis Chichester's iconic yacht, which he sailed into the history books in 1967, was suddenly brought back from the brink of being declared 'a total loss'. It was an unforgettable and emotional moment for all involved.

All the stories in this book are a celebration of the human instinct for survival – battling against the elements and the odds – even if in all these cases the yachts were a 'total loss'.

This is not a pessimistic book, as Jack Coote acknowledged in the preface of the original edition 23 years ago. It's not intended to discourage anyone from setting sail in a well-found boat having made sound preparations. Neither are the stories morbid or voyeuristic. In fact, the only loss of life among the 40 incidents in this book is aboard two yachts: the 25ft yacht *Ouzo*, run down or swamped by a P&O ferry in the English Channel in 2006, and *Hooligan V*, which lost her keel.

We may never know what really happened in the case of *Ouzo*, but the loss of Rupert Saunders, James Meaby and Jason Downer, all in their mid-thirties, was a tragedy which threw a spotlight on a host of valuable lessons which may help save lives in the future. The death of Jamie Butcher, 27, on *Hooligan V*, also led to a comprehensive investigation by the Marine Investigation Branch into the reasons for metal fatigue and how such accidents can be avoided in the future.

Why make mistakes when you can learn from the hard-won lessons and experience of those who sailed before you?

The surviving sailor who loses a yacht, for whatever reason, has lost a partner in great adventures. As Frank Mulville wrote in '*Girl Stella*'s Going': 'A boat . . . has a soul, a personality, eccentricities of behaviour that are endearing. It becomes part of a person, colouring his whole life with a romance that is unknown to those who do not understand a way of life connected with boats. The older a boat becomes, the stronger the power . . . people look at boats with wonder and say "She's been to the South Seas", or "She's just back from the North Cape", and the boat takes on a reputation in excess of that of its owner . . .

A boat is always there – you never stop worrying about her whether you are aboard or ashore . . . Men lie awake worrying about their bank balances, their waistlines, their wives, their mistresses actual or potential; but sailors worry about boats.'

For Mulville the loss of *Girl Stella* was 'a dead weight of responsibility that settled heavily on his shoulders . . . a score that could never be wiped clean'.

For Michael Richey there could also be 'no going back' after the loss of *Jester*. As he watched her recede into the distance, 'looking as trim and pretty as ever' he realised how much he had loved her. 'Men personalise their boats as no other artefact. I felt I had failed her, that I should have stayed with the boat . . . It was one of the unhappiest moments of my life,' he recalled.

The chances of having to 'abandon ship' are as small as being involved in a plane or train crash. A reasonably competent yachtsman can expect to sail for a lifetime without having to face the kind of dramas described in the following pages. Nevertheless, it can happen, and perhaps that's why the awful finality of the term 'total loss' holds such a fascination for most sailors. Yachts are lost at sea for many reasons. Some are strange and unexplained. But I am grateful that the survivors of such losses have been willing to share their experiences through their genuine desire to pass on lessons which can benefit us all.

PAUL GELDER

ACKNOWLEDGEMENTS

THIS BOOK COULD NOT HAVE BEEN compiled without the co-operation of many people. The original idea came from Julian van Hasselt, when he worked for Kelvin Hughes. The late Peter Tangvald had once intended to put together a similar book and generously shared some of his research with Julian, who did some preliminary work before handing the project to Jack Coote, who edited the original edition in 1985. In 1999 I took over the second edition following Jack's death in 1993.

The editors of sailing magazines on both sides of the Atlantic have given permission to use extracts from their publications. Among those who wrote accounts specially for the book are Jason Baggeley, whose *Ana* was lost in the 40th anniversary Singlehanded Transatlantic Race in 2000, and Gavin McLaren, who survived the horrific gas explosion aboard *Lord Trenchard*. Stuart Quarrie, navigator of *Griffin* in the notorious 1979 Fastnet Race, also wrote his account specially for the book, as did Ann Griffin *(Northern Light)*.

Yacht club journals often contain exciting, well-written accounts of incidents experienced by members and the following editors and contributors are to be thanked: the editor of the *Royal Cruising Club Journal* and Alain Catherineau for his part of 'Fastnet Rescue', and Brigadier D H Davies (acting on behalf of the late W H Tilman) for '*Mischief*'s Last Voyage'; as well as Peter Phillips for 'The End of an OSTAR'; the editor of *The Silhouette Owner* and Clementina Gordon for 'Bad Luck in Boulogne'; *Lowestoft Cruising Club Journal* and George Harrod-Eagles for '*Song* – the Final Episode'. I would like to thank Doris Karloff for her patience and assistance on research concerning incidents in the Pacific Ocean. I would also like to thank Liz Piercy, my book editor, for her patience and care with many and various revisions and updates from the last editon.

For permission to use excerpts from books, I have to thank Martin Eve of Merlin Press and the late Frank Mulville for '*Girl*

Stella's Going' and the family of Phil Weld for the extract from *Moxie – the American Challenge*, a book which is a collector's item for any sailor's library.

Yachting Monthly writers Miles Kendall, Chris Beeson, Dick Durham, and James Jermain all provided valuable input and knowledge for some of the lessons to be learned from this book. Alastair Buchan and Miranda Delmar-Morgan also contributed to the chapter on the loss of *Ouzo*.

Graham Elliott *(Hooligan V)* which lost her keel, Peter Crowther *(Galway Blazer)*, Hugh Cownie *(Keelson II)*, Niels Blixenkrone-Moller *(Nuts)*, Joe Bass *(Sea Crest)*, Micheal Dresden *(Wahkuna)*, Peter and Zara Davis *(F2)*, Bill Clegg *(Linan)*, Richard Wood *(Eclipse)*, Mike Richey *(Jester)*, Bob Shepton *(Dodo's Delight)*, Paul Newell *(Chartreuse)*, John Passmore *(Lottie)*, and Noel Dilley ('That Sinking Feeling') were also generous in sharing their experiences so candidly. Jacques Demarty wrote a dramatic account of the loss of his Bowman 40 *Fleur de Mer* on a reef in the Caribbean, while Phil Kerin shared the painful loss of his Falmouth Quay punt, *Dunlin,* in 'Abandoned!' For all the authors who took the trouble to share painful memories we owe a debt of gratitude that we can learn from their experiences.

COLLISION

RUN DOWN OR SWAMPED?
THE *OUZO* MYSTERY

Yacht	*Ouzo* (Sailfish 25)
Skipper	Rupert Saunders
Crew	James Meaby and Jason Downer
Bound from	Bembridge, Isle of Wight to Dartmouth
Date of loss	21 August 2006
Position	south of Isle of Wight, UK

Being run down by a big ship is a sailor's worst nightmare. The scenario sometimes involves fog or crossing shipping lanes. But in the case of the 25ft yacht Ouzo, *a fatal chain of unseen factors led to the deaths of three sailors on a summer's night off the Isle of Wight in Britain.*

ONE OF THE LAST PEOPLE to see *Ouzo* afloat was Bill Mitchell (46), proprietor of the Bembridge boatyard AA Coombes on the Isle of Wight, where the yacht had been based for 25 years. At around 1930 on Sunday 20 August 2006, Bill was walking his dog along the beach when he saw the 25ft navy blue GRP sloop a quarter of a mile off-shore. She was in the Bembridge Channel motoring out towards St Helen's Fort.

Bill was confident the yacht was in good shape. He had fitted out the Angus Primrose-designed Sailfish 25 three months earlier. All her navigation lights – masthead tricolour, port and starboard lights on the pulpit and stern light, plus steaming light – were working when the yacht was launched at the end of May. *Ouzo* did not have a liferaft, but she did have an inflatable dinghy. The crew were experienced sailors. Skipper-owner Rupert Saunders (36) was setting out on a night passage to take part in Dartmouth Regatta Week. His crew were two friends, James Meaby (36) and Jason Downer (35).

At 2230, a mobile phone call from one of the crew confirmed her last known position as Sandown Bay, as *Ouzo* sailed south of the Isle of Wight, beyond the range of Southampton VTS radar, and into one of the biggest maritime mysteries of recent times.

The first sign that something had gone tragically wrong came 38 hours later. At noon on 22 August the body of a man wearing a lifejacket was found floating in the sea 10 miles off the SE coast of the Isle of Wight. It was later identified as James Meaby. Next day, the bodies of the two other crew were recovered 10 miles south of the Nab Tower.

Despite an extensive search of 95 square miles of seabed for the wreck, using the Royal Navy, merchant ships and aircraft, no wreckage was ever found and exactly what happened on that fateful night is still shrouded in mystery. It is known that *Ouzo* had DSC VHF radio, a one million candela flashlight, a compressed air canister foghorn, an octahedral radar reflector, distress flares and a deflated three-man inflatable dinghy stowed in a locker.

Voyage Data Recorder (VDR) records from all ships in the Solent that night were traced and examined and a detailed inspection was made of the hull of P&O ferry *Pride of Bilbao*, looking for paint samples and scratches. A ship one mile away travelling at 20 knots will take just three minutes to reach a yacht.

The Marine Accident Investigation Branch's (MAIB) report into the loss of *Ouzo* was a 174-page dossier which cost more than £150,000 and took seven months to complete. It made chilling reading for yachtsmen and pieced together the events on that night.

The 37,583 tonne P&O ferry *Pride of Bilbao* had left Portsmouth bound for Spain, via the eastern Solent, over two hours late, at 2325, due to a technical fault.

At 0022 approaching the Nab Tower, the ship's captain gave orders for full ahead, the normal procedure. At 0030 he handed control of the vessel over to the Second Officer Michael Hubble (61) and told him he would be in his cabin should he be needed. At 0059 there was a changeover of lookout on the ship's bridge and a couple of minutes later a radar check revealed no close targets. A course change was made from 221° to 243°. This was to take three minutes using the electronic autopilot. At 0107, the ferry's lookout on the port side spotted a dim white light off the starboard bow and then a brighter red light. The ferry was travelling at 19 knots.

The Second Officer used the joystick to turn the bow of the ferry. The lookout saw a yacht with two white sails passing down the starboard side. The Second Officer altered course again, the other way, thinking the ferry's stern might strike the yacht. After seeing a light off the stern, he believed the yacht was safely clear and continued on course across the Channel.

Inspectors from the MAIB spent several nights at sea on the *Pride of Bilbao* reconstructing what happened. In varying conditions, they checked blind spots on the bridge and gave out questionnaires to passengers to check for clues. The ferry lookout's eyes were tested and his prescription glasses sent for tests by experts. The ferry's radar was also investigated.

The report concluded that the ferry's course alteration at 0101 that night may have confused *Ouzo*'s crew about the ship's intentions. Visibility was good and although it was a dark night, the ferry was well lit and approaching from astern, not obscured by *Ouzo*'s sails.

The report added: 'Any attempts by the yachtsmen on *Ouzo* to attract the ferry's attention were ineffective as the watchkeeping officer and lookout only saw the yacht's lights at the last minute' – when it was too late.

The fatal chain of factors on the bridge of the ferry, which are believed to have contributed to the tragedy, included the following: the lookout was wearing the wrong sort of glasses, with photochromatic lenses, which darken in light and affect light transmission in low light levels. When the Second Officer altered course, he used the autopilot joystick. If, instead, he had used the override controls, the ship would have changed course much more swiftly, though the 1,490 passengers aboard might have felt the forces of gravity.

FIVE FACTORS WHICH COULD SAVE YOUR LIFE

Below are five key factors and recommendations involving the P&O ferry:

1 The yacht didn't show up on the ferry's radars because GRP yachts the size of *Ouzo* have poor radar reflectivity, even with a radar reflector displayed (which was believed to be the case: *Ouzo* had an octahedral reflector). The radar signal is reduced further in moderate or rough conditions. At least one of the ferry's radars was adjusted using automatic clutter control.

Recommendation: Ships' radars should be routinely switched to manual clutter control to check for small targets.

2 There were poor blackout procedures on the ferry's bridge. Light pollution affected the vision of both lookout and watchkeeper. The red light in the chart room was switched to white because the Second Officer found it gave him headaches. Some blackout curtains were not drawn, further impairing night vision.

Recommendation: Keep stray light to a minimum.

3 The lookout first saw *Ouzo* when he'd been on the bridge for nine minutes. His eyes were still adapting to the dark – a possible reason he didn't spot *Ouzo* earlier.

Recommendation: Handovers should be 15 minutes long, so a lookout's eyes are better adapted to the dark. It takes 10–15 minutes to get full night vision.

4 After the incident, the ferry failed to stop, assist or communicate with the yacht. The officer saw a light astern, but this didn't mean *Ouzo* was safe. Her battery compartment was well-protected and her lights may have been lit despite being swamped or capsized with crew in the water in desperate need of help. The lack of an aggrieved VHF radio call from the yacht may have indicated she was not safe.

Recommendation: The effect of a large, fast ship passing close to a small boat can be dangerous . . . every effort should be made to ensure the safety of small vessels after a near collision.

5 Research commissioned from the Institute of Ophthalmology showed the lookout's photochromatic glasses stopped at least 20 per cent of light transmission.

Recommendation: Such glasses should not be worn by bridge lookouts at night.

WHAT HAPPENED ABOARD *OUZO*?

The loss of *Ouzo* was a puzzle that was the talk of yacht club bars for many weeks. Was she swamped? Why wasn't she seen until the last minute? The MAIB inspectors used a sister ship to reconstruct *Ouzo*'s probable track from Bembridge and to assess the yacht's survivability in various swamping scenarios.

Coastguard computer software was used to calculate the drift of a partially submerged 25ft yacht, as well as the bodies of the crew. James Meaby's body drifted 40 miles in wind and tide. The MAIB inspectors tested the most commonly used radar reflectors as well as yacht navigation lights. They also investigated the psychological impact of collision at sea on lookouts and watch officers, and whether or not 'denial' was a factor in this case.

Here are 10 key factors uncovered and some safety recommendations:

1 Masthead tricolour navigation light lenses, similar to *Ouzo*'s, are prone to crazing, reducing their efficiency. Bulbs fitted can be accidentally replaced with ones of lower luminosity.
Recommendation: Yachtsmen should check lenses and make sure bulbs are constantly bright, knocking the lens case and moving the wires to simulate movement.

2 In a yacht heeled more than 5°, the horizontal intensity of her navigation lights may be decreased. *Ouzo* was probably close-hauled and heeling to 20° or more, so her masthead light may well have been compromised.

3 Even if *Ouzo* had deployed her octahedral radar reflector, it would not have been very effective in the 'clutter' of moderate sea conditions.
Recommendation: Fit the best radar you can afford. Consider the Sea-Me active radar reflector, which came top in a group test conducted by *Yachting Monthly*.

4 *Ouzo*'s crew didn't have time to send a MAYDAY by VHF radio, or to fire distress flares. Without a liferaft or EPIRB, the survival of *Ouzo*'s crew depended on their physical fitness, clothing and lifejackets. All three were physically fit and in good shape. The attention they gave to their choice of clothing was impressive: under high-quality waterproof jackets and trousers, all three wore warm fleece garments on trunk and legs over normal indoor clothing. All wore 150N lifejackets. One was of the auto-inflation type, two were manually inflatable, but none had crotch straps or lights.

The crew weren't declared missing until almost 40 hours after the collision, when the first body was found 10 miles south of the Nab Tower. It is estimated that James Meaby survived for at least 12 hours and his crewmates for only three. Why? Because Meaby had fitted his lifejacket more tightly.

Survival expert Dr Frank Golden wrote: 'All three lifejackets were fully inflated at the time of recovery but none were supporting the body in the optimal position to assist survival. Two bodies were found face down in the water, supported only by their lifejacket waist strap under their armpits. Their heads had slipped through the collar as they hung vertically with the lobes floating on the surface.

James Meaby's angle of flotation was still nearer the vertical, so that when consciousness was eventually lost through hypothermia, the neck muscles were no longer able to support the weight of the head. Had lifejacket crotch straps been fitted and secured, it would have helped all three crew to float nearer the horizontal than vertical, significantly increasing their survival chances.

Given the water temperature (18°C), the relatively benign sea conditions, and the amount of insulation *Ouzo*'s crew were wearing, all three would have survived for some time (6–12 hours) had they been able to float in the desired semi-reclining angle. But buoyancy was lost as air trapped between layers of clothing was slowly displaced by water. Survival strategies are limited in water below body temperature. As body temperature falls, muscle function is compromised and the physical effort of holding on to the lifejacket collar becomes impossible. Unless the wearer can keep his airway clear of the water, death from drowning rather than hypothermia will happen.

Because *Ouzo* was lost without an alarm being raised, it is debatable whether crotch straps would have made a significant difference to the tragic outcome.

Recommendation: Fit crotch straps (optional extras with most lifejackets) which can significantly increase survival time. They are not expensive and can be retrofitted, regardless of model. The British Standards Institute (BSI) may make them standard on lifejackets.

5 Lifejacket spray shields will extend survival time in breaking seas

but will only be of value if crotch straps are also used.

6 None of the lifejackets had lights. A light, a waterproof torch or personal mini-distress flares could have alerted one of the many craft in the area that night. Additional hand-held Cyalume light sticks can be held up to attract attention. Their higher vantage point – at the end of a raised arm – may be easier to locate in a seaway, but their use should be in conjunction with, and not instead of, an approved life-jacket light. Other forms of lighting may also be considered, eg water-proof strobe light or torch, some hand-held types of flares (eg mini-flares or self propelled flares).

7 A waterproof hand-held VHF radio could have sent a MAYDAY from one of *Ouzo*'s survivors.

8 An EPIRB or a Personal Locator Beacon (PLB) could also have raised the alarm. Some EPIRBs release and activate automatically when immersed in water. A mobile phone in a waterproof pouch might help.

9 *Ouzo* did not have a liferaft rigged with an automatic hydrostatic release unit.

10 A safety knife readily accessed on a lanyard round the neck could have assisted with disentanglement from lines, etc. In cold water, hand function becomes impaired rapidly. If buying safety equipment ensure that no fine movement is required to activate it.

The MAIB report concludes that some of these factors 'would have dramatically increased the crew's chances of survival'. The report was not intended to determine liability or apportion blame, but to learn the lessons to prevent future accidents.

TIPS FOR BETTER NIGHT VISION

Not many sailors realise how long it takes for eyesight to adapt to darkness. Dr James McGill, a yachtsman, honorary consultant ophthalmic surgeon and a member of the RNLI Medical and Survival Committee, commented:

'Coming from bright lights, we all know that everything initially is totally blank. Night vision doesn't really begin to improve significantly in less than 10 minutes. The full process of dark adaptation takes up to 30 minutes. After being in a brightly lit area (like a chart room), a medium-sized masthead light one mile away will not be seen until after 14 minutes' dark adaptation.

'Wartime bomber pilots wore red goggles to aid dark adaptation for at least 30 minutes before going outside for a night flight. Yet yacht crews often go on watch straight from a bright environment. A quick dash down to the galley to get a hot drink will ruin night vision. A few seconds' exposure to white cabin lights will reduce dark adaptation to zero. The whole process of dark adaptation has to start again.

'The older you are, the longer it takes to adapt to the dark, and the less effective your night vision. Compared to a 20-year-old, a 60-year-old will take 11 minutes longer to fully adapt to darkness.

'Colours are also not seen equally easily during dark adaptation. After 10 minutes in the dark, green is the colour most difficult to see.

'If your crew wear glasses on watch at night make sure they are not using photochromatic lenses. These can reduce night vision by 20 per cent, even for fully dark-adapted eyes. If your crew wear glasses in daytime, make sure they have an up-to-date prescription.'

RULES TO OBSERVE ON NIGHT WATCH:

1 Cabin lights should be minimal, carefully controlled and preferably red.

2 Cabin and chart table lights should be shielded from on-watch crew. Use a red light by the chart table.

3 At least two crew should be on watch, so that if one goes below someone fully dark adapted can keep an effective lookout.

4 At the change of watch, at least one member of the old watch should stay on deck for at least 15 minutes until the new watch is fully dark adapted.

5 Make sure masthead or steaming lights don't affect crews' night vision.

6 Keep a good lookout astern, as well as ahead.

7 An old standby is to keep one eye closed if going below, to preserve some night vision.

COLLISION COURSE IN THE DEADLY 'BLIND ZONE'

The *Ouzo* tragedy echoes the unsolved loss of another yacht seven years ago, the 28ft Twister, *Tuila*, which inexplicably disappeared with the loss of four lives in the North Sea in the summer of 2000. Adam Clackson (58) and three crew in their twenties were sailing home from Holland to Harwich, Suffolk. No wreckage was found for many months, but two weeks later three bodies were recovered. At the inquest in 2002 an open verdict was recorded and the MAIB said the most likely fate was being run down by a big ship.

There are strict rules on visibility for watchkeepers on big ships. But sailors will be alarmed to know that 117 vessels were detained for 'bridge visibility deficiencies' in 2003, the latest year in which statistics were available. The area covered was European coastal waters and the North Atlantic basin. Also in the last 10 years there were 89 reported collisions or near misses between merchant vessels and yachts.

How many sailors realise that the watchkeeper on the bridge of a big ship moving at 20-plus knots may have a 'blind zone' of up to 500m ahead, with 10° either side of the bow – the same area as 12 football pitches.

The bows of a VLCC (Very Large Crude Carrier) may be up to 90ft above sea level and it has been calculated that 'the blind zone' from such a vessel can cover an area equal to more than 10 football pitches. Yachts sailing inside this deadly zone are virtually invisible and risk the fatal consequences of a collision.

Tricolour masthead lights, like those displayed by *Ouzo*, may be seen at sea on a dark night in the sight line of a watchkeeper on a bridge, but they can be lost against the confusion of shore lights. Some experts say you are better off using pulpit and stern lights when sailing off the coast. Sidelights for yachts under 12m are required to be visible for just a pitiful single mile. For vessels under 50m the figure rises to two miles.

MAIB research reveals that over 58 per cent of collisions and groundings, over a five-year period to 2004, can be attributed to single-handed bridge watchkeeping. The same study concluded that lookout standards in general are poor and that late detection, or failure to detect small vessels, is a factor in many collisions.

Most vessels keep a lookout visually or by radar. According to the MAIB 81 per cent see the vessel they hit before the collision and 47 per cent see the other vessel in time to take avoiding action.

Ships on a collision course appear reluctant to give way until the last moment, and instead of making an obvious course alteration – as required by the rules – they tweak the helm to give the least possible CPA (Closest Point of Approach). Course changes must be big enough (a minimum 30°) to show up clearly on radar.

In the ideal world, every big ship would have an attentive look-out scanning the horizon, but too often the lookout is regarded as a luxury and given duties away from the bridge.

The MAIB makes it clear that human error plays a role in collisions, with examples like the report of a watch officer with an unrestricted view ahead (as well as an electronic chart and radar) who didn't see the ship he hit until after they collided; and the mate, who told his captain they might have hit something: he wasn't sure, because the radar was full of clutter, but they had in fact just collided with a 23,000-tonne bulk carrier.

Accident reports of collisions are a history of inaccurate radar plotting, distractions, and plain ordinary mistakes. Radar pictures make it easy to believe that a safe speed in fog is the same as that on a clear day. One vastly experienced master told investigators he didn't usually reduce speed when encountering restricted visibility. Another declared he considered 17 knots a safe speed in 200m visibility.

Commercial ships face big pressures to arrive in port on deadline. Any change of course or loss of speed could cut into the ships' owners' profits.

WHAT CAN THE SKIPPER DO?

The ultimate lesson from the *Ouzo* tragedy is that the yachtsman's best chance of averting a close-quarters situation from which there may be no escape is to act sooner rather than later. With fast-moving shipping around, a yacht skipper may feel like a blindfolded man in the middle of the M25. Failure to peer to leeward beneath the genoa, scan the horizon and glance astern regularly has led to many a ship 'coming out of nowhere'. The onus is on the yachtsman to be as vigilant as possible and never assume he's been seen. He should do everything he can to make his vessel as visible as possible. Having radar helps, but a small craft is an unstable platform.

James Stevens, RYA Training Manager, also points out that: 'We would advise yachts in the open sea not to get in the position where the ship is the give-way vessel.'

A yacht might be the 'stand on' vessel crossing a Traffic Separation Scheme (TSS) but the reality is that it would be suicidal to stand on one's rights and rely on a technicality from the give-way vessel. There are many apocryphal stories of tankers and container ships arriving in port with a yacht's mast or rigging hanging from their bow anchor like a toothpick – the big ship's crew didn't even know they had hit something.

Yachts under bare poles are difficult to spot. A GRP or wooden yacht does not give a good echo on a radar screen and heavy rain or rough seas degrade radar capabilities. The ARPA (Automatic Radar Plotting Aid) systems used by ships require return echoes on 50 per cent of their scans before they start plotting a signal. Acute heeling on a yacht reduces the effectiveness of her radar reflector – and her lights.

There have been many suggestions for making boats more visible, from making the top third of mainsails a bright orange to adding a retro-reflective band and making dodgers and sprayhoods brightly coloured. The human eye is naturally attracted to movement and a flashing light will be seen long before a fixed light. Some experienced sailors say a strobe has a lot to recommend it and fitting one is easy. Most electronic stores sell replacement waterproof strobe lights for burglar alarm boxes. But a strobe is not a substitute for normal navigation lights and should only be used in emergencies.

The MAIB say 'Yachtsmen should not hesitate to attract the attention of ships' watchkeepers by whatever means available.' This specifically includes calling on VHF radio, illuminating sails with spotlights and, as a last resort, directing the light at the bridge.

Don't shirk on engine maintenance or set off low on fuel. You can't sail yourself out of trouble if there's no wind.

An AIS (Automatic Identification System) receiver gives the name and details of nearby vessels of 300 gross tonnes and more, but the MAIB cautions that 'it is not an anti-collision aid'. AIS transponders will trickle down to small craft but they will contribute to the spectre of 'information overload' and icon-cluttered screens.

A proper passage plan and a mental picture of what the tide will be doing at any given time is essential. White collision flares should be kept handy, clipped to a bulkhead.

FOOTNOTE

At a trial at Winchester Crown Court, Michael Hubble (the officer of the watch on the P&O ferry *Pride of Bilbao*) was cleared of all charges relating to the deaths of the crew of *Ouzo*. The jury cleared Mr Hubble of manslaughter and were unable to reach verdicts on charges under the Merchant Shipping Act, that he engaged in conduct as a seaman likely to cause death or serious injury. The judge therefore instructed the jury to return 'not guilty' verdicts. The jury had also heard that *Ouzo* was close to a 3,500-tonne coastal tanker, *Crescent Beaune*, and not the *Pride of Bilbao*, at 0140 BST on 21 August. The captain of the tanker, Alastair Crichton, told the jury he had broken the law when he failed to have a proper watch on his ship's bridge that evening.

two

ANATOMY OF A COLLISION

Yacht	*Wahkuna* (Moody 47)
Skipper	Michael Dresden
Bound from	Diélette to Hamble, Southampton
Date of loss	28 May 2003
Position	25 miles south-east of Portland, Dorset

Skipper Michael Dresden's £400,000 Moody 47 Wahkuna *was run down and sunk in May 2003 after a collision with a 66,000-tonne P&O Nedlloyd container ship in fog in the English Channel. The MAIB report on the incident said that only one of 19 other vessels in the area had reduced speed in the fog.*

EXPERIENCED OFFSHORE YACHTSMAN Michael Dresden (67) was still in shock after his one-year-old boat sank within minutes, leaving him and his four crew drifting in a liferaft 25 miles south-east of Portland, Dorset.

'When a 907ft ship weighing 66,000 tonnes bears down on you out of the fog in mid-Channel it is not a good experience,' he said. 'The first 10ft of *Wahkuna* was pulverised. It was like an explosion. We were then pushed sideways by the ship as we passed along her side, before she disappeared into the fog.'

Mr Dresden, a Yachtmaster with 41 years' sailing experience and more than 120 Channel crossings, was returning from Diélette, on the west side of the Cherbourg peninsula, to his mooring on the Hamble when the collision happened.

Wahkuna departed in good weather conditions: wind variable Force 1 to 2, calm sea state and visibility three to five miles. Once clear of the Channel Islands, a compass course of 012° to 015° was set towards the Needles Fairway buoy, under autopilot. Mr Dresden and the crew, all members of the High Sea Sailing Club in north-west London, were in the cockpit. The crew had qualifications ranging from RYA Offshore Yachtmaster to Day Skipper.

Wahkuna was making a speed of about 7.5 knots. Her position was plotted every 20 minutes by one of the crew. At about 0930, visibility began to deteriorate and, at times, reduced to about 50m. In addition to switching on the automatic fog signal, Mr Dresden instructed the crew to raise the mainsail to increase visibility. He and one other crewmember constantly monitored the radar, which was set to the six-mile range.

Wahkuna was fitted with a Raymarine R70 3cm (M)ARPA radar display in the cockpit and a Raymarine R80 display at the chart table. Only the cockpit display was monitored during the incident. Two targets were detected about a quarter of a mile apart, bearing approximately north-east at a range of six miles. They were visually tracked until the range had decreased to three miles, at which point Mr Dresden assumed *Wahkuna* was on a collision course with the nearest vessel.

He and a crewmember took manual control of *Wahkuna* and slowed her down to under two knots. Then, the engine was disengaged to bring her to a stop. At that point both the skipper and crewmember agreed that the ship would pass ahead at a distance of 1.5 miles. Soon after, one of the crew recalled hearing a fog signal and saw the bow of a large container vessel looming out of the fog at about 50 to 60m to port. To try to avoid a collision, the skipper came hard-to-starboard and ahead on the main engine.

But the container vessel's bulbous bow struck the forward part of *Wahkuna*'s port hull, demolishing the first 3m of her bow. *Wahkuna* rose up 2m on the ship's bow wave and slalomed down her starboard side, stern-first for some 75m, before sliding back into the sea. The container vessel's stern passed, leaving *Wahkuna* wallowing in her wake.

One of the yacht's crew read the word 'Monrovia' on the vessel's stern. Another recorded the GPS position. Mr Dresden opened *Wahkuna*'s forward cabin door to find water pouring in and told the crew to don lifejackets and collect food and water. The engine was put in astern and the yacht began making stern-way at a speed of about half a knot through the water, reducing the flood of water.

But *Wahkuna* was still sinking. Instructions were given to deploy the liferaft. After collecting flares and an EPIRB, the crew abandoned *Wahkuna* for the liferaft. Soon after the yacht sank by the bow. In the liferaft, the EPIRB failed to work – the light indicating normal operation didn't illuminate. The crew's mobile phones were also out of range. It was some five-and-a-half hours later that one of their distress flares was seen by *Condor Express*, a high-speed cross-Channel ferry. The crew were landed in Guernsey and taken to hospital for a routine medical examination.

Mr Dresden was interviewed by officials from the Department for Transport's MAIB and the Maritime and Coastguard Agency (MCA). He submitted his own 32-page report of the incident to the MAIB.

His insurers, Groves John Westrup (GJW), paid out in full, eight days after the accident, and pursued a claim against the ship for reimbursement of the insurance money and the loss of equipment on board the yacht for which Mr Dresden was not covered.

Following enquiries, two MAIB inspectors travelled to Hong Kong to interview the captain of the P&O Nedlloyd ship *Vespucci*, which is registered in Monrovia, who admitted seeing the yacht on his radar. Blue paint marks similar to *Wahkuna*'s were found on the vessel's starboard bow.

The MAIB report praises the 'good fortune and the last minute evasive action of Mr Dresden, which probably reduced the damage' and saved the lives of his crew.

P&O NEDLLOYD *VESPUCCI*'S STORY

The 66,000-tonne container ship was on the second day of a passage from Antwerp to Singapore, via Port Said. She was travelling at 25 knots in thick fog when *Wahkuna* was detected at a range of five to six miles on the port bow. Automatic Radar Plotting Aid (ARPA) showed her course was northerly, speed 6.5 knots. The master estimated the yacht would cross eight cables ahead.

However, at a range of between 1.5 and 2 miles, *Wahkuna* slowed quickly and the ARPA vector indicated she had also altered course towards north-east. Her speed by ARPA reduced to zero. This concerned the captain, who immediately started the second steering motor and ordered the Second Officer, then Officer On Watch (OOW), to change to manual steering. This was done, but neither course nor speed was adjusted. The CPA (Closest Point of Approach) of *Wahkuna* was then two cables on the port side and the captain was uncertain of her intentions.

He reported that *Wahkuna* was never seen to be lost in the radar ground wave or clutter and that her range by ARPA was not less than two cables. As *Wahkuna* passed, the captain saw her radar trail pass two cables astern. The time was shortly before 1100. When *Wahkuna* was between one and a half to two miles astern, her course and speed by ARPA was about 075° at 3 knots. *Wahkuna's* contact was cancelled from ARPA and the ship continued on passage. The lookout on the port bridge wing did not see or hear anything, and the captain was completely unaware that a collision had occurred.

MAIB VERDICT

The MAIB concluded that three actions by the ship, two by the yacht and two by both ship and yacht caused the collision.

VESPUCCI'S ACTIONS:

1 The high speed of the container vessel: a safe speed for *Vespucci* would be one which allowed the vessel to stop within the visibility range of 50 to 100m. But since it would have taken three cables to stop the vessel, even at slow ahead, such a speed was impracticable and was not an option if steerage was to be maintained. At 25 knots, however, the possibly tired captain, who had been on the bridge for 14 hours, had less than five minutes to assess the situation and react to the yacht's unexpected action using potentially inaccurate data. Also, the vessel could only have been stopped after 2.4 miles, which was beyond the yacht's position.

2 Acceptance by *Vespucci's* captain of too small a passing distance: when *Wahkuna* was first detected, the captain was content with her crossing eight cables ahead. He did not consider this to be a close-quarters situation and took no action. As the vessel was transiting in thick fog at high speed, the captain's acceptance of such a small passing distance was inappropriate. Given the manoeuvrability of his vessel, and the light traffic density, either a bold alteration to starboard within the sea room available or a reduction in speed could have easily been made. Either course of action would have prevented the collision, but neither was taken.

3 Undermanned bridge: the ship's bridge team comprised the captain, Second Officer and a rating. In the prevailing conditions of visibility, the positioning of the rating on the bridge wing was appropriate to maintain an oral and visual lookout. By not having a second rating available on the bridge to act as helmsman, however, in accordance with his standing orders, the captain had no alternative but to use the Second Officer as helmsman after changing to manual steering. As a result, a valuable second pair of eyes was lost, which could have been used to enhance the radar lookout – either at long range, to allow the captain to safely reduce his range scale, or at short range, to provide a second opinion on the situation.

WAHKUNA'S ACTIONS

1 A misunderstanding about COLREGS: there was a misunderstanding about which collision regulations are applicable in fog. The skipper thought he was the 'stand-on' vessel, but such a status does not exist in the COLREGS during restricted visibility. In fog, the onus is on both vessels to take 'avoiding action in ample time'.

2 The inability to use radar effectively: *Wahkuna* had two radar displays with 10-target tracking, selectable target vectors, target risk assessment with danger alarm, history plots, target speed, course, CPA and TCPA (Time to Closest Point of Approach) calculations. During the events, when the cockpit display was monitored, none of the features listed were used.

The MAIB report stated: 'Neither the skipper nor crew fully understood or appreciated the information that could have been provided by the equipment.' As the vessels eventually collided without *Vespucci* altering course or speed, it is evident that had the yacht not reduced speed, she would have passed safely ahead of the container ship. The actions taken by the yacht were based on an inaccurate assessment of the situation by radar and confused the bridge team on *Vespucci*, as well as putting the two vessels on a collision course.

BOTH VESSELS' ACTIONS

1 Failure of both vessels to keep an effective radar lookout: *Vespucci*'s captain couldn't have constantly monitored the radar bearing of the yacht when he first became aware of its speed reduction. Had he done so, it might have caused him to question the information on the target provided by ARPA. His decision to take no action was based on incomplete or scanty radar information.

When *Wahkuna* was virtually stopped in the water, her skipper estimated that the radar contact of *Vespucci* would pass 1.5 miles ahead as a result of his action. His assessment, however, was also based on scanty radar information because the yacht's crew didn't know how to use the radar's automatic plotting facilities and a manual plot was not made. After making the assessment that the container ship would pass ahead, it was apparent that a radar lookout was not maintained. Had it been, it would have been evident that the ship was closing rapidly, and avoiding action could have been taken sooner.

2 Over-confidence in the accuracy of ARPA: several factors reduce the accuracy of the speed and bearing calculation carried out by ARPA equipment. Given that the captain and the OOW were content with a CPA of two cables, they were probably unaware of the accuracy parameters of their radars. Likewise, had *Wahkuna*'s skipper been able to use his Mini (M)ARPA effectively, he might have realised that his action of reducing speed substantially increased the probability of a collision.

■ LESSONS LEARNED

The MAIB recommended that the RYA and BMF (British Marine Federation) should act to improve yachtsmen's radar knowledge.

Yachtsmen should be aware of the following frightening statistic from the MAIB report: 'According to shipping traffic monitored by Jobourg Vessel Traffic Service (and recorded by radar surveillance), out of 19 vessels in the vicinity at the time of the collision only one reduced speed because of the fog.'

The owner of *Vespucci* instructed all its vessels to proceed at a safe speed at all times, especially in restricted visibility. This was to be audited on a regular basis by the company.

Speed input for all ARPA installations should be derived from the vessel's log. This would enable water-based information, the correct format for anti-collision avoidance, to be displayed. Ground-based radar information, derived from GPS for example, is affected by set, and drift can have an adverse effect on the accuracy of radar plotting.

A safe CPA in the open sea is considered to be at least one mile.

It has been suggested that guidelines be issued to help ships' captains to better understand and manage fatigue.

The yacht's EPIRB had been tested the month before and stored down below. Had it worked properly, the time the crew spent in the liferaft (in shipping lanes and in fog) would have been reduced. The makers have been asked to review design and quality control to ensure corrosion and battery failure do not occur and to ensure existing beacons are checked, rectified and modified if needed.

The MAIB found that commercial pressure might have influenced the *Vespucci's* captain in his decision to proceed at 25 knots in such conditions. The owners of the vessel denied such pressure was applied.

three

SUNK IN THE NORTH SEA

Yacht	*Laughing Gull III* (32ft GRP fin-keeled)
Skipper	Menko Poen
Crew	Victor Poen
Bound from	Lowestoft, UK to Scilly Isles
Date of loss	June 2004
Position	25 miles north-east of Ramsgate

Dutch father and son Menko Poen (49) and Victor (13) found themselves adrift in their liferaft when their 32ft yacht sunk after a mystery collision 25 miles north-east of Ramsgate in 2004. Amazingly, they spent 8 hours in one of the busiest shipping areas in the world before rescue. Despite firing several red flares at ships within sight, it was ultimately the smell of smoke from the flares, not the sight of them, that brought rescue.

Menko started sailing at sea almost 30 years ago, and has extensively cruised the North Sea, the Channel and the Baltic, mostly singlehanded. He took part in the North Sea Race and the Driehoek Noordzee.

MY SON VICTOR AND I set sail from Lowestoft, on the East Coast of the UK, on the afternoon of 29 June, heading for Ramsgate on our way to the Scilly Isles, where the rest of the family planned to join us for a holiday. Our yacht, *Laughing Gull III*, was a 32ft GRP fin-keeled boat built in 1981 in Amsterdam.

The weather was a squally SW Force 6 to 7, veering and easing to a westerly Force 5. Keeping clear of the sandbanks in the Thames Estuary, I plotted our position on the chart regularly. Although it was wet and windy and hard work in the squalls, it was also exhilarating sailing. We were 25 miles north-east of Ramsgate and I was on watch, while Victor rested in his bunk below, when at around 0130, I heard a bumping sound and the boat's speed dropped.

She was also pushed to port. Although this seemed consistent with the conditions, I felt something was wrong. I turned my head and listened, waiting for the sound to come again. But it didn't. I leaned through the companionway and asked Victor if he had noticed anything. He told me he'd heard a sound like a loud knock on a door and had also noticed we were pushed to port.

Still not sure what had happened, I checked the bilges and saw to my horror they were full of water. I couldn't see any damage and the keel bolts seemed fine. Soon the water level was above the floor and, despite bailing with a bucket, it continued to rise, pouring into my boots. I checked the seacocks. If something was wrong with them, I could stop the flow with a wooden plug. But they were OK.

This meant there must be damage to the hull itself. I continued bailing and considered pulling a sail around the outside of the hull to try and stem the flood. But with a fin keel, it was unlikely I'd get the sail close enough to the hull to have any effect. I thought of breaking off the cupboards and interior fittings to inspect the hull for damage, but the water was pouring in so fast there wasn't time.

By now, water was up to my knees and rising. I told Victor we had to abandon the yacht. I stressed there was nothing to be afraid of and we discussed what had to be done: sending out a MAYDAY, firing flares (if appropriate) and preparing the liferaft.

I didn't want to go on deck to lower the sails in case this caused the boat to capsize, so I trimmed them to steady the movements. I sent Victor into the cockpit to help stabilise the yacht and started to send the first MAYDAY on VHF radio Channel 16. I had an instruction booklet handy to remind me of the procedure. I also had the yacht's name written out in the phonetic alphabet.

I transmitted five to ten MAYDAYs, but with no response. By now, I realised, the batteries were completely underwater. As I was transmitting the last MAYDAY, the water was up to my chest as I sat at the chart table, and the switchboard was half underwater. Before I left the cabin, I wrote on a piece of paper that the crew had abandoned the sinking yacht and were all OK – in case *Laughing Gull III* was found afloat.

I carried the liferaft from the front cabin into the cockpit, wading through the water in the saloon. On the horizon, I spotted two ships. I fired two parachute flares and lit one red hand-flare. Although I estimated the ships were only a few miles away, they didn't respond. Not all our hand and parachute flares worked, although they were almost brand new.

We deployed the liferaft, after carefully checking the instructions. We tied it to the stern and dropped it overboard, yanking the rope to activate automatic inflation when it was about 10m away. We pulled the raft against the stern and I told Victor to jump carefully. It was a horrifying moment! Then I followed him, remembering the phrase: 'Only use your liferaft when the step into it is a step upwards'. I can assure readers that we were just in time!

The only things we took with us were two torches, a knife, my passport and credit cards. Everything else we left behind.

At 0210 we cut the liferaft loose from *Laughing Gull III* – an emotional moment, as it meant a final goodbye to my yacht. Until then, I was still hoping for rescue by a lifeboat or any other vessel with an electrical pump. The weather was fair: it was dry, the wind was westerly Force 5, with good visibility and a moon shining through the clouds. I remember thinking it was beautiful sailing weather.

It was almost High Water and the tide was soon going to turn with the north-going ebb. Taking into account the tide and our approximate position, I realised we were slowly drifting towards the Traffic Separation Scheme (TSS). I looked back at *Laughing Gull III* and could still see her masthead light. Just before sunrise the light suddenly disappeared, meaning that she had sunk, or the batteries had gone dead.

With a water temperature of only 9°C it was cold in the liferaft. Keeping up our morale was my number-one priority. I was completely soaked and my muscles were aching. I was also very tired, but I was still capable of thinking clearly. Victor was in a bad condition: severely seasick and unable to swallow water. He had to pee and he asked me where he should do it. I told him I had just done so myself a moment ago in my trousers and the warmth on my legs had been very welcome. We both tried to sleep for a while, or at least we closed our eyes.

When we noticed vessels in our vicinity, we fired red parachutes and hand flares. Although the ships were close – we could see their navigation lights reflected in the water – they didn't respond. After sunrise, more ships in the TSS became visible. They were moving to the SW and, as the wind was blowing us to the east, there was a risk of being run down.

I looked at the liferaft's solitary paddle, which was very small. I decided to wait until the ebb, which would push us in a N to NE direction. By paddling, with the help of tide and wind, I hoped we could move to the NE, alongside the TSS. I calculated that the ebb would start running again at about 1400. So I still had time to rest. Then I heard an aeroplane above us. I regretted that I hadn't had time to grab our emergency bag with the orange dye, which would have coloured the water to draw the aircraft's attention. I also lacked a mirror to give light-signals to ships. A hand-held VHF would have been useful, too. Most of the time I kept a lookout, with one of my hands holding Victor's ankle to reassure him I was there.

The silhouettes of the ships in the TSS had been visible for some time when I saw a dot on the horizon slowly becoming a vertical line, then changing into two larger lines and finally transforming into three even larger lines. It was a ship with three masts, slowly heading SW and closer than all other vessels. This could be our opportunity!

We still had one red hand flare, two orange smoke signals and three white parachute flares. I reasoned that I had to wait until the ship was close enough but, on the other hand, our liferaft still had to be visible when looking ahead from the ship's bridge. I waited for the right moment before using our last two orange smoke signals and our last red hand flare.

Almost immediately after using the red hand flare we saw the ship's three masts becoming one. The ship had turned in our direction! We were saved and we embraced each other! After eight hours adrift in our liferaft, we were taken onboard the Norwegian Tall Ship *Sørlandet* on her way to Dunkirk at 1010. Dover Coastguard and the French authorities were informed. Victor and I were offered hot drinks and a meal, dry clothes and even a bunk, but, above all, a lot of understanding, warmth and kindness. Later, the crew of the *Sørlandet* told me that they could smell but not see the smoke from our flares, being on our leeside. When the *Sørlandet* arrived at her port of destination, Dunkerque, my family was waiting to take us home again to the Netherlands.

■ LESSONS LEARNED

Be mentally prepared for shipwreck. Be prepared for failures, but maintain morale and, above all, don't panic.

Have the VHF MAYDAY procedure at hand, including your ship's name in the phonetic alphabet.

Being able to drop the mainsail and take all speed off the yacht might have reduced the flood of water.

Make sure you have your emergency grab bag in a place where it can be easily found. We left ours behind, with its orange dye and signalling mirror. A hand-held VHF radio in a water-proof pouch would have been useful, too.

Have the liferaft stowed on deck, if possible, or in the cockpit or a locker. Stowing it in the forward cabin is not the best place. There might not be time to carry it through the saloon if there's a collision or a fire aboard.

Reading the instructions for deploying your liferaft when you are abandoning ship is not the best time! Find time to rehearse your emergency procedures on a normal sailing outing.

Make sure you have wooden plugs tied to the seacocks and they are the right size.

Make sure your bilge pump is not blocked by debris.

Do you have an emergency kit aboard so you can make provisional repairs of the hull?

Don't count too much on VHF radio Channel 16. These days a DSC VHF is better. And an EPIRB (Electronic Position Indicating Radio Beacon) is even better. A Search and Rescue Transponder (SART) also improves your chances of detection by search and rescue. Be prepared for the fact that even brand new hand and parachute flares may not work.

Even with just two of us, we found space in the four-man liferaft limited and suffered cramp and fatigue.

RUN DOWN, OR RESCUED?

Yacht	*Nuts* (Danish Bandholm 28)
Skipper	Niels Blixenkrone-Moller
Crew	Rikke and Rasmus Blixenkrone-Moller
Bound from	Los Llanos, Tenerife, for Barbados
Date of loss	18 December 1999
Position	1,600 miles from Barbados

Danish schoolteacher Niels Blixenkrone-Moller, his wife Rikke and son Rasmus (11) were on a year's sabbatical and crossing the Atlantic when their rendezvous with a tanker went disastrously wrong.

ON 19 JUNE I SET SAIL from our home port of Nappedam on the east coast of Jutland, Denmark, with my wife, Rikke, a psychologist, and our 11-year-old son, Rasmus, aboard our 28ft yacht *Nuts*, a sturdy Danish Bandholm 28 design.

An uneventful North Sea crossing was followed by a rainy sail across Scotland, via the Caledonian Canal. From the island of Ghia we sailed to Ireland and then cast off from Kinsale for a five-day crossing to north-west Spain and down the Spanish and Portuguese coasts to the Algarve.

In the Canary Islands we became part of the cruising community, planning to cross the Atlantic. The ARC (Atlantic Rally for Cruisers) sailors were busy preparing their yachts for the departure deadline. But we, and many others, believe that choosing your departure day should be done on the spot and not set a year in advance. Thus it was not until 7 December that we finally left Los Llanos, Tenerife, bound for Barbados.

By this time, Herb Hilgenberg's Atlantic weather SSB radio net and others suggested that we should sail SSW to at least 20° N to find the trade winds.

With a south-east wind we logged between 106–124nm each day, always hoping for a nice easterly. On the tenth day we discovered that both our batteries were too low to start the engine. We hoped our solar panel would feed one battery sufficiently to do the job. Otherwise we had enough dry-cell batteries to power our hand-held GPS and torches.

We hadn't seen any ships since the first day. But at midday on the eleventh day we saw a large tanker approaching. We thought this was an opportunity to get assistance – either to get our battery charged, or to obtain a new battery.

We contacted the tanker by hand-held VHF and although the radio contact was poor, they were prepared to help us. Our position was 18° N and 35° W. It was a sunny morning and we were sailing at 5 knots on a heading of 240°.

The tanker manoeuvred in a large circle and we thought they would stop on our port side to give us a lee from wind and waves. The sea was not rough, but the swell and waves were one to two metres.

But as the tanker approached, we were surprised to see steps lowered on its port side. We thought they had decided to send over a small boat. VHF communication was not working. But soon they were on our starboard, leeward, side, just a few metres away. Heaving lines landed like small bombs all around. Cries of 'Make fast!' and 'Get closer!' were in the air.

Although we were uneasy, we tied the heavy lines fore and aft, expecting to be able to stay off the ship's side by steering off.

Suddenly, we were sucked along the iron wall towards the huge tanker's rudder. To prevent disaster, we were pulled forward. Our mast banged against the giant.

In seconds the situation had changed. Our masthead lights and the mast's starboard spreader had gone. The teak cap rail was crushed and the pushpit bent.

With 1,600 miles to go to Barbados our yacht was now disabled.

In desperation we climbed the vertical steps to board the tanker. We were surprised to learn that we had been 'rescued' and 'saved'. The Arab and Pakistani crew seemed to feel that Allah had helped us.

We, however, felt that bad seamanship by the tanker's captain had severely damaged our yacht.

As the last of my family arrived on deck, I asked if *Nuts* could be craned aboard. The captain welcomed us aboard, but also informed me that our yacht would have to be abandoned as he refused to take her aboard as deck cargo. I asked if I could go back aboard *Nuts* with a volunteer sailor to salvage our personal effects. My wish was granted. But as we were on our way down the ladder, the second bridge officer came running and stopped us, saying, 'Is there really anything there worth risking lives for?'

All we had managed to bring with us were four carrier bags containing wallets, camera and films, but not much else. Now we were forced to abandon our lovely home, plus much valuable equipment aboard – including scuba diving gear, the liferaft, dinghy, outboard engine, plus three months' provisions and treasured possessions, like our diaries.

The captain asked if he could sink *Nuts* as a hazard to shipping. Instead, it was agreed that she would be left adrift and a sécurité message was broadcast. We informed Herb Hilgenberg's Atlantic radio net. Finally, we told friends over the SSB not to expect us in Barbados.

Soon we were shown to our new quarters – our home for the next 12 days – and we heard the ship's main engine start. The tanker was en route from America to Angola.

By now a strange double reality had developed. The tanker's logbook recorded 'Rescue operation'. But from our point of view we had been 'run down'. The captain insisted we had been 'lucky' to meet them.

Whatever our confused feelings, the friendliness and helpfulness of the tanker's crew were overwhelming. We were given shoes, clothes, toothbrushes and even Christmas presents for our son Rasmus.

On the evening of 28 December, 14 miles off the coast of Angola, we were told a helicopter would take us off the tanker on the morning of the 30th. The captain did not let us have our passports until I signed a paper saying that I was prepared to pay all expenses for our return to Denmark.

The helicopter arrived while the tanker was at anchor near a place called Soyo, an hour by plane from Luanda. We had been told by the captain that his company would pay for our journey home and then invoice us later.

However, once ashore we were told we had to pay on the spot for our tickets. Luckily, we were able to make arrangements with our bank in Denmark. Later that morning we flew from Soyo to Luanda, where we caught a flight to Paris, finally arriving in Copenhagen on 31 December. The cost of our return flights, including the help of an agent in Angola, totalled US $6,959.

A month later, on 2 February, the Danish Coastguard informed us that a Norwegian vessel had sighted *Nuts* at position 43° W and 19° N and had lifted her aboard. She was now on her way to San Cristobal, Panama.

There she was landed and a local agent inspected her and informed our insurers, Pantaenius, of the damage: *Nuts* had been dismasted and the starboard side of the hull had suffered a rupture one-and-a-half metres long by a metre. The pushpit and pulpit had been torn off. The yacht was insured for 300,000 Danish krona, but unfortunately, our onboard equipment was not covered separately.

■ **LESSONS LEARNED**

With a young child aboard, and 12 days from Barbados, Niels still feels that he didn't make a wrong decision calling for assistance, although he admits 'we had enough dry-cell batteries to power our hand-held GPS and torches'.

Sailing literature is full of horror stories involving small yachts having disastrous close encounters with big ships – either by design or accident. Invariably, the yachts are severely damaged.

Any experienced ocean sailor will tell you to give the widest possible berth to any ships that might approach too close, perhaps out of curiosity. Forces like drift, suction from prop wash, and wind eddies will guarantee you surrender all control over what happens next.

Sound preparation of yacht and confidence in your seamanship should mean that, even facing engine failure and flat batteries, you can complete an ocean passage safely under sail.

It was not until *Nuts*'s batteries went flat that Niels discovered the crank handle to handstart the 17hp Volvo engine could not be turned, because movement was restricted by the construction of the galley.

As back-up against power failure next time, Niels could add a separate generator, bigger solar panels, or even a towing generator. Having full insurance for equipment and personal effects aboard is also a sound idea.

ANATOMY OF A SINKING

Yacht	*Sea Crest*, a Brewer 44
Skipper	Joe Bass
Bound from	British Virgin Islands to Venezuela
Date of loss	16 June 1998
Position	two days south-west of US Virgin Islands

As a circumnavigator and highly experienced yachtsman, Joe Bass thought he was prepared for any emergency. Yet he found himself in life-and-death circumstances, battling unexpected challenges. 'If my experience can help one couple face a similar situation better prepared, this account will have been worth the effort,' he said.

RECENTLY, I RE-CROSSED THE ATLANTIC once again in *Sea Crest*, my Brewer 44. After three years in the North Atlantic and the Mediterranean, I looked forward to the warmer seas and reliable trade winds of the Caribbean. I finished a re-fit in the British Virgin Islands and then it was time to sail to hurricane-free Venezuela, by way of Bonaire. Because my crew was called back to the USA, I decided to singlehand to Bonaire. *Sea Crest* was perfectly rigged for solo sailing. Between fully crewed voyages, I loved singlehanding as a way to 'stretch' my sea legs and become one with my boat on the open ocean.

COUNTDOWN TO COLLISION
14 June: At 0700 I weighed anchor and sailed out of St Thomas and set a rhumb-line course directly for Bonaire, some 400 miles distant.

The winds were perfect, 20 knots out of the south-east, and the sailing was magnificent. *Sea Crest* was in her element on the open seas. *15 June:* Once again *Sea Crest* sailed beautifully. Everything was right. It was one of those days which cruisers remember as sheer perfection. *16 June:* The last day of her existence dawned with heavy clouds coming in from the south-east. The forecast was for a 'tropical wave' to move through the area, bringing squalls with heavy rain and gusts of up to 35 knots. Around 0900, squall after squall began passing through, bringing intense rain and high winds. Visibility grew more limited. By 1100, the frequency and strength of the squalls had increased. I furled the working jib and changed it to *Sea Crest's* normal heavy-weather rig – double-reefed main and staysail. She sailed comfortably in 9ft seas, rising and falling gently as they swept past beneath her. We were 'snug and cosy' for the conditions and if it hadn't been for the limited visibility, it would have been an exciting sail.

At 1300, the squalls increased once more in frequency and wind speed. Heavy rain was driven horizontally towards us and there was very little visibility. I was down below monitoring the radar for any traffic.

Sea Crest charged ahead, riding well and comfortably, as I switched the radar from one range to another, watching for any signs of traffic. In one particularly strong squall, the wind speed indicator shot up to 38 knots, as she heeled sharply and moved ahead.

At that moment, *Sea Crest* rose up on what seemed to be a particularly large wave and came down into the trough. As she fell, heavily heeled over, I heard a loud bang. It was a rending, hard sound, unlike any I've ever heard from waves hitting a boat. She shuddered and veered off course, as though being bodily pushed or shoved aside. The autopilot quickly brought her back on course and as she continued sailing, the bilge alarm started its shrill warning signal.

I rushed up on deck to see what I had hit. Because of driving rain, the high seas and forward momentum of the boat, I could see nothing.

I hurriedly clipped on my safety harness and moved around the deck, looking over the sides from bow to stern for any sign of damage to the hull above the waterline. I could find none.

I dropped the staysail, made my way back to the cockpit and brought *Sea Crest* upwind, hove-to. I examined the leeward side of the hull, but I could see no sign of any damage above the waterline.

Rushing back down below, I opened the engine-room doors to inspect the bilge area. Every sailor's nightmare had come true. The bilge was rapidly filling and the water was already up to the engine block. I had to find the source of the inflow . . . and fast.

I moved through the cabin, pulling up the floor hatch covers to inspect the through-hull fittings. They seemed secure. But the bilge pump wasn't keeping up with water rushing in.

To my surprise, I quickly discovered that once the source of the water inflow was covered by rising water, it would be almost impossible to find, unless it was a big 'gusher'. My only hope was to find it by feel. I tried to trace the direction of the inflow and follow it back to its source. But with the boat both rolling and pitching, there was no 'direction' to follow – only turbulence.

I soon realised that 75 per cent of the possible area of damage, the underwater hull, was completely inaccessible from inside the boat due to the flooring, furniture, glassfibre liners or the four fuel and water tanks.

I abandoned the futile search for the source of the leak to return to the engine room to get the portable high-capacity bilge pump I stowed there for just this kind of emergency. It had been used only once, in mid-Atlantic, when I answered the distress call of a 27ft wooden yawl which was sinking. This high-capacity pump saved the boat. Now, I desperately needed it to save *Sea Crest*.

I lowered the pump's intake into the bilge, ran its three-inch discharge hose out of the nearest opening port, secured it to a stanchion and directed the flow overboard. I hurriedly connected the electrical leads to the engine-starting battery with crocodile clips. The pump immediately started throwing water out at a high rate. It worked! The water level appeared to be dropping slightly. It had fallen two inches, from the top of the engine block. Clearly the breach in the hull was not large. With the pump working and buying me time, I started a systematic search for the damaged area. The pump was definitely reducing the water level, which meant the inflow was less than the pump's discharge. There was hope.

I grabbed my boat-saver 'umbrella' – a heavy canvas device which in its 'closed' mode is shoved through the hole in the hull and, once through, opened up like an umbrella and pulled tightly back against the outside of the hull, secured there by an adjusting clamp on the inside.

I had kept it ready to use, as well as underwater epoxy and a 'collision mat' – a heavy canvas with grommets, made for just this use.

I desperately searched every area of the hull I could reach, feeling and probing, hoping to discover any discernible rush of water or apparent direction of flow. But as *Sea Crest* rolled and pitched in the large seas, rising water was thrown about in every direction.

By the time I gave up this unsuccessful effort and got back to the pump, I was in for a terrible shock. The pump had been stopped most of this time – blocked at its intake. The water level was now covering the engine and spilling out into the cabin. The blockage was caused by oil absorbent pads stowed in the engine room. The pads had fallen into the deep bilge and were now clogging the pump's intake. I tried to pull them out, but they were very heavy in their soaked state and came apart, leaving a pulpy mass.

I cleared the intake and re-lowered it, only to see it clog moments later. Cardboard boxes with filters and engine parts disintegrated in the rising water, turned into pulp floating on the surface and clogging the intake. Every time I had to stop to unclog the intake, the water level rose.

As long as I could keep the pump's intake clear, I gained on the water level. 'I can save her!' I kept thinking to myself. But the pump repeatedly clogged and the water level rose. When I stopped to search for the source of the inflow, the water level rose still further. I was astonished at the incredible amount of debris and paper that was now floating on top of the rising water. The cabin sole hatch-board covers, which I had removed and replaced while checking the through hulls, floated up and off and became deadly hard-edged 'surfboards' and battering rams, being hurled from side to side on top of the water, as the boat rolled and pitched. One knocked the crocodile clips off the battery, stopping the pump. The clips seemed adequate at anchor but were all too easily dislodged when hit by floating debris. It became clear they needed to be much larger and stronger. I was losing the battle. I switched the battery leads to the separate and much higher 'house' battery bank, which was still above water. Repeatedly, the pump intake clogged.

I was losing the battle. I realised I was going to need outside help to save *Sea Crest*. I have always been reluctant to call for assistance, but I urgently needed a larger, petrol-powered pump – one that was not so vulnerable to clogging. I started a series of MAYDAY calls on VHF channel 16, hoping to reach a ship within range.

There were no replies. I turned the radar on to the 24-mile range, but there was nothing. I was out there alone. It was time for urgent action to get help. I grabbed the EPIRB 406 and taped it to the aft rail and activated it. Returning below, I made a distress call on the SSB emergency frequency. Getting no response and with water rising up my legs, I switched frequencies to WOM, the commercial high-seas marine operator in Miami, and they responded immediately. They relayed my position and situation to the Coast Guard and I went back to the pump. Then, I was confronted with another unexpected discovery – one which almost proved fatal.

As water rose above floor level, all ten cabin sole hatch-board covers had floated off, leaving ten large gaping holes hidden under the surging water. As I went forward to search again for the source of the leak, my right leg plunged deep into one of these gaping holes up to my knee.

My leg was jammed solidly under the water; wedged firmly between the top of the fuel tank and the bulkhead. I couldn't get it loose.

If I couldn't free myself, I would go down with my sinking boat. I realised I had to relax my foot and leg and slowly move it about, rather than pull it straight out by brute force. With great effort I managed to take a deep breath, relax and slowly move my foot and leg about. I lost some skin, but after ten of the longest minutes of my life, I was free.

An hour had passed. From now on I had to move about most carefully. There was no cabin sole left, there were only holes . . . traps. The scene around me was one of chaos and destruction. I faced the shock of seeing my beautiful home transformed into a disaster area. The emotional distress was traumatic.

With every roll of the boat, hatch boards were thrown back and forth in the surging water. As the water rose, two heavy engine-room doors floated off their pintles and joined them. Just to remain standing in the rising water, as it surged from side to side with every roll of the boat, was difficult. To work in this situation was almost impossible. I had to use one arm to fend off the doors and hatch boards hurtling across the cabin with every roll. To do all this, and find and deal with the inflow and pump would have kept a full crew busy, much less a solo sailor or a cruising couple.

Though I had not yet thought of abandoning ship, it was now clear I had to face that reality. I launched the Avon liferaft and attached it to the aft rail. I was then faced with a cruel choice. If I took time to salvage my most important possessions it would keep me away from the pump intake, and almost certainly guarantee the loss of *Sea Crest*. I chose to put all my faith and effort into saving my boat. It was going to be all or nothing.

Two hours after the collision, I heard a great roar overhead and rushed up on deck with my hand-held VHF radio – an essential piece of equipment in such a crisis. The rescue aircraft had arrived from Curaçao. The pilot said he was going to fly off on a circular route to search for any vessels within range. I told him I needed a vessel with a large portable pump. When I returned below, the water was up to my waist. I had a battle to stay on my feet, avoid traps in the sole, fend off debris and keep the pump unclogged. The next 90 minutes were a blur.

The aircraft returned and the pilot told me that the nearest ship was about 60 miles away and would arrive in 2–3 hours. I told him I was going to keep trying to save the boat but would board the liferaft and cut loose only at the last moment before she went down. I have always said that my boat would have to leave me, by going under. I would not leave her. But, of course, I never really believed it would happen.

Several hours later, I heard the pilot calling on the VHF. A Norwegian ship, *Heros*, was arriving on the scene and he said I should immediately leave *Sea Crest*. I spoke to the captain. He didn't have a suitable pump on board. That news was the death knell for *Sea Crest*.

I went below one last time, grabbed my wallet, passport and ship's papers, put them into a plastic bag and secured it to my lifejacket.

That's all I could take from what had been my home for several years. I had gambled that I could save it all. It had been so close. But it had not worked out that way.

I paused on the aft deck to bid farewell to *Sea Crest*. As the seas lapped over her decks, I stepped into the liferaft. I had poured my life, my work, and my worldly possessions into her. It was all going down with her. I didn't then, or now, regret that I gave her my best effort. She deserved at least that.

The captain explained the rescue procedure by VHF. I cast off from *Sea Crest* and the liferaft was driven by seas and winds towards the sides of the now stationary ship. As I watched the crew lowering the rope ladder, I heard them shout, 'Look out!' The same seas and winds driving the raft towards the ship were also pushing *Sea Crest* towards me. The ship and *Sea Crest* were going to collide – and I was caught between them.

The crew saw it before I did. I turned to see *Sea Crest* go down into the trough of a large wave. As she rose on the crest and was about to be thrown violently against the ship's side, I jumped from the liferaft back onto *Sea Crest*'s now awash deck – just in time. The liferaft was folded over and crushed by the violent impact of the two hulls. When *Sea Crest* drifted back away from the ship, the liferaft popped back to shape. As my yacht drifted away and sank beneath the waves, I grabbed the rope ladder and climbed to safety clutching the plastic rubbish bag containing my worldly possessions.

AFTERMATH AND OBSERVATIONS

The captain of *Heros* and I discussed what I may have hit. Some of the crew had seen semi-submerged logs in the area. We thought it was a partially-sunken container or logs. Both are often lost off ships in bad weather. I have seen several half-sunken containers as I've sailed around the world. Off Cape Trafalgar, near Gibraltar, I saw one directly ahead, with only its edge sticking up above water. I turned just in time, missing it by not more than 25ft. It's not an empty sea out there. During the same period that *Sea Crest* was lost, two other yachts sunk in the Atlantic after colliding with submerged objects. One shipping report states that more than 1,000 containers are reported lost at sea each year. Many others are not reported. How many remain semi-submerged is anyone's guess.

Be prepared, it can happen to you – far out to sea or on a coastal passage. I was prepared for storms, gear failure, close encounters with ships or other mishaps. But the shock of hitting a submerged object caught me mentally unprepared. I thought collisions only happened with ships and I always kept watch for traffic and used radar fitted with a very loud alarm when sailing singlehanded.

You must have both a plan and equipment ready in the event of a sudden catastrophe. The hand-held VHF was crucial in communicating with the aircraft and the rescue ship. The portable high capacity bilge pump almost saved my boat. It could very well save yours. Built-in bilge pumps are often inadequate. An investment in a portable pump is not only extra insurance for your vessel, but could save any stricken sailboat you encounter.

Obviously, you must have an EPIRB 406. No one should go offshore without one. But it must be registered properly, with telephone contact numbers. I was very surprised to learn that the EPIRB did not give my position to rescue authorities on the first pass. They had to call the telephone numbers I gave on my registration. They reached my son who informed them I was sailing from the Virgin Islands to Venezuela. This helped them determine my location before the additional passes required for a fix – time you may not be able to afford. By this time, the rescue co-ordination centre had been informed of my SSB MAYDAY call with my exact position.

For the EPIRB system to work, you must register it and provide 24 hour telephone contacts if possible. And back it up with VHF or SSB calls if possible.

■ LESSONS LEARNED

Though I have circumnavigated and sailed full-time for more than 10 years, I faced surprises I was not prepared for: I was amazed how difficult it was to trace the source of the inflow once the water level was above the source. Three-quarters of the possible area of damage was inaccessible from inside the boat due to the flooring, furniture, fibreglass liners, etc. I had only a few precious minutes before this happened. I should have made that search my first priority. It probably cost me my yacht. But my first instinctive reaction was to rush up on deck and see what I had hit. Then, I took time to carefully inspect the hull above the waterline.

By the time I got back below, the water level was already above the inflow source. That made it impossible to find the breach in the hull. Finding the source of the breach must be your first action. Everything else can wait.

You have only a short time to decide your actions. The first five minutes are the most crucial.

Set your priorities now . . . in advance. Be sure your mate or crew is as familiar with the procedure as they are with the man-overboard drill. Your earliest actions will be your most effective.

The cabin sole hatch-board covers became deadly hard-edged 'surfboards' and battering rams as the boat rolled and pitched.

Another danger was that all ten cabin sole hatch-board covers floated off, leaving ten large gaping holes hidden under the surging water so that I almost lost my life by stepping into a hole. Secure yours in advance. This is vital in case of a capsize, of course, but few people think of it in the event of taking on water. Also put as many of those boxes and paper products as possible in waterproof plastic bags. I never expected to see so much pulpy paper floating and submerged . . . and it proved devastating to the pump's operation.

I have always sailed with a small brass plaque next to the navigation. It reads: 'Hope for the best. Organise for the worst'.

So, expect trouble. Do your planning and preparation now.

THAT SINKING FEELING

Yacht	*Solaris*
Skipper	Noel Dilly
Bound from	Azores and Madeira
Position	off the coast of Casablanca

Noel Dilly, an eye surgeon in London, has been sailing for more than 45 years. In this account he describes the sudden holing and sinking of Solaris, a 36ft charter yacht off the coast of Casablanca.

It was a beautiful starlit night with virtually no wind and just a gentle Atlantic swell running. We were a few miles off Casablanca, on a return voyage from the Azores and the Madeira Islands. We had just begun to round the headland with the lights of Casablanca harbour in sight when there was a bang as the hull hit something under water.

We brought the yacht on to a reciprocal course, but after about 10 minutes there was a second thump, much gentler than the first because she was travelling much more slowly. However, the usual precaution of pumping immediately after hitting something revealed that we had taken on water in the bilges. They had been dry after the first strike. A shout from forward revealed that water was welling up through the floorboards. The next shock was that it was not possible to remove the floorboards to try to locate the source of the leak.

Amazingly, they had been screwed down at the last refit. Worse still, the weight of inrushing water was buckling the floorboards and bending the screws so that they could not be turned with a screwdriver. It was imperative that we remove the floorboards if we were to stand any chance of saving the yacht. First we used a winch handle and then a large hammer to try to smash through the boards, but they were of quality teak and the hammer hardly dented the surface!

The biggest screwdriver we forced into the gap between the boards bent when it was used as a lever. By now the board was under water and efforts from inside the yacht became futile. We decided we would have to tackle the leak from the outside.

The bilge pumps were doing their best, but the boat was filling visibly. What had not been taken into account was the action that had been going on above decks while the battle was being fought below. The engine was still running, and as it was obvious to the rest of the crew that we were in danger of sinking, they had steered the yacht towards the apparent safety of the shore.

The swell was breaking on the beach and we were pitching about in the beginnings of the small but frequent waves. Our attempts to get underneath the wildly gyrating bow proved hazardous and only a half-hearted attempt was made to find the leak. While this was going on, the water level had reached something vital, stopping the engine. Then the boat started settling quite rapidly. We tried draping a sail under the bow, but this did nothing except sink the bow – the extra weight up forward caused an increased rush of water. The entire crew then moved their combined weight to the stern, but still the hole remained below the waterline. With no wind, no engine, and sinking with no chance to stop the leak, it seemed a good idea to consider abandoning ship.

The idea had hardly been mentioned when one of the crew, who was obviously under considerable stress, threw the liferaft overboard. It was not much more than 200m to the shore, and it would have been much easier to have pumped up the inflatable dinghy. However, as the liferaft was inflated and ready we decided to use it.

The crew went gingerly below to collect their valuables and put on extra clothes. Surprisingly, everyone reappeared in smart 'going ashore' gear. The valuables were hastily thrown in the rucksack normally used for shopping, which was put in the raft; then everyone climbed in.

With the canopy doors open, the paddles were used to head the liferaft towards the shore. However, as the liferaft entered the breakers it capsized and we were washed overboard. Then we realised that the vital rucksack had been lost. Bedraggled, we swam the liferaft up the beach, and stood up dripping to face a car full of Moroccan policemen.

Fortunately, they had seen the yacht slipping beneath the waves. But bureaucrats are bureaucrats the world over and the full entry formalities still had to be fulfilled. The senior policeman then asked what we would like to do.

The skipper announced: 'Take us to the best hotel in Casablanca!'

Just after midnight, five dripping yachtsmen were deposited in the hotel's foyer. A haughty and obviously horrified manager surveyed us and saw that we had no baggage. Drawing himself to his full height he demanded: 'And how do you intend to pay?'

The skipper then fished a sodden handkerchief from his top pocket and ceremoniously unwrapped an American Express credit card.

'That will do nicely, sir!'

It was at that point that everyone fell about laughing.

Next morning, intent on salvage, we went down to the beach where the yacht had been washed ashore. The hole in the bow was not much bigger than a fist. If only there had been a wrecking bar aboard to smash our way through the floorboards.

■ LESSONS LEARNED

The single most startling, but I suspect almost universal, fault that this incident revealed was that no emergency plan had been agreed before or during the cruise. The distress, although dire, had not been communicated to anyone. No one had been delegated to send a MAYDAY, nor to inflate the dinghy. Certain sensible things should be agreed from the outset.

The skipper with a few words can decide who launches the liferaft and who sends the MAYDAY, should the need arise. Dilly says that on his own yacht he has the whole format for the MAYDAY message written on a notice alongside the radio so that even the most inexperienced crewmember knows what to do.

Immediately after striking anything below the waterline, or falling off a large wave, it is a good idea to pump the bilge. This way you have a dry bilge as a starting point from which to assess if you are making water when you try to pump later. Or, of course, you may not be able to pump the bilges dry, which will signal that you are taking a significant amount of water aboard.

If you start taking in water, close all the seacocks. 'It was an amazing sight to see water siphoning through the marine toilet once the basin lip was below sea level. Water rushing into the cockpit via the cockpit drains was probably the last straw that provoked the panic launch of the liferaft,' says Dilly.

Never, ever screw down the floorboards. Use toggles or latches. It is prudent to think about how you would get to the below-the-waterline hull of your boat. Most people who consider this problem end up buying a lump (club) hammer and a wrecking bar to add to their tool kit. The item frequently forgotten is a substantial pair of bolt croppers to free a mast that has fallen overboard. Research reveals that this is the most common cause of being holed below the waterline.

How big a hole would sink your yacht? There is a whole science of fluid dynamics, but a reasonable estimate is that if the hole letting in the water is bigger than the smallest part of the bilge pump pipework, then, unless you can make the hole smaller, you will surely sink.

A good engine-driven bilge pump will shift about 40 gallons per minute under ideal conditions. The average hand-operated one is about half that amount. Bilge pump ratings in the manufacturers' claims are usually for 60 pumps per minute against no resistance, and with no need to lift the water (to a particular height above sea level) before discharging it. A head of 7ft will halve the output. Any length of piping will rapidly reduce the efficiency of the pump, as length of pipe plays an important role in generating the resistance against which the pump is working.

Just to depress you further, you cannot pump faster than the time it takes for the pump to fill and empty. Otherwise the pump loses efficiency. Next time you pump your bilges just time a complete cycle. The classic 'frightened man with a two-gallon bucket' will shift about 20 gallons a minute. That involves lifting and throwing 20lbs of water every six seconds. One way of working-out to keep fit!

It is a reasonable assumption that the flow of seawater through a hole is directly proportional to the fourth power of the radius of the hole. A two-inch hole will let in four times as much water as a one-inch hole would in the same time. Do not make the hole bigger by exploring it, if you can avoid doing so. Any means of decreasing the size of the hole will be richly rewarded by a big decrease in inflow. Do not despair if you seem to be getting nowhere pumping the boat out after you have plugged the hole. There is an awful lot more water about than is visible, and a great deal has to be shifted before there is any visible fall in the water-line.

Do not, repeat do not, make for the shore. In this incident, the breakers were dangerous and had the boat remained in calm water, she might have been saved. Breakers are no place for small liferafts. Even an inflatable dinghy would have had problems.

A surprising problem arose after the liferaft capsized. Two crewmembers had been wearing automatically inflating lifejackets; once they were thrown in the water the jackets inflated. As designed, the jackets turned them face up. It proved extremely difficult for them to overcome this righting tendency so they could swim to the shore.

seven

THE LOSS OF A 'FRIEND'

Yacht	*Yondi* (T24)
Skipper	Peter Jackson
Bound from	Plymouth for a daysail
Position	five miles south of the western end of Plymouth Breakwater

---

Peter Jackson began sailing in the Solent as a Sea Scout aged 12. Years later, a spur of the moment decision to go for a sail ended in disaster when his yacht Yondi *struck a submerged object off Plymouth and began to sink.*

IT WAS NEAR THE END OF SEPTEMBER, and I should have been sailing west with my son on what would probably have been the last trip of the season. But the forecast had predicted gales, so the trip was postponed and I decided, instead, to change the filters on the engine. When I'd finished, I should have gone home. Instead, I decided to give the engine a test and *Yondi* and I were soon heading out into Plymouth Sound.

There was a fresh breeze blowing from the north-west which meant that although the wind was about Force 5, the sea remained fairly calm. Since I was already late home I decided to throw caution to the wind and have a short sail. Soon we had cleared the breakwater and were heading for the open sea. *Yondi* was going perfectly and we were both thoroughly enjoying ourselves. She was a heavy boat with a deep keel and needed a good wind to go well. Conditions were ideal and she was flying along at near 7 knots. Soon we were well on the way to the Eddystone Lighthouse. What time did I say I'd be home?

I'd just left the tiller to prepare the sails to go about and return home, when there was a tremendous crash and *Yondi* seemed to stop dead. I was thrown forward on to the cabin bulkhead. I thought we must have collided with another vessel, but nothing was in sight. I was very confused. I knew that there were no rocks in the vicinity, and then I saw it: a huge log – no, a tree – just under the surface of the water. It was about 30ft long, and around 5ft in diameter, covered in weed and goose barnacles.

I went below to look for damage and was surprised when I found no big holes in the hull. In fact, I could find no damage at all, except for a slight seepage of water into the bilge pump. I wasn't concerned as the electric pump could easily deal with it. I felt it prudent to return to harbour as soon as possible, so rather than make a long beat back against the wind, I dropped sail and started the engine. As I had not replaced the cover on the bilge sump I could see the water level from the cockpit, and soon noticed that the level was slowly rising. I wasn't worried as I had a large capacity Whale bilge pump I could use if the electric pump couldn't cope. Although the sea was reasonably calm, there was a swell running and without sails *Yondi* was rolling.

After about 10 minutes the water level had reached the top of the sump, so I started using the bilge pump, quickly reducing the water level. I examined the sump again but still couldn't see any holes or cracks. I deduced that the water must be seeping up around the keel bolts, which had perhaps been loosened by the impact of the tree on the keel. I realised that, if this was the case, the movement of the boat was likely to exacerbate the leak and I could see no way of stopping it. The water level was now rising steadily and I was using the bilge pump continuously. Unfortunately, I was no longer able to keep the level within the bilge and water was beginning to slop around the floor of the cabin. I still felt that I would be able to reach Plymouth safely, as I knew *Yondi* would have to be nearly full of water before she would sink. Then matters took a turn for the worse.

The water reached the lower lockers where all of our tinned food was stored and the labels were being washed off and sucked into the pump strainer, slowing its efficiency.

Although I cleared the strainer several times, it blocked almost immediately and the water level was climbing quickly. I decided that I needed help. A quick look around showed no other vessel in sight. I went to the VHF radio and made a MAYDAY call. We were five miles south of the western end of Plymouth Breakwater.

The Coastguard responded immediately and calmly. Help was on its way. I put my lifejacket on and went to inflate my dinghy which was on the foredeck. I'd just started inflating it when the lifeboat called to obtain a radio fix on my position. I'd started inflating again when another yacht called to ask me to fire a flare so he could do the same. This I did, burning my hand in the process.

Once again, I turned to the dinghy, but now the Coastguard called again for an update. The water seemed to have levelled out but I realised this was only because it was filling the full volume of the hull. The cabin was now a dangerous place. Every time *Yondi* rolled, all kinds of floating debris was being thrown around the cabin, and the force of the water was so strong that I was unable to unblock the pump strainer again. Fortunately, I had installed the radio so that it could be operated from the cockpit and, surprisingly, it was still working, although the batteries had long been under water.

The first help to arrive was a fast rigid inflatable boat (RIB) from Fort Bovisand Diving Centre with three fit young men on board. They were soon bailing with buckets. When another RIB from the same centre arrived it was decided to pass lines under *Yondi*, attached to these boats, to try and keep her afloat. The bailing seemed to be making no difference to the water level.

There were now several boats standing by and the lifeboat arrived. They launched their dinghy to bring a large petrol pump over to *Yondi*. I felt a big sense of relief as I was still very uncertain about being held up by those RIBs. *Yondi* was a very heavy boat. This relief didn't last for long, however, as the lifeboatmen couldn't start the pump. It was decided to bring the lifeboat alongside and use its internal pump, even though this meant casting off from the RIBs.

We were alongside the lifeboat and I was just taking the hose from a crewmember when the coxswain ordered us all to leave *Yondi*. No one moved. This time we were given the same order in much stronger and louder language. This convinced us. As I went to do so, my lifejacket became entangled with one of the rear mast stays and for what seemed a lifetime I was firmly attached to the boat. Eventually, I freed myself and jumped into the sea. I turned immediately and was just in time to see the top of the mast and the new, expensive furling foresail disappearing under the water. *Yondi* sank like a stone, leaving just a few pieces of debris floating on the surface. There was nothing to show that my beautiful boat had ever existed.

I was soon on board the lifeboat, being given a hot drink. Perhaps only those who have owned a boat, and used it as intensively as I did, can begin to understand my tears as I stood on the pontoon at Clovelly Bay Marina as the sound of the Plymouth Lifeboat's powerful engines receded in the distance. Certainly some of the tears were due to release of the tension of the past hours, but there was also a feeling of having lost a close friend, with whom I'd shared so much; encounters with dolphins, quiet anchorages, learning new skills. *Yondi* had been so much a part of our lives over the past four years; now she was gone for ever. Months later we were still remembering lost items aboard, but the saddest loss was our log book, describing all the adventures we had shared.

We first saw *Yondi* in an open barn on a farm in the middle of Gloucester, where her owner had been replacing much of the wooden cockpit and fitting a new diesel engine. She was a T24, built in 1965 by D C Perfect of Chichester.

■ LESSONS LEARNED

Although Peter Jackson cleared the bilge pump strainer several times, it blocked almost immediately and the water level was climbing quickly. When the water reached the lower lockers, where all the tinned food was stored, the labels were being washed off and sucked into the pump strainer, slowing its efficiency.

Fortunately, Jackson had installed a VHF radio so that it could be operated from the cockpit and, surprisingly, it was still working, although the batteries had long been under water, when he sent his MAYDAY.

THERE SHE BLOWS

Yacht	*Pionier* (32ft sloop)
Skipper	Gordon Webb
Crew	Jennifer Webb, Tony Keeney, Peter Flockemann, Willi Schutten
Bound from	(racing) from Cape Town, South Africa to Rio de Janeiro, Brazil
Date of loss	23 January 1971
Position	approximately 1,600 miles west of Cape Town

The South African yacht, Pionier, *sunk after striking a whale while racing across the South Atlantic. The following extracts are from an account written by Anthony Hocking after interviews with* Pionier*'s crew. The 1971 Cape to Rio race started on 11 January and the 'strike' occurred when* Pionier *was eleven days out from Cape Town.*

TONY KEENEY WAS ON WATCH, sitting among the cushions in the cockpit behind the wheel as midnight approached. It was a dark night, with only a sliver of moon and a few brave stars appearing through the cloudy haze. Tony had been there since 2200, alone while the other four rested below, reading, sleeping, plotting. Since the second day *Pionier*'s crew had been watching alone, two hours at a time through the day and night. Gordon Webb, *Pionier*'s skipper, was due to relieve Tony at midnight.

Gordon took control, standing with one hand on the wheel looking out into the blackness ahead while Tony eased himself from the cushioned seat beside him, en route for his bunk. He had been at the wheel most of the day. There was not much to say. Both Gordon and Tony knew the implication of the position report. *Pionier* was placed to win, the wind was right, they were heading straight for Rio. Almost, though neither of them would have dreamt of suggesting it out loud, the race was in the bag.

Suddenly there was a shuddering crash. *Pionier's* bow shot high, arching out of the water in the darkness ahead, pointing to the stars as she crashed into some terrible obstruction. As she plunged down again, a fraction of a second later, there was a second bang, a sickening smash, this time from under the hull, as *Pionier* was hurled bodily to starboard.

The men struggled to keep their balance; there was not much light around. The binnacle light was on, there was light filtering from the cabin, a token glimmer from the sky, the stern light. Gordon looked aft, as *Pionier* fought gamely to recover from the cruel shock. In the glow of the stern light he saw the huge tail fin of a blue whale, 2.5m across and forked, strong, majestic and now disappearing into the deep.

Tony had seen it too, just. Halfway into the cockpit, he had turned at the two crashes, and though he was low in the boat, he could see the end of the tail over the dodger and the life-buoys, as it dipped slowly out of sight.

The boat lurched crazily as dazed wits gathered. Gordon still held the wheel, Tony was standing in the hatchway. Down below, Willi in the fo'c's'le had taken the full force of the first blow; Jennifer, the wife of the skipper, the second. Willi thought the boat had hit rough weather and wondered where it came from. Jennifer had felt the impact of the second blow under her head. She was thrown up and half out of her bunk, and she let her feet fall to the deck to steady herself.

It was then she felt the water. Creeping up through the cabin planks, from down somewhere by the keel, she could feel it lapping her ankles as the boat heeled over under full sail. She screamed her discovery up to Gordon on deck. Gordon and Jennifer eased up the cabin planks to see if they could find the leak. But it was coming in too fast. Gordon told Peter Flockemann to get on to the radio.

Peter tuned the transmitter to 2182 kHz, the distress frequency.

It was supposed to be left free for emergencies like this one, and all ships were supposed to keep a watch on it. But there was the usual cacophony of messages broadcast in abuse of the international agreement. Peter could hear a conversation going on, by the sound of it not far away. He switched on the transmitter and began broadcasting the MAYDAY. *Pionier* was sinking, he called. He gave the position they had calculated most recently, 24°30'S, 07°06'W. There was no response.

The water was swirling knee deep in the saloon by this time. Gordon had read somewhere of a way of saving a holed ship with sails, by draping them over the side and allowing suction to pull them into the hole and seal it off. He outlined the plan to Tony and Willi, and they set about the job. There were two spinnakers in the cockpit, and they took one from its bag and draped it over the port side. The boat had lost way by now.

But still the water poured in. Now it was waist deep in the cabin. Gordon was out in the cockpit, taking the liferaft from its cover. He pulled the inflation trigger, it opened with a loud hiss, and he put the raft over the side. He shouted down to Jennifer to cut free the plastic jerry cans of water lashed to the legs of the saloon table below, the extra water *Pionier* was obliged to carry in addition to the water in her tanks, to comply with the race rules. She tossed four of the jerry cans to Willi up in the cockpit.

Jennifer's next thought was of food. She scrambled to collect all she could find in the provision lockers and pass it to Willi on deck, who by this time had the liferaft alongside. Jennifer took over the radio, and had time to shout out two more MAYDAY signals before the radio went silent as the flooded batteries died.

Willi had remembered to grab flares before going up on deck. He took a full box of them, ordinary hand-held flares, unfortunately, rather than the parachute flares he had been looking for. And he grabbed an heirloom from the days when he had sailed his first yacht, *Falcon*, years before. His one and only smoke flare.

Tony's thought was of clothing. He had read an article on liferaft survival which had advocated clothing as protection both from heat and cold, and it was this thought that drove him to the nearest clothes locker. He grabbed armfuls of whatever came to hand. Sodden jerseys and trousers, anything, he passed them to Willi in the cockpit. Peter, equally practical, found a sleeping bag and a bottle of whisky.

Gordon ordered everyone on deck. The boat was sinking fast. Willi was in the liferaft, holding it to the gunnel of the yacht in the heavy swell, still wearing nothing but his underpants. Gordon told Jennifer to climb in with him, after her Tony, after him Peter. Gordon suddenly remembered their passports. He knew they were in a wallet down below. He went down, the cabin almost full of water, and dived down to the locker where they were kept. He found them, surfaced, and found, too, his precious sextant and navigation books floating by. He took them in his arms and climbed into the liferaft – able to step straight from the gunnel into the shelter, so low was the yacht.

The liferaft stood off some way, for the yacht was rolling over. Slowly she dipped at the bows, further under water as the pulpit disappeared, and as she heeled over, as if in final, tragic salute, a short somewhere on the electric panel produced the last cruel joke. All *Pionier*'s lights flashed on, her masthead lights, the navigation lights, the lights on her spreader, and over she rolled, sinking under the waves as, like a whale herself, she showed her underside, deep fin keel with rudder still intact on the skeg – and the long, jagged rip in her hull which told *Pionier*'s crew what they needed to know: that they could never have saved their ship. The yacht disappeared, and they were alone.

There they sat, in the dark. They had a torch, but to conserve its batteries they used it only sparingly. They had brought one packet of cigarettes, and a box of matches. But the matches were soaked in seawater and would have to be dried out. Some tried to sleep, ignoring the cramp of legs intertwined uncomfortably with four other pairs. Every so often came an unnerving hiss of escaping air from the raft.

At dawn with light to see what they were doing, they began to organise their raft. The sail they had brought as a sea anchor was already trailing overboard. Gordon decided the three white plastic jerry cans should be trailed as well, once he had made sure their plastic caps would not let in seawater. Fresh water being lighter than salt, they would float. So the jerry cans were tied together with a rope, and gently let into the water.

Conversation turned to food, and the five investigated the

contents of the sailbag. Tins galore, boxes of dehydrated vegetables, broken eggs in their boxes, muesli breakfast cereal, the sodden packets spilling their contents; even a hunk of Christmas cake wrapped in tinfoil and a jar of honey. Jennifer set about preparing something. Her eye fell on Gordon's sextant box, the sextant was ejected, and the box became a serviceable pot. She mixed the muesli cereal and some broken eggs into a tasty paste, with Christmas cake to follow. Nobody noticed the tang of salt water.

Breakfast over, they opened the liferaft's emergency survival pack. First, they found a hand pump for the raft, with instructions which, among other things, explained the disturbing hisses of air they had heard in the night. These had come as air was let out of the raft to counteract its heavy load. There were sponges, to help in drying out the raft, which was ankle deep in water from the night before. There were six 3-pint tins of water, and a can-opener, with a measuring cup. Instructions with the water advised regular rationing. No random drinking, but instead a cupful early in the morning, one at noon, and a third at night. Though they had plenty of water in the jerry cans, Gordon decided they would follow the directions. Glucose sweets, an emergency medical kit and a funnel to catch rainwater completed the provisions.

There was not much conversation. Gordon had told them at the outset they were in quite a spot. They were way off the normal shipping lanes, and it would be a miracle if their MAYDAY signal had been picked up. The rest of the fleet would not miss them as a number of yachts had not been heard of in days, in most cases because of the failure of their generator plants. So it might be weeks before anyone thought of mounting a search for them. On the other hand, they had plenty of water, the means of catching more, and clothing and covering enough to shelter them. They knew that even without food they could survive for weeks on the water alone.

What was suggested openly was that it would not be long before a few legs were amputated and thrown overboard. All were in agonies of cramp, unable to move their legs without dislodging the whole arrangement of the raft. But nobody complained.

Noon arrived, and it was getting hot. Somebody had tossed a sodden sheet into the raft, Jennifer's tropical sleeping bag – an ordinary sheet sewn double along three-quarters of its length. They had a couple of large sombrero hats with them too. One way of keeping the watchkeeper cool during his 20-minute agony was to soak the sheet in seawater and drape it over his back and neck, while he wore one of the hats. Noon was the time for more water rations, and each received his measure from the cup. Nobody wanted food.

So the watches went on through the afternoon, 20 minutes turn and turn about, the raft bobbing to the top of the swell and giving a view for three miles around, and then dropping back into a hollow. The watchkeeper wearing his sheet and his hat, the other four cowering in the shelter, without speaking. On the raft's canopy, all the clothing there was room for, drying in the sunshine. And the precious matches, being dried for the pleasure of the packet of cigarettes still to be smoked.

Tony was sitting outside again, passing in to the others the clothes that had been drying in the sun. Then someone asked for the matches. Tony did not smoke, but he looked for the matches and found they had disappeared. It looked as if they had gone over the side. With disgust the others resigned themselves to survival without cigarettes, and the apparently useless packet was thrown overboard. Two minutes later the matches turned up – among the dried clothes in the liferaft.

Scanning the horizon for a sail, the shapes of clouds had played cruel tricks with the hopes of the watchkeepers, so much so that they had taken to looking many times before daring to believe their eyes. And each time it had turned out there was nothing there. But when Tony noticed a movement on the horizon, as the liferaft rose to the top of a swell, he felt a curious burst of excitement. It was a new shape, to the north-west. But it was far distant, and he knew he could be wrong. He looked to the south, to the east, looking for a sail, anywhere but to the north-west. But he had to look again. This time he was sure there was something there. What looked to him like goalposts, the derricks of a big bulk carrier, or tanker, perhaps. But he wanted to be sure.

He carried on watching as the liferaft rode the swells, watching as the ship came closer. He could see his 'goalposts' clearer now, and he was sure it was a ship. But still he said nothing. He watched as the ship emerged clearer from the mist on the horizon, and looked again at the approaching rain squall, getting dangerously close. He could see the ship's bows and her bridge. His heart was beating fit to burst, but he stayed quiet, until he was confident there was hope of rescue, and his eyes were not betraying him. He called Gordon.

'I think there might be something over there,' he said, leaning towards the opening in the canopy.

The atmosphere was electric as Gordon slowly crawled across the craft, its bottom heaving, and knelt in the opening to see what Tony had spotted. He was not over-optimistic. Clearly there was a ship, but he estimated she would pass three miles away. Tony had been watching it for some minutes now. He told Gordon he felt she had changed course. Gordon did not allow his hopes to rise too high.

The three left inside the shelter were hanging on to every muttered word that passed between the two men. The ship was five miles away.

Gordon thought quickly. How could he attract the ship's attention to the tiny ball of orange adrift between swells? He was revising his ideas of how far away the ship would pass. As she came closer, he thought it might be something like two miles. But she was still far away.

There was suddenly pandemonium on board. The box of white flares Willi had saved was useless in daylight, and this was a blow. The only hope rested with the old orange smoke flare. Gordon pulled its triggering mechanism and flung it through the air. It landed nine metres away and worked, scattering bright orange smoke over a wide area of ocean. But the wind scattering the smoke kept it only half a metre or so above the sea's surface, and for all but a fraction of the time it was as invisible to the ship as the raft itself. If they could not see the ship, how could it see the liferaft?

But the ship kept coming, and Gordon was beginning to agree it might come close after all. Peter and Tony grabbed two bright orange jackets which had been salvaged with the clothes, Jenny's and Willi's, part of the crew's uniform. They stuck them on the two short paddles that had come as part of the liferaft kit, and began waving them furiously through the opening of the shelter, waving till their arms refused to work more and dropped in exhaustion. And it was then the ship responded with three long blasts of her whistle.

Jennifer burst into tears and flung herself at the necks of each man in turn, her husband first and then Willi, Peter and Tony, and on each face there was a smile as big as it could take. They were cheering, everyone was talking at once. Everyone realised they had been rescued without going through any ordeal at all, only 16 hours in the water when they had feared they might be there for ever.

Up came the ship, more than 13,000 tonnes of her, rusted and wave-worn. A ship they would not have spared a second glance if they had seen her in harbour. But now she was the most beautiful ship they had ever seen. A bulk grain carrier, and on her bow they could read her name: *Potomac*. She manoeuvred to within 100m as they wriggled eagerly in what seemed an eternity, waiting for their deliverance. On deck they could see the crew making ready. A pilot's ladder was lowered over the side, and deckhands were standing ready with a rope. Others were swinging a lifeboat overboard, still on its davits. On the bridge stood several officers, one of them with a loud-hailer. He tried to shout down instructions to them, but his words were carried away on the wind.

The *Potomac* came up close. A line was thrown across, but missed the raft. As it was thrown, a rain squall, which had been threatening all afternoon, arrived. Driving rain forced them back under the canopy, even finding its way through the air vents. The sky grew dark, the sea green and the swells white-capped. The *Potomac* lost way and had to start her engines. Their wash swept the tiny liferaft astern to her, and away into the gloom. The *Potomac* disappeared, ahead, over the swells half a mile away.

'They'll lose us,' cried Jennifer. The smiles disappeared as new anxious thoughts crowded in. The squall was dangerous. It was as if the sea had reacted in fury as it saw its victims all but snatched from its clutches, and was taking its revenge on them. But they could see the *Potomac* circling round, and she came up from behind, this time further away. They watched as the lifeboat on its davits was lowered into the water, with its crew of seven aboard. And they watched as it crossed the swells separating them from the ship.

The sea was rough and it was a dangerous manoeuvre as the lifeboat chugged in to relieve the excited survivors. But soon it was alongside and brawny arms helped first Jennifer, then each of the men into the lifeboat. Peter carried the bottle of whisky with him, still all but full as they had consumed only a part of it on the raft. The other things were left on the raft, which was towed to the ship behind the lifeboat. And the survivors met their rescuers.

They were Americans. The *Potomac* was from Portland, Oregon, on America's west coast, and was on her way to Cape Town. In command of the lifeboat was the man they had to thank for their deliverance, Third Officer Roy Newkirk. He had been on watch on the bridge, soon to be relieved, when he saw the tiny orange dot in the distance, three miles off the port bow. He thought it might be a buoy drifting. But he did not want to take chances, and told the *Potomac*'s master about it. Vernon Hansen, from America's Deep South, had been asleep in his cabin, but climbed to the bridge immediately. Through binoculars it was obvious the orange dot was a liferaft, and Hansen ordered a change of course. But there was no sign of life aboard. Just then Hansen spotted the trail of orange smoke from Gordon's flare. It drifted over a wide expanse of water. 'There's life all right,' he told Newkirk.

He ordered a lifeboat to be prepared and Newkirk himself asked to be put in charge of it. He wanted to find out what people were doing out in the middle of nowhere where nobody ought to be, he explained.

The lifeboat pulled alongside the ship, heaving in the swell, and the crew helped the survivors grab the scramble net and clamber up the deck, a vertical climb of 24m. Jennifer and Gordon went first, Jennifer a little worried about the bikini bottom she was wearing as its elastic had broken. She had tied a piece of string to it taken round her neck as a kind of suspender. Willi went next, hampered by his injured leg and clambering up with the strength of his arms. Peter and Tony brought up the rear, and the lifeboat was winched back on deck.

■ LESSONS LEARNED

The international distress frequency 2182kHz is supposed to be left free for emergencies and for all ships to keep a watch, but as the crew of *Pionier* discovered there is often a cacophony of messages broadcast in abuse of the rules.

Gordon had read of the method of saving a holed ship by draping sails over the side and allowing suction to pull them into the hole and seal it off. Theory is all very well, but you need almost perfect conditions to put it into practice.

Pionier was obliged to carry extra water in addition to the water in her tanks, in order to comply with the race rules. But this is a good idea in all circumstances, in case the tanks become contaminated, or spring a leak.

The next problem was that the parachute flares could not be located. Willi managed to grab a full box of hand-held white flares. But, ironically, it was 'an heirloom from the days when he had sailed his first yacht, Falcon, years before' that proved to be the crew's salvation . . . His one and only orange smoke flare.

Tony's thought was of clothing. He had read an article on liferaft survival which pointed out that though fresh water was a high priority in survival at sea, almost as high was shelter. It had advocated clothing as protection both from heat and cold. Tony grabbed armfuls of sodden jerseys and trousers, anything. Something that Willi, wearing nothing but his underpants, would be grateful for later.

When a ship was sighted in daylight, all hopes rested with the orange smoke flare. It was the trail of orange smoke that prompted the rescue ship's skipper to remark: 'There's life all right.'

FAILURE of GEAR or RIGGING

THE NIGHT OUR KEEL FELL OFF

Yacht	*Hooligan V* (Max Fun 35)
Skipper	Ed Broadway
Crew	Jamie Butcher, John Charnock, Graham Elliott, Will Robinson
Bound from	Plymouth to Southampton
Date of loss	4 February 2007
Position	seven miles off Start Point

Graham Elliott (48), one of the crew aboard the Max Fun 35 Hooligan V, *describes the night when she lost her keel, capsized and one of her crew died.*

I SHOULD HAVE BEEN in my sleeping bag, safe and warm below deck, not clinging to the hull of an upturned yacht in the darkness of a winter night. *Hooligan V* had sailed from Plymouth on Saturday 3 February at about 2300. The five of us onboard were returning her to Southampton after a winter refit. At midnight we began watches and I led the first.

Conditions were good and we enjoyed some wonderful sailing. The recent bonding of the deck and hull joint seemed to make the yacht feel 'stiffer' and more powerful. The owner, Ed Broadway, 61 – a vastly experienced yachtsman and offshore racer – helmed for the first hour of my watch and then went below. Nothing untoward occurred, although we reefed the main twice as the wind increased to 25 knots. The weather forecast was for an easterly Force 5–6.

At 0300, after a brief handover discussion, John Charnock took the helm and the watch from me. We could clearly see Start Point lighthouse abeam to port about seven miles off. Visibility was good; a full moon with broken cloud. We were on port tack, heading further offshore, meaning no navigational issues were likely.

Of the five aboard, all were experienced yachtsmen, although the two youngest – Jamie Butcher, 27, and Will Robinson, 18 – were new to *Hooligan V*. I went below, keen to get some rest but John soon called me back. We needed another reef in the mainsail. Jamie and Will, in the cockpit with John, were unfamiliar with the boat and it was easier for me to do it.

I was surprised another reef was needed as helming had up until then been fine. I asked Jamie and Will, who aspired to join our racing team, to furl away some more jib, as I began preparing for the third reef. This would mean re-using the first reefing line, a practice common to many yachts. I suggested to John he reduce the heel by pinching a little. We weren't racing, after all. I was leaning on the boom so easing the mainsheet was delayed for a few moments.

Without warning, the heel increased as though the yacht was broaching . . . 70, 80 and then 90° of heel. John shouted, 'She'll come back!' I, too, expected the mast to rise again, but the roll continued and, after a momentary pause, the sails disappeared below the waves.

At about 110° of heel I stepped off to starboard into the shockingly cold water. I was not wearing a lifejacket but had full offshore gear on, including boots. I looked up to see the port side of *Hooligan V* come down close to me as the hull overturned. Will surfaced beside me.

There was nothing to hold on to along the side of the upturned hull. It was so cold I decided against kicking off my boots. I glanced up and noticed that the keel was missing. Will and I swam towards the stern where we met John. We discussed the fact that two were missing and agreed that they must both be inside the yacht. We knew skipper-owner Ed had been asleep below, but Jamie had been in the cockpit.

At that stage I found it very difficult to swim. Waves broke over our heads and I began to swallow seawater. I remember thinking that this did not look good. I considered our options. They were: climb onto the upturned hull, or retrieve and inflate the liferaft, which was tied to the cockpit floor at the transom. The motion of the hull and lack of anything to hold on to meant that climbing was impossible.

Before long, two yellow plastic flare pack boxes appeared. Someone inside the yacht must have sent them out as they were usually kept below in a locker. Will swam after one and managed to bring it back to the yacht. Five minutes later Ed surfaced, gasping for air.

Was Jamie inside, we asked? 'No', was the reply. Ed had not seen him. Will opened a box and took out three red parachute flares before the box filled with water and sank. John, wearing a lifejacket, fired two of them and Will fired the third.

John, as a former Army Officer, had fired flares before but he still found himself unfamiliar with them. The first one went not much higher than horizontally, although he could be forgiven as his head was under water at the time.

I did assume that the two lifebuoys would float free of the upturned yacht but they didn't. We could see the attached lights flashing under water. Nothing buoyant floated free.

I began cutting the lines around the liferaft with the knife I had in my pocket. It was difficult, as the stern was rising and falling due to the wave motion and my fingers quickly became numb with cold. I learned later that the seawater temperature was 10°C. The cold began to tell. Initially work was urgent, if not frantic, but I then began to feel more relaxed about it and then, frankly, I didn't care very much what happened. I began to feel lightheaded and lost any sense of urgency. I didn't know it then but I was experiencing the first stages of hypothermia.

I cut a few lines, including the painter, and just after I dropped the knife for the second time, without recovering it, the liferaft came away in my hands. I turned the valise over a few times until I found the inflation pull cord. I pulled some line free and attempted to tie it to the backstay, which was under water. I gave the valise to Will and told him to swim away until it inflated. After hearing the pop and hiss, what a wonderful sight I saw.

Will pulled himself into the inflated raft and we both pulled at the painter. The raft slowly moved towards the stern of the upturned yacht. Having seen the raft inflate, John began to swim towards it, with Ed hanging onto his shoulders.

John had not realised that it was now attached to the yacht and missed it by some margin. As the raft got closer to the yacht I made a grab for it and Will helped pull me in. John then called for assistance. I expected to find a throwing line in the liferaft, but if there was one I couldn't see it. The only help I could give, as the liferaft blew downwind, was to point out to John that he was near the liferaft's drogue (sea anchor). I suggested he grab it and pull the two of them towards us. This helped and eventually we pulled them into the raft.

There was plenty of water inside and it took quite a while to bail it out. We also fired all the flares we found inside. Eventually, ships came closer. We were in the water for more than half an hour. Much longer and we would have started to lose people. Ed, with little clothing on, was almost unconscious by the time we managed to get him into the liferaft and has no recollection of some of these events. Whilst in the liferaft, Will inflated his lifejacket. We did not realise he had one on and it did not occur to him to inflate it earlier. It shows how rational thought is difficult in these circumstances. Soon we could see a couple of ships approaching us, illuminating us with searchlights. Neither of them seemed to want to take the lead in recovering us. I presume they expected a lifeboat to pick us up.

The liferaft painter parted and eventually the wind blew the raft down onto RMS *LAAR*, a German ship with Russian crew. It must have been about 0500 by then. At the top of a wave we scrambled aboard – fortunately the freeboard was only a metre or so – and we were grateful for the consideration shown by the crew. The Russians offered Ed a hot shower. Fortunately, we knew better and warmed him slowly in a bed until a medic arrived from one of the now numerous vessels around us.

Jamie's body was later recovered with his lifejacket inflated. It is my belief that he was unable to leave the upturned cockpit, and there were no air pockets. The four of us found it hard to come to terms with this tragic news. I knew Jamie for less than a day before he was drowned, but having read what other people have said about him I am sure that he would wish all sailors to share any lessons learned.

Hooligan V was a well-found, well-run and successful racing yacht. The skipper had a policy that all racing crew pass the ISAF Offshore Racing course and the Sea Survival course. I should have been wearing a lifejacket myself that morning and I intend to be more conscientious in future. However, I intend to change to one that has to be manually inflated.

There were many things that were crucial to our survival, our proximity to ships and the position of the liferaft being at the top of the list. Many people keep rafts below decks or in a locker, and until now I have kept the liferaft on my own yacht in a locker, mainly because of its weight. In the future it will be more accessible. I also have a buoyant grab bag for my flares, which will not be kept in a locker.

Keel loss is extremely rare so we need to keep this in context, but we also thought it would never happen to us.

FIN AND BULB KEEL FAILURES

There have been various keel failures with traditional stub-and-bolts keels, such as Simon le Bon's *Drum* during the 1985 Fastnet and *Martela* in the 1989–90 Whitbread, but proportionately these keels suffer far fewer failures than more modern racing yachts with fin and bulb and canting keels, which place huge stresses on the fin at the pivot point.

Tony Bullimore's carbon fin on *Exide Challenger* snapped off at the hull in the Southern Ocean during the 1996–97 Vendée Globe Round the World Race. The entire fin and bulb dropped out of Mike Golding's *Ecover* 51 miles from the end of the 2004–05 race and also Nick Moloney's *Skandia*. Dame Ellen's former *Kingfisher* suffered a similar fate in the South Atlantic during the same race.

Max Fun yachts are built in Holland. And they're fast. In the right conditions, 20 knots is easily achievable. This is partly because they are so light. The Max Fun 35 weighs just 3,000kg and nearly half of that lies in the bulb at the base of the fin, 2.15m below the surface. The main and 100 per cent jib total 72.2m^2 and the spinnaker, at 145m^2, doubles that.

Hooligan V's letterbox keel failure was under investigation by the MAIB as this book went to press.

■ **LESSONS LEARNED**

Don't stow your liferaft inside a locker as it won't be accessible in a capsize.

Learn how to activate your flares in the dark. Live firing exercises are best. Check with the RYA for a sailing school course.

Which lifejacket is best for you? If you have inexperienced crew make sure they know the implications of wearing an automatic one. Statistically you are more likely to be hit on the head by the boom than lose your keel, so automatic may be best.

If you wear a harness, practise unclipping it in the dark. Will wore one with double clips at one end, but had it on the wrong way round. He had to undo both clips from his lifejacket before he was free.

Make sure your grab bag/flare pack floats and will not sink if filled with water.

Secure a long line so it doesn't float away.

Go on a sea survival course. It might save your life one day.

ten

WHY WE HAD TO SINK OUR YACHT

Yacht	*F2* (Hunter Legend Passage 450)
Skipper	Peter Davis
Crew	Zara Davis
Bound from	from Las Palmas, Canaries, to St Lucia, Caribbean
Date of loss	December 2002
Position	1,200 miles west of Canaries

Peter Davis and his wife Zara set off from Las Palmas in the Canaries with the 2002 Atlantic Rally for Cruisers fleet to realise a dream by sailing to the Caribbean island of St Lucia. Seven days later, in the middle of the ocean, they were forced to deliberately sink their boat.

WHEN WE TOLD FRIENDS we were buying a yacht to sail around the world, they knew we would take it in our stride. Zara was the British women's windsurfing champion 2000 and had done a little offshore sailing with her father as a young girl. She had caught the sailing bug and had always said that one day we were going to cross the Atlantic. Her decision was reinforced by the death of her mother at 54 and, soon after, her father at 62. They had intended to retire and live on a boat in the Med, and we knew then that we had to follow our dreams while we were young.

We started looking for a bluewater cruiser and went to the Southampton Boat Show with a shortlist of new and second-hand boats, including Oysters, Hallberg-Rassys and Moodys. On the

Internet, we finally found *F2*, a Hunter Legend Passage 450, and fell in love with her. She was only 18 months old and had been fitted out to a high standard, with watermaker, generator and even a washing machine. Being 13.49m (44ft) long, she fitted the bill of a comfortable long-distance cruiser, set up for short-handed sailing. She cost £158,000 and we spent a further £30,000 on equipment.

We signed up for every course available and began our steep learning curve. We took our RYA Competent Crew and Day Skipper exams, plus courses in sea survival, VHF and SSB radio, radar, first-aid and a Ship Captain's medical course. Zara passed her Yachtmaster theory, but hadn't sailed enough miles to be eligible for the practical exam.

Our initial plan was to leave in 2003 with the Atlantic Rally for Cruisers (ARC), but when I took redundancy from my job and Zara found someone to manage her osteopath surgery, there was no reason not to cast off in 2002. So, in August 2001, we sailed from Plymouth, allowing three months to get to the Canaries for the start of the ARC in Las Palmas. The only crew aboard was Ellie, our German shepherd dog.

During our shakedown cruise we visited some lovely places, our first landfall being La Coruña in northern Spain, three and a half days across the Bay of Biscay from Falmouth. From there we visited a variety of ports, including Bayona, Cascais and Lagos. Our longest passage (476 miles) was from Lagos to Porto Santo, Madeira.

Arriving in Gran Canaria in October we made our final preparations for the Atlantic crossing. The start, on the third Sunday in November, was spectacular. An armada of 217 boats set off on the 2,700-mile crossing to St Lucia in the West Indies. Light winds of 6 to 8 knots gave us a gentle ocean baptism – until we got to the bottom of the island and the wind turned southwesterly, 30 to 40 knots. We reefed down and *F2* coped well. The conditions forced about 40 yachts to turn back but, although tired, we were pleased to sail on.

Two days later the wind eased and veered northeasterly. *F2* was taking the big seas in her stride. Every day we transmitted our position so friends and relatives could follow our progress on the ARC website. Without pushing ourselves or the boat we were pleased with our 49th position.

We were 1,185 miles from Gran Canaria, taking it easy, doing about 6 knots and well reefed in the big seas. Our caution was underlined by the tragic news of fellow ARC sailor David Hitchcock, who had lost his brother Philip overboard their yacht, *Toutazimut*, and been unable to recover him. 'There but for the grace of God go us,' we thought.

Then, on day seven, disaster struck. With no warning, we lost steerage way and the helm went slack. There was no bang or collision impact to suggest the rudder had been damaged. The boat simply went through 180° and started going round in circles. We shipped the emergency tiller, but it had no effect. I donned a snorkelling mask and harness and, from the sugar-scoop stern, dipped my head in the water to see what had happened. My eyes must have been on stalks. Where once our rudder had been, there were now just a few strands of glass fibre.

After putting out a PAN PAN call on the VHF and SSB, we contacted Falmouth Coastguard and the ARC organisers on our satellite phone. We then set about making a jury rudder. For instructions, I referred to an offshore cruising guide and lashed a floorboard to a spinnaker pole. It was no mean feat while lying beam on to 4m (13ft) seas. The trouble was that the angle between the pivot point on the rail, where we lashed the pole, and the edge of the sugar scoop, was too shallow. The rudder blade was out of the water in the swell and even when it was immersed it failed to steer the boat. With her narrow, fin bulb keel, *F2* simply went round in circles.

With nightfall coming we feared a knockdown or a rollover. We couldn't get her head to wind so we tried streaming a drogue off the stern, but despite using all our lines (more than 400m [1,312ft]), plus three buckets and our No 2 genoa, *F2* still lay beam on to the swell. Putting up our storm jib, however, stopped us rolling and gave us some forward motion.

Still fearing a knockdown, we went below and battened down all the hatches, spending a scary and uncomfortable night being battered by the ocean swell. Before dawn, two ARC yachts, *Muskrat* and *Little Women*, arrived and stood by until daybreak. Then two more yachts arrived – *Aida* and *Sarema*.

Peter Thomson, skipper of *Muskrat* and a former SAR helicopter pilot, took us in tow heading for a rendezvous with *Tenacious*, the

Jubilee Sailing Trust's Tall Ship and the biggest boat in the ARC. She had full workshop facilities on board.

Even under tow and with a drogue line over the stern, *F2* veered through 90°. The towline snapped several times and eventually Peter suggested we used a rope round the mast leading to a chain through the bow roller. We padded the chain with towels and this worked for some time until the bow roller was so damaged that we had to stop for fear of breaking the forestay.

Fortunately, *Tenacious* came over the horizon and the captain, John Fisher, took charge. His engineer, Peter Stonehouse, and 'chippy', Paul Brent, transferred to *F2* in a RIB. They decided the only option was to remove *F2*'s rudder stock and take it back to *Tenacious*'s workshop. They were optimistic that they could come up with an effective repair.

It was too dangerous for anyone to stay on board *F2*, so we were invited to return on the RIB to spend the night on *Tenacious*. Ellie came, too. *F2* was left to drift through the night with a parachute anchor and drogue out to slow her down. Her navigation lights were also left on.

The boys in the workshop toiled away all night and by 1700 next day had fabricated a makeshift rudder from a scaffolding pole, some box steel and one-inch plywood. Using a rope as a 'mouse', the new rudder stock was floated in. It was too dangerous for us to go back to *F2*, so we spent another night aboard *Tenacious*. This meant a second tough night for Peter and *Muskrat*'s crew, who were hove-to in case they were needed.

By now we had contacted our insurance company, James Steel, of Rayleigh in Essex, who was sympathetic to our plight. The company's engineer, Barry Goldsmith, liaised with *Tenacious* over payment for their efforts and approved the jury rudder being fitted.

At first light the next day we reboarded *F2* with renewed hope that we could sail her to the Caribbean. For the next four days we sailed in convoy with *Muskrat*. Finally, happy we were making headway, albeit very slowly, we no longer felt we could hold *Muskrat* up and released them from sailing in company with us. As long as we kept the speed down, *F2* was all right. The jury rudder was a little erratic, probably due to being less streamlined than the original, but running under twin headsails allowed us to steer the straightest course and put less stress on the rudder. It was dusk on the fourth day and the swell had increased when the steering suddenly went slack. A feeling of dread overtook us. Checking underneath the boat, I discovered that jury rudder number two had broken off.

We had been running a safety radio net and knew which boats were behind us and how far away they were. We put out a PAN PAN call and *Muskrat*, 52 miles ahead, immediately altered course to beat back to us. We spent another uncomfortable night rolling beam on to the swell.

By first light, three ARC yachts – *Muskrat*, *Lorrigray II* and *Toutazimut* – were circling us. It was very reassuring. We were making water but the bilge pump was coping. With 1,400 miles to go and drifting south-west at just 1.5 knots, Venezuela was our most likely landfall. However, it was a dangerous coastline for which we had no charts, even if we could get some steerage way. By now we'd tried towing and fitted two jury rudders, both of which had failed. Weather conditions concerned us, too. Who knew what would happen in a week's time, let alone six weeks?

Following a long discussion with Peter on *Muskrat* we decided to abandon ship. We had rescue boats all around us but we couldn't ask them to stand by any longer. They had already acted beyond the call of duty. Our lives were more important than our yacht so, reluctantly, we took the heartbreaking decision to abandon her, after checking with our insurers.

To prevent *F2* being a danger to shipping, we had to sink her. *Muskrat*'s crew ferried Zara and Ellie across to *Lorrigray II* in their RIB, leaving me to cut the engine cooling water inlet pipe, plus the generator and watermaker pipes. I also removed the log transducer and water gushed in. Windows and hatches were left open to avoid airlocks keeping the boat afloat. Now it was my turn to be ferried across to *Lorrigray*. As I looked back, *F2* was already low in the water. We gave her position to Falmouth Coastguard and the ARC office.

Our passage to St Lucia was completed aboard *Lorrigray II*, which crossed the finish line with *Muskrat*, and we received an amazing welcome from our fellow ARC participants. *Muskrat* later won the coveted Spirit of the ARC award.

INSURANCE CLAIMS AND SALVAGE

Peter and Zara Davis contacted their insurance company by satellite phone to see if scuttling their boat would prejudice their claim. Leading marine insurer Chris Knox-Johnston considers that onus on scuttling a boat 'remains with the owner'. It is not for the insurer to order an owner to scuttle a boat – although he can recommend it. However, if *F2* had been left to drift as a derelict and caused damage to another vessel it would then have been the job of that vessel's insurers to prove that Peter and Zara were legally negligent.

'Peter did the right thing in contacting his insurer because had he not done so he might have been faced with the task of proving it was an "insured peril",' Knox-Johnston said. 'I do not believe this case has set a precedent. It is all about marine law and that law is the same for the *QE2* as it is for this yacht.' Peter and Zara's insurance company paid up in full after the incident. Rules of salvage also apply in this case: anyone, other than the owners, who had managed to get *F2* across the Atlantic could have claimed salvage.

THREE WAYS OF RIGGING JURY RUDDERS

1 Steering oar: most people's first choice, but it can be difficult to rig efficiently and is hard to use. A tiller/rudder works at a mechanical advantage of about 6:1. A steering oar is at a disadvantage of 1:3, which means that 18 times more force may be needed to move the oar than the tiller. The 'oar' can be made up of a spinnaker pole or the boom, with a flat panel (locker door or floorboard) lashed to its end. The 'blade' must be weighted (with something such as chain) to sink the oar and lashed firmly to a strong upright (pushpit leg or backstay) to stop the natural tendency of the blade to twist to the horizontal. In use, it may be easier to control its vertical angle with the topping lift and to 'steer' with lines led to the sheet winches. Good chafe protection, such as carpet, is vital.

2 Trailing pole: easier to set up than the steering oar, this method is effective for boats that are easily steered. The spinnaker pole or boom is weighted at one end and trailed astern with a topping lift support. The inboard end is clipped to the backstay and steering bridles are led forward to sheet winches. A pole across the transom with blocks can improve the lead.

3 Vertical jury rudder: this jury rudder is more elaborate than the previous two and requires more materials to set it up. However, for a longer-term solution it is probably the most effective. It requires a stout tube (plastic drainpipe or in extreme conditions a section cut from the boom/spinnaker pole) to be lashed vertically to the transom or hull side and braced fore and aft and athwartships. Inside this is inserted the jury rudder, a pole forming the 'stock' with a blade (floorboard, etc) lashed to the bottom and a tiller on the top.

JURY RUDDER TOO BIG

Luhrs Marine are the builders of the American Hunter Legend boats and of *F2*. The managing director of their UK base, Stephen Cutsforth, said Luhrs Marine talked to Peter and Zara Davis during their ordeal and advised them on how to make a jury rudder. However, the shipwrights on board the Tall Ship *Tenacious* made the blade bigger than was necessary. 'Our engineer said it would break and I'm afraid it did', said Cutsforth. He said that the company had been 'extremely happy' with the original rudder design. *F2* had been extensively used before Peter and Zara Davis bought her and if a previous owner had unwittingly hit an object it could have fractured the rudder post, leaving it weakened.

'She is a well-balanced boat – you can take your hands off the wheel and she will steer. With the right sail plan and the correct distribution of weight on board she could have been brought back, although getting it right is a little tougher on a boat with a centre cockpit.'

■ LESSONS LEARNED

An Atlantic crossing should not be taken lightly. It's not all tradewinds and sunny days, even though some sailors may think that joining the ARC is like 'crossing the ocean by numbers'. It's a big ocean and a dangerous place, as demonstrated by the death of crewman Philip Hitchcock lost overboard in this race, the first ARC death in its 17-year history.

For their next cruising yacht Peter and Zara will avoid narrow fin keels with a bulb. The boat's rolling motion was very uncomfortable and water was getting through the aft hatches until they sealed them with tape.

Next time they would question the weight aft of dinghy davits, outboard engine (on bracket), plus satellite aerial and other equipment which may have accentuated the rolling motion.

Peter and Zara are now looking for a boat with a longer keel and a skeg-hung rudder. A sugar-scoop stern is far from ideal when it comes to rigging a jury rudder.

There is not much they could have done differently. Many experienced sailors agree that they made the right decision to abandon ship while they had the chance of being rescued.

FOOTNOTE

This was the first case of a yacht being deliberately sunk on the ARC after rudder failure. The second incident involved a Sun Odyssey 43, which was sunk in the 2006 ARC. The story, 'Pulling the Plug', appears on page 77.

eleven

PULLING THE PLUG

Yacht	*Zouk* (Sun Odyssey 43)
Skipper	Caroline Nicol
Crew	French, mixed crew of six
Bound from	the Canaries
Date of loss	December 2006
Position	1,000 miles east of Martinique

Caroline Nicol, a young French skipper, had to sink her yacht when a mid-Atlantic tow from the Tall Ship Tenacious *proved impossible.*

CRACK! THE SOUND WASN'T LOUD, but it shattered the hopes of an easy Atlantic crossing. The crew of *Zouk*, a Sun Odyssey 43, looked astern in dismay to see their rudder floating away.

Caroline was now faced with the enormity of the situation. The 31-year-old skipper and her six crew had to find a way to steer the yacht the remaining 1,000 miles to landfall in Martinique, in the French West Indies. She consulted the boat's owners, the Glenans Sailing School in France, and set about jury-rigging a rudder. Caroline and her crew tried different systems but after five days of drilling, lashing, screwing and bolting she gave up. The four-metre waves and 25-knot winds were simply too powerful and they couldn't control the boat. On Friday 7 December, with food and water running low, Caroline put out a distress call.

The Maritime Rescue Co-ordination Centre (MRCC) in Martinique picked up the call and asked for help from boats in the area. *Tenacious*, the Jubilee Sailing Trust tall ship, was 240 miles away and responded. Amazingly, almost exactly four years earlier, during the 2002 ARC *Tenacious* came to the rescue of *F2*, who also lost her rudder mid-Atlantic. The ship's captain at the time removed the rudder stock and took it back to *Tenacious*'s workshop, where a new jury rudder was fabricated, then floated in. It lasted four days before failing. Owners Peter and Zara Davis were forced to sink their boat and finish the rally on another ARC yacht. What would happen this time?

Tenacious lay to the east of *Zouk* and her captain, Barbara Campbell, set sail for the stricken yacht. The square-rigger's 36 crew (twelve of whom had physical disabilities, including three wheelchair-users) trimmed the sails to squeeze out every knot of speed they could.

On board *Zouk*, Caroline tried to slow the rate of drift. The crew dragged a sail from the stern but the bow still swung wildly as the yacht rolled and yawed: the stove fell off its gimbals twice. All they could do now was wait.

Two days later, at 1600, a lookout on *Tenacious* spotted *Zouk*'s bright orange storm jib on the horizon. A RIB was launched and Second Engineer Steve Garrett went onboard *Zouk* to help set up the tow. A bridle was made with lines running forward from the main cockpit winches forward through at the bow.

Now Barbara had to manoeuvre *Tenacious* close enough to pass the towline across. The first attempt nearly ended in disaster. *Zouk* veered through 180° just as the tall ship approached and was almost dashed against the 177ft-long (54m) hull.

Tenacious approached again and used a line-throwing rocket to fire a messenger line across *Zouk*'s deck. The aim was good and soon 200m of mooring line linked the two boats. An anchor and 10m of chain was streamed from the yacht's stern to reduce her slewing.

At 1800, Steve returned to *Tenacious*, bringing three of *Zouk*'s crew with him. Standing on the tall ship's deck was an incredible relief for them after the maelstrom of the previous days. 'Our rescue ship could have been an ugly, smelly, rusty freighter but, instead, the ship we saw coming to our rescue was a sumptuous pyramid of white sails; a dreamboat,' wrote crewmember Philippe de Fleury to Barbara after the event. 'Your magnificent, professional crew came to the rescue with amazing efficiency. At that moment of difficulty and emotional distress for us, the warm and generous welcome will be something I shall never forget.'

Tenacious began towing at 1800, heading for Antigua at three knots. *Zouk* darted around at the end of the tow-line. Within the next three hours, two of the three tow-lines parted as the yacht zig-zagged in *Tenacious*'s wake.

Barbara doubted the final line would last long and told Caroline to call her on VHF radio when it parted. 'I felt desperately sorry for Caroline,' recalled Barbara. 'I told her that when I looked astern the next morning I wanted to see her there. She almost laughed and cried at the same time.'

At 0115 the tow parted. *Tenacious* hove-to, slowing to 1.2 knots. Barbara called *Zouk*, telling Caroline to set whatever sail would make the motion more comfortable in the 3.5m swell. 'I told her that we wouldn't abandon her, and that we'd come back in the morning.'

It was clear that towing the rudderless yacht in large, following seas was impractical. Caroline was prepared to carry on, but the rest of *Zouk*'s crew wanted to abandon ship. Her French owners liaised with the rescue centre in Martinique and told *Zouk*'s crew to abandon her and board *Tenacious*.

Barbara told them that *Zouk* would have to be scuttled as she would be a hazard to shipping if left afloat. The owners spoke to their insurance company who agreed that the yacht should be sunk. The call was put through: 'Sink *Zouk*.'

At first light, a RIB transferred the remaining crew off *Zouk*. Caroline put on a brave face, but beneath it all she was very emotional and exhausted. The RIB made seven runs, removing anything buoyant, all pollutants and any items of value. The process was exhausting, explained Barbara: 'Each time the RIB came alongside we had to be hove-to so as to create a good lee. In between, we had to catch up with *Zouk*, which was still drifting downwind.'

Just after noon, *Zouk*'s seacocks were opened, the paddle wheel log prised out and all cupboards, hatches and deck openings left open so that no air could be trapped inside. Water flooded in and, 45 minutes later, the salvage crew abandoned ship. Five minutes after that *Zouk* sank, her skipper sitting alone on *Tenacious*'s foc's'cle, quietly watching.

■ LESSONS LEARNED

The reason for *Zouk's* rudder failure is unknown. None of the crew reported a collision. Skippers should thoroughly inspect the rudder at every haul out and before any long passage. Remove the rudder every three years or so to check the stock and bearings.

Plan what you will do if you lose your yacht's rudder. Identify the equipment you could use to jury-rig a temporary steering system and carry suitable tools and spares.

The total loss of the rudder meant that *Zouk's* stern slewed around uncontrollably. This motion massively increased the loads during towing and made the inevitable chafing even worse.

Caroline rigged a textbook towing system but, faced with large seas and fresh winds, it failed. Barbara noted that *Zouk's* mast was only deck-stepped; had it been keel-stepped she might have tried putting a tow-line round the mast.

Rigging a towing bridle from the anchor chain is one way to combat chafe.

The decision to scuttle a yacht is one of the hardest a skipper can make, but leaving a yacht adrift creates a potential shipping hazard. If possible, check with your insurer before abandoning ship. Yachts left drifting are still the responsibility of the insurers and could land them with great expense. 'If a yacht insured by us hit, say, the *QE2* and bent her prop shaft, that would be a bill we would have to pay,' explained a spokesman at Pantaenius. As a rule of thumb, only yachts worth more than £100,000 are worth salvaging.

twelve

SINK AND SWIM

Yacht	*Linan* (22ft Alacrity)
Skipper	Bill Clegg
Crew	none
Date of loss	June 2003
Position	Moray Firth, Scotland

This account by lone sailor Bill Clegg describes his nine-hour survival ordeal when his 22ft yacht mysteriously began taking on water and sank during a local cruiser race across the Moray Firth in Scotland in 2003.

WHEN I PUT TO SEA in *Linan* for a June weekend race in the Moray Firth, I believed her to be in a sound condition. I had bought the 22ft Alacrity trailer-sailor whilst 'between bigger boats'. I'd renewed all the skin fittings on her hull, replaced the standing rigging and bottle screws and bought a new mainsail and furling foresail. I had also fitted her with a new 4-hp Suzuki outboard engine, with an electrical charging system. I had also equipped her with a GPS, depth sounder and log, a hand-held VHF radio, plus a fixed VHF, which was waiting to be fitted. For safety I had parachute and hand-held smoke flares, plus a Danbuoy and a spare automatic lifejacket.

The Moray Firth Cruiser Race, held for local clubs, starts outside Findhorn Bay and finishes at the harbour at Cromarty and covers a distance of about 12 miles. On the morning of the race I set off single-handed and made my way out to the Firth to prepare for the start. The weather was foggy with a heavy swell and a fresh wind.

I was well prepared and wearing lots of layers of suitable wet weather gear. With the prevailing weather conditions, and since I was sailing solo, I decided not to go on deck to raise the mainsail and used only the furling headsail.

The race started at noon and we crossed the start line near the end of the fleet, averaging 4.5 knots. After 90 minutes, visibility was down to about half a mile and by now the land wasn't visible. To get a bearing, I decided to alter course north-west to pick up the headland and the entrance to the Cromarty Firth through the channel at the Souters. I sighted land and the east cardinal buoy at the area known locally as the Three Kings. I headed in this direction to sail parallel to the coastline and make the entrance to the Cromarty Firth.

I then noticed that the motion of the boat had changed. She seemed to be dipping at the bow and not responding as usual to the helm. I looked down below and to my horror discovered about two feet of water in the cabin and cushions floating around.

It wasn't possible to find where *Linan* was leaking, nor did it seem sensible to waste time trying to use the manual bilge pump. I had a serious problem and I decided to radio for assistance. Over the next 10 minutes I broadcast three MAYDAY calls, but had no response. I grabbed a parachute flare and fired it to leeward. A second flare failed to work and I threw it overboard. Next, I tried two red hand-held smoke flares in succession. By now the yacht was wallowing badly and was very difficult to handle. I knew I was in a serious predicament.

Having failed to attract attention, I decided to make for land under power. But within a few minutes, because the boat was so low in the water, the outboard was swamped by a wave and stopped. I couldn't re-start it. Now the only alternative was to sail for the shore. But before I could get the sails set, a large wave swamped the yacht, she capsized and was left lying on her side.

I climbed onto the side of the hull holding onto the stanchions. Caught up in the rigging and afraid of being injured or dragged down with the yacht, I grabbed the spare lifejacket, which had automatically inflated, and started to swim for the shore, which was about a mile away.

Just 30 minutes had gone by since my initial discovery of the leak. It would be another two and a half hours before I made it to shore. My multiple layers of clothing helped reduce the initial shock of the cold water, but nevertheless cramp set in, first in one leg, then the other. This eventually eased but it was only because I was wearing proper foul weather sailing clothes and using a second, spare life-jacket for extra buoyancy that I survived so long in the water. My confidence was also boosted by having worked in the offshore oil industry and been on many sea survival courses.

I was lucky to be on a lee shore at slack water, as otherwise I might have drifted out into the Firth with virtually no hope of making land. Getting tired trying to swim, I rolled on to my back but the waves came over my head and filled my mouth with water. By using a combination of dog paddle and breast stroke, the distant hill tops gradually got closer, though it seemed to be an eternity before I was scrambling over the rocks onto the beach.

After ascending an almost sheer face of about 200ft, with just ferns, bracken and the odd rock for handholds, I was met by an almost impenetrable forest of thick gorse bushes. The only way through was to crawl on my stomach, dragging myself along. I passed out with exhaustion a couple of times – all I wanted to do was go to sleep but I thought this might be fatal so I carried on and eventually arrived at the summit, a total height above sea level of 650ft. It had taken me almost six hours after my three hour swim.

I found a small track and walked over the brow of the hill to a small loch. Desperate for a drink, I tried some of the dirty water, but immediately spat it out. It tasted foul. Continuing over fields and climbing fences, I saw in the distance a white farm. I knocked on the back door and heard somebody moving behind it. I learned later that the farmer's wife feared there were poachers about and was afraid to open the door. When she did so, she saw the distress I was in and called for her husband. The couple helped me into their warm kitchen and pulled off my sea boots and sailing clothes.

I was given a hot mug of sweet tea and a cigarette. The couple contacted the police and Coastguard in case a search was being made for me, and called a doctor, who ordered that I shouldn't eat or drink for fear of secondary drowning.

Before I was taken to Raigmore Hospital in Inverness, to be treat-ed for hypothermia and exhaustion, I phoned a friend in Nairn who had been in the yacht race to tell him I was safe. I discovered that no-one even knew I was missing. But then I wasn't an official race entrant. After an overnight stay in the hospital I discharged myself.

At home, going through my post, I found a letter from my insurance company advising me that temporary cover on the yacht had expired. The company had previously requested details of equipment and serial numbers on board, and I'd delayed sending the completed form and payment for the full cover. I was therefore not insured for the loss of *Linan*, which was a double blow.

■ LESSONS LEARNED

The hand-held VHF radio was working, but its range was limited. I should have had the main VHF connected, with a masthead aerial. Then my MAYDAY might have raised the Coastguard.

No-one saw my distress flares in the thick mist, but they are still a vital part of any yacht's safety inventory.

I should have had an inflatable dinghy onboard.

I should have handed in my race entry form at Findhorn – then the organisers would have known I was missing.

In the future I will have an EPIRB onboard.

If I hadn't been as well prepared with foul weather sailing clothes and lifejackets I wouldn't have survived so long in the water. Going on a survival course is a good idea. Having done so myself I had the confidence that I could cope.

It's a good idea to have a spray-shield attached to your lifejacket. It will cover your face and protect you from breaking waves and inhaling water.

Make sure your insurance policy is up to date.

We've all read lots of stories in the press about mobile phones being used to alert rescue authorities. It's a good back-up, but no substitute for a proper VHF radio. I had my mobile phone with me but forgot it was in my pocket. I'd tried to use it earlier but wasn't getting a signal.

thirteen

THE END OF AN OSTAR

Yacht	*Livery Dole* (35ft trimaran)
Skipper	Peter Phillips
Bound from	Plymouth, England to Newport, Rhode Island, USA, in the 1980 Observer Singlehanded Transatlantic Race
Date of loss	28 June 1980
Position	about 700 miles east of Newport

Livery Dole *was one of the 88 starters in the 1980 OSTAR race, in which trimarans gained the first five places. But Peter Phillips, a police sergeant from Plymouth, was not so fortunate.* Livery Dole *had been 21 days at sea when she flipped over.*

I HAVE JUST OVER 700 MILES to go to the finish. By 0500 the wind is up to about 35 knots and I have three reefs in the main and the No 2 jib. *Livery Dole* is not at her best. She is doing 6–7 knots but slamming and dipping the lee float well under the water. The weather float is another problem. The seas are so big that every now and again a wave hits the up float with alarming force.

Not much later, I have the fourth reef in the main and the storm jib, and I have got the speed down to 4–5 knots. I try to hold at that but as *LD* is such a lightweight trimaran I may have to run off under storm jib or heave-to for a spell. The seas are the biggest problem. I reckon they are 12 to 15ft with heavy breaking crests. It's about 0600 and I look up on deck. Not much different. I hear a roar behind me and look back to windward. There is a big wave, much bigger than the others, coming towards me with a vicious, already breaking top. It hits the windward float and throws it in the air. The tri is virtually standing on its starboard float with the mast along the surface of the water. I am convinced we are going right over and will capsize. The wave picks up the main hull and then moves upright but the down float goes on up and the windward float gets slammed back down on to the water with an almighty crash. I hear a crack and to my utter surprise the whole front section of the windward (port) float has snapped off. The wave crashes on through and we are nearly capsized again.

We are still afloat, but for how long? She is sailing on the good float but slamming so badly I ought to heave-to, but I cannot because the other float will fill and capsize us. The windward float and front crossbeam are taking a terrible bashing. The seas crash into the open end and put undue pressure on the crossbeam. The broken edge is right at the crossbeam and the bolts are beginning to tear out. If the remainder go, the float will come off and fracture at the rear beam by pressure alone. There is little doubt: I am in trouble.

I start to get things organised in case I have to leave the tri, but almost immediately there is a crack and part of the front crossbeam is broken off by another wave. I go on deck and cut the liferaft straps and pull it out ready to go if need be. The problem is that I cannot launch the raft at this speed, about six knots again, but I cannot reduce too much for fear of a capsize to windward by wave action. I tune my radio into the distress frequency, ready for use. The front end of the port float is breaking away from the beam. I broadcast a MAY-DAY and give my position several times. Fortunately my navigation is up to date and I reckon my position to be 42°20' North and 54°10' West. I get a part confirmation from St Lawrence Coastguard that they have got my message, but they want the name of the yacht and the nature of the trouble. I give it to them.

Suddenly the lee (down) float is pushed up by wave action. The open end of the windward float digs into the water and we stall. We begin to capsize to windward. I grab the emergency beacon from my bunk and jump up through the hatch. We are going over to wind-ward. I throw the liferaft over the side and operate the 'panic' button on the Argos satellite transmitter. The tri is almost over. I climb up and jump over the side into the water near the liferaft, hanging on to the emergency beacon. The mast hits the water, momentarily stops, and then carries on going. Then it's upside down – completely inverted. The whole process has taken only seconds.

I grab the liferaft painter and pull it several times. It inflates right way up. I put the beacon inside and get in myself, leaving the liferaft painter still attached to *Livery Dole*, which is still floating, but low in the water. The damaged float has already torn itself off and is attached just by the bracing wires. I try several times to get into the tri through the safety hatch to get more food and water but the big seas break and wash me off. It is obvious that with these seas I am not going to succeed. I make my way back to the liferaft and get into it. I set the emergency beacon going and put it in the water on its line. The pulsating light is operating well and that makes me feel a whole heap better. If a search does get under way soon and my position is correct it will help them locate me. I close the canopy on the liferaft to conserve body heat as hypothermia and exposure are the real killers in situations like these.

I decide to stay in the liferaft attached to the tri for as long as is possible. If people are searching it will give them a bigger target to look for. She looks in a terrible state and I feel very sorry about what has happened and for all the people involved in the project from beginning to end. It should have never ended like this.

I decide to wait until the weather moderates and then try to gain access yet again. I get most of the water out of the liferaft and curl up on the floor for a bit of wet and uncomfortable sleep. I wake up after maybe a couple of hours; I don't really know as I didn't even have time to pick up my watch from the chart table.

I look out and there is a problem. The starboard float has completely snapped off with most of the crossbeams and the main hull has gone deeper in the water by the escape hatch. The seas are no better but I am going to have another go at getting back aboard.

I pull myself in and climb back on the bits of crossbeam – there isn't much of them left – but try as I may I cannot get to the hatch, I just get washed off every time by the seas. I eventually get back into the liferaft somewhat exhausted by the effort.

About an hour later I hear an aircraft. I look outside and see a Search and Rescue plane flying straight for me. What luck, and so soon. He flies over the top and straight on. I watch for him to turn but he goes out of sight and I am puzzled. I wait for him to return but no such luck. He should return if he is homed in on the emergency beacon. The beacon is lying around the back of the liferaft so I pull it into sight. The flashing light is NOT working. No wonder the plane went on. I check the beacon battery connections and everything. It looks okay but isn't working. Just my bloody luck – my MAYDAY was received, the plane is there but he has no beacon to home in on. Visibility is not good and I doubt that he will see me from the air.

I take stock again. Without the beacon, rescue will take a lot longer. I am going to have to last without the food and clothing, but I will stay attached to the tri for as long as is possible, to aid identification. *LD* is now lower in the water.

Later the visibility improves – I have no idea of the time but it is still light. The tri is very much lower in the water and the main hull is trying to roll over. I cannot risk staying attached any longer so I cast off and gradually drift away from it with the wind. I have never seen such a sorry looking mess, and yet to me she was a beautiful-looking craft. I gradually lose sight of her in the swell and I am pleased when I can no longer see her.

The weather has eased, as is always the way. The swell is still large and I cannot see much chance of being spotted, particularly from the surface, but I hope and get ready to spend a cold wet night in the raft. Funny thing, I haven't noticed the lack of food and water yet. I shut up the raft and try to sleep to conserve energy. I hear aircraft and look outside. There are two Search and Rescue planes flying in circles not far from me. They are about 50ft off the water and obviously conducting a visual search. I am elated. Their circles are coming closer to me all the time. As they reach me they pass over several times and show no signs of having spotted me. I can't let the chance go. I get three red flares ready and wait until one of the aircraft is flying straight at me. I light all three flares at once and stand up and wave at them. Nothing and then YES – something is dropped from the plane. It hits the water and goes off; a smoke marker. He has got me. I suddenly feel on top of the world. The plane approaches again, very low this time. I wave and can see the pilot wave back. It is a Canadian plane and I notice that the other is American. More smoke markers around me and I begin to feel secure and relieved. Even if I don't get picked up for a couple of days it doesn't matter. I can wait.

The American plane begins a long run in and makes a drop. As the items hit the water two dinghies inflate about 600ft apart and are joined by a floating line. I am going downwind towards the centre of the rope. A great drop by the pilot. Packs are floating attached to the dinghies. They are obviously survival packs and I presume it means that there are no ships immediately to hand and I am in for a wait.

I decide to help things along and paddle my way towards the rope. I eventually reach it and pull myself along and secure my life-raft to one at the end of the line. I pull in the survival pack containing space blankets, water and sweets and begin to get myself sorted out for a stay. The plane still circles around replacing the smoke markers, and it is comforting to have him there.

Later I look up and see a ship approaching. This is great. I am not even going to have to spend a night in the raft. I can hardly believe my luck. As it comes closer I see that it is a container ship well loaded. It slows up and then comes forward until the bow protruder picks up the rope between the two rafts only feet away from me. Lovely positioning. This brings my raft alongside the starboard side of the ship. It isn't rough but in the liferaft I am moving up and down quite a bit. The scramble nets are in position near the stern and ropes along the side. I learnt later from the captain that the ship's boats were crewed ready for use if needed. I catch hold of one of the ropes and begin to pull myself along the ship's side. The gangway is being lowered ahead of me and that looks like a very civilised way of going aboard. Someone is at the bottom of the gangway ready to help. I approach slowly because of the up and down movement. There are lots of people to help. The liferaft comes up, one step and I am on the gangway. The man at the bottom catches hold and pushes me past him, and in seconds I am on deck and it's all over.

■ LESSONS LEARNED

On the subject of multihulls in heavy weather, the late Rob James, author of *Multihulls Offshore*, considered it best to keep sailing as long as possible. 'I am firmly of the belief that it is the correct thing to do, even to windward.' But he also added: 'The most likely event that may cause one to give up the effort, is damage.'

This is what happened to *Livery Dole*. Peter Phillips reported doing 6–7 knots in his lightweight trimaran, but slamming and dipping the lee float well under water. The seas were so big that every now and again a wave hit the up float with alarming force.

Having taken the fourth reef in the main, to reduce speed, a wave much bigger than the others came along and carried away the front section of the windward float.

Several accounts in this book blame extraordinarily large waves with breaking crests for disasters. Some waves are of a size and shape that there's no defensive tactic to prevent damage.

Livery Dole had a safety hatch in her main hull, and after taking to his liferaft, Phillips tried to use the hatch to enter the cabin to get more food and water, but big seas washed him off. Abandoning ship in a hurry after the capsize, he only had time to throw the liferaft over the side and hit the panic button on the satellite transmitter. Fortunately he had already broadcast a MAYDAY and this, together with the use of flares, resulted in his eventual rescue. He was lucky his MAYDAY got through, so that he was able to give an accurate position, since his EPIRB failed to work and he had no food or water in the liferaft.

Wisely, he decided to stay in the liferaft attached to the trimaran for as long as possible to give SAR a bigger target to look for. But when the tri was lower in the water and trying to roll over he could not risk staying attached any longer and cast off, drifting away with the wind.

STRESS of
WEATHER

fourteen

THE CAT WITHOUT NINE LIVES

Yacht   *Team Philips* (120ft catamaran)
Skipper   Pete Goss (39)
Crew   Andy Hindley (32), Alex Bennett (24), Graham Geoff (40),
                   Paul Larsen (30), Richard Tudor (34) and Phil Aikenhead (55).
Bound from   Totnes, Devon, on sea trials
Date of loss   10 December 2000
Position   900 miles west-north-west of Land's End

She was the most revolutionary yacht built in Britain to date and captured the imagination of the British public. She was the nautical equivalent of the Starship Enterprise – an exotic, revolutionary craft that challenged the philosophy of ocean racing. With a budget of £4 million, Pete Goss used Star Wars technology to build a giant state-of-the-art 120ft rocket ship – 'the wildest piece of kit that anyone has seen on water!' he claimed.

LAUNCHED ON THE RIVER DART, in the quintessential English town of Totnes, Devon, in January 2000, she was bigger than the centre court of Wimbledon, but weighed no more than 44,000lbs. The 70ft-wide catamaran was set to contest the fastest non-stop ocean dash around the globe, The Race – a no-rules, no-limits global drag race for the most hi-tech yachts on the planet. The prize was a million dollars and Pete Goss was Britain's brightest hope. Computer predictions suggested he could do it in 65 days. The Jules Verne record stood at 71 days 14 hours and 18 minutes.

Tragically, *Team Philips* never even got to the Barcelona start line.

The catamaran's designer, Adrian Thompson, had gone 'back to nature' for the concept. He looked at birds of prey, fish and evolution – 'the best designer in the world'. But since evolution takes millions of years, Thompson used a computer – 'to speed things up a bit!'

'If you watch a dolphin, it cuts through the water with minimum drag,' he said. 'Think of a grasshopper and an elephant. One is frail, but nimble. The challenge for us was to develop something slender, lightweight, but strong.'

But it wasn't strong enough.

'Have you ever seen a fish with a flat top? Have you ever seen a sea-gull's wing with supports?' enthused Goss. 'I don't think of it as a boat . . . this project is more like something from aerospace or Formula One racing cars. I want the trailblazers of tomorrow to learn from what we are doing today,' exclaimed Goss, Britain's new all-action hero, an ex Royal Marine, who adopted an 'open house' policy as half a million people visited the shed to see the craft take shape.

Team Philips, named after her Dutch title sponsor, was built of exotic materials like Kevlar (used for bullet-proof vests) and titanium metal. The structural engineering was by Martyn Smith, who designed the sharp end of Concorde. The 135ft unstayed wing masts were like a section of massive aircraft wing. *Team Philips* was designed to sail at over 40 knots (47mph) and the pod in which the crew slept and ate had to be mounted on rubber shock absorbers. On a yacht of this size, you'd expect a crew of 10–15. *Team Philips* was designed for a crew of six, including Goss, to keep down weight, with reduced stores. The entire boat was controlled by just four winches.

Wave-piercing technology, developed for high speed boats used by the Special Forces, meant the vessel would fly a hull out of the water in just 12 knots of wind. At top speed (over 40 knots) the yacht would be clocking almost 50mph. If you laid all the carbon fibre filaments in *Team Philips*'s structure end-to-end they would stretch to the moon and back 200 times.

In March 2000 – days after her maiden voyage and the naming ceremony in London by Her Majesty Queen Elizabeth – *Team Philips* left Dartmouth and headed into the Atlantic for sea trials to the cheers of 100,000 well-wishers. Twenty-four hours later she was being towed into the Isles of Scilly supported by air bags after a catastrophic structural failure. In winds reported to be no more than 24 knots and, with seas of 5–6ft, a 45ft section of the port hull had snapped off. The starboard hull was also cracked. It was an agonising moment in the history of British yachting. And for those who had followed one of the most professionally managed campaigns it was a terrible blow. The craft was unceremoniously towed back to the building shed in Totnes where the problem was identified as a failure of the unidirectional carbon strakes (strips) that run the length of each hull.

The bonding of the carbon laminates to the honeycomb Nomex core had not worked.

But never one to give up, Goss, acknowledging that his project was at the cutting edge of technological advances, repaired her. *Team Philips* was relaunched on 25 September, only to suffer another devastating setback two weeks later with a broken bearing at the base of her port mast which saw her limping back home for a second time.

The final twist to the saga came on the morning of 10 December, 2000, after Goss and his six-man crew set off from Dartmouth on Saturday 2 December to sail around the British Isles. All had seemed to be going well on this 'third time lucky' outing as the team gingerly took the giant catamaran on its Atlantic shakedown cruise.

'We wanted a stern test of the boat before setting off for the much more settled conditions of the Mediterranean, so we dived in with both feet by heading 60° north,' said Andy Hindley, First Mate.

They rounded the north of Scotland in a Force 8 and Goss said *Team Philips* felt strong and safe, despite the uncomfortable seas. He decided they would continue west into the Atlantic. With navigator Hindley regularly in contact with shoreside weather expert and router Lee Bruce, they planned to stay in favourable following winds to the north of the relentless depressions.

The crew were not pushing the boat. Generally they were broad-reaching with one reef more than they needed while they got used to handling the huge cat. The acceleration of the boat proved remarkable. Coming out of tacks boat speed would leap from single figures to more than 20 knots in around three seconds. The speed topped 35 knots.

Ultimately *Team Philips* was heading for the Mediterranean and the start of The Race. The plan was to hook round the west side of a depression that would take them into the more regular westerlies to the south and provide them with a favourable wind angle to lay Gibraltar.

But a large depression with 70-knot winds was hovering over Newfoundland 350 miles away and was forecast to remain there for 24 hours. On board *Team Philips* the crew were expecting to see 35–40 knots and were waiting for the wind to veer to the south-west and then west as they crossed the front preceding the depression. They saw the barometer drop as expected as they touched the eastern extremity of the depression.

The sea was becoming increasingly lumpy and confused and as *Team Philips* headed south the crew wondered why the wind hadn't veered. Instead of staying static, the east side of the Newfoundland depression defied the forecast and became elliptical, creating three separate intense mini-depressions, often known as 'bombs'. At lunchtime on Saturday 9 December, *Team Philips* was in the northern part of one of these. Over the course of three hours the barometer, already dangerously low, dropped by a further 18mb in three hours. 'We didn't really know why it was happening,' said Goss, 'but we knew we were in something pretty big.'

The intense low was kicking up waves from a third direction, the east, adding further confusion to the sea. 'We were in this cauldron of very big waves with lots of energy, completely unpredictable,' said Goss. 'There was no way of working out where it was coming from or where it was going. Occasionally in the cockpit you could see these very, very high rogue waves which would shoot off at twice the speed of all the other waves.'

The crew, thinking the depressions would head north-east, set a course to the south-west to get into a more regular wave pattern. But the boat took a hammering. The central pod, slung high above the waterline between the catamaran's two crossbeams, was being slammed by waves.

At the height of the storm the impact of three waves in quick succession ruptured the pod at the bottom of the winching cockpit, just forward of the aft beam. Despite the pod's carbon fibre construction, the split began to grow larger and whenever a wave struck, the gap would open by as much as three inches.

The structure of the pod was disintegrating and the crew were concerned that if the catamaran endured these conditions for much longer the pod might collapse into the water, taking the accommodation and all their navigation and communications equipment with it. It might also rip off the aft steering cockpit along with the vital hydraulics for the steering system.

With someone on the helm they could survive the conditions, but if they lost their steering they would be utterly at the mercy of the sea. The catamaran had emergency tiller bars which fitted to the top of each rudder stock but the crew did not feel they would be able to control the boat with these in the prevailing conditions.

As they came more under the influence of the depression, the waves became larger but more regular and the wind more ferocious. The anemometer four metres above the deck showed 56 knots but the sea state indicated it to be closer to 70 knots. This lasted for eight hours and Goss described it as one of the worst storms he'd ever seen.

They turned the boat around and ran before it. At the outset of bad weather they had dropped the mainsails and streamed warps, including their 300yd long 1in anchor line and their sea anchor. Even dragging all this and with the wing masts feathered fore and aft, the boat speed recorded was 32.5 knots.

'We had huge breaking seas. At times we had the transoms 20ft under water with the waves lapping over the steering cockpit. At times we had the bottom of the rudder tips, which have a 6ft draught, about 10ft out of the water,' said Goss.

With the centre pod becoming increasingly unsafe, the crew were huddled in the starboard hull in their survival suits with their grab bags. The most valued items on board at that moment, reported Mark Orr, Managing Director of Goss Challenges, were their Musto Gore-Tex socks and a hot cup of tea. The hull is normally used for stowage and is a rabbit's warren of bare carbon bulkheads and structural floors. It was not designed as living accommodation, particularly in a storm.

Meanwhile, Goss remained resolutely on the helm, keeping the boat on track down the waves, with Hindley at the chart table in the centre pod liaising with Lee Bruce and feeding Goss regularly with mugs of sweet tea. By this time the Maritime Rescue Co-ordination Centre at HM Coastguard in Falmouth had been alerted and were monitoring the situation. It was not looking good.

The crack in the pod was getting worse. Although the wind was beginning to ease, the waves remained large and another depression was forecast to strike within 10–12 hours. It seemed unlikely that the pod would survive another battering. If they lost the steering there was every chance the boat would capsize during the next depression. If the crew ended up in the freezing North Atlantic in mid-December it was likely that someone – possibly all of them – would die. Some of them, Goss included, had young families. They were heading north-east, away from the shipping lanes, and the longer they left it, the longer it would take to rescue them.

At 2355 GMT Goss agreed with the MRCC that they should issue a MAYDAY, with a view to abandoning ship. At the time *Team Philips* was lying at 52° 44'N 28° 12'W, 900 miles west-north-west of Land's End. *The Hoechst Express*, a 294m 67,680 tonne container ship belonging to the German company Hapag-Lloyd, responded to the call.

On board *Team Philips* the Inmarsat Mini-M satellite radio had been ripped off the deck after it had become entangled by a flailing sheet. The Inmarsat A satcom terminal on board the *Hoechst Express* was not functioning so communications between the vessels and the MRCC were carried out by Inmarsat-C telex. To help with communications, the MRCC asked the RAF to scramble a Nimrod from their base in Kinloss, Scotland.

At 0400 Captain Edzard Ufer on board the *Hoechst Express* had *Team Philips* on radar and soon after was in VHF communication with Goss, working out how they would go about the rescue. With the large sea still running it was hard to locate *Team Philips*. The RAF Nimrod dropped a green flare to indicate her position. Expertly Captain Ufer slowed his massive ship, passed *Team Philips* and spun the *Hoechst Express* around and brought her to a standstill, leaving the catamaran in her lee.

With no sails up and still streaming lines *Team Philips* had been sailing at nine knots but in the lee of the ship's 79ft freeboard she slowed down and, with the help of the starboard engine, Goss was instructed to manoeuvre her along the starboard side of the ship.

The wind may have dropped but a 30ft sea was still running. Warps were dropped down to the boat and an attempt was made to secure her alongside but the rise and fall between the two vessels was some 30–40ft. 'There was one particularly big wave when we were perhaps 50ft away and this breaking crest came between us and we lost sight of her. That gives you some idea of the sea state,' explained Goss.

With the mooring lines slack, *Team Philips* was moving fore and aft considerably, occasionally crashing into the ship as her 135ft-tall port unstayed mast slapped against the ship's hull like a giant fly swat. The brunt of the impacts was taken by the bulbous cockpit around the foot of the port mast but one bang bent the tip of her port bow.

Rope ladders were dropped down from the ship's main deck along with a net. The ship's crew would not open the lower pilot door for fear that *Team Philips* would damage it. By 0550 the first crewman had clambered to safety. This involved waiting for the catamaran to be on the peak of a wave and then hurriedly climbing the ladder before the next wave came along, or before they were swatted by the mast. As sailmaker Graham Goff climbed the ladder, the mast slammed into the hull just four feet away from him. Twenty-five minutes later all the crew, including Goss, who was the last to leave, were safely on board the *Hoechst Express. Team Philips* was cast off and left to fend for herself in the North Atlantic.

The crew had left one wind generator working and the Inmarsat C terminal was switched on. This enabled their shore team to poll the position of the boat. Positions from the stricken catamaran were being received for some time after she was abandoned.

On 13 January 2001, a beacon signal was picked up by satellite and confirmed at regular intervals. Goss Challenges, working with Falmouth Coastguard, began a second extensive air search in a corporate jet aircraft chartered for £10,000. Despite good visibility, Goss and his logistics manager Nick Booth had no sightings.

So ended the short career of this popular ill-fated craft of the 21st century.

'I think she'll turn up somewhere, eventually . . .' said Mark Orr. 'She could go north or south. She could turn up in the Arctic pack ice, or drift to the west coast of Ireland.'

FOOTNOTE

Just as Mark Orr predicted, wreckage from *Team Philips* was washed ashore six months later as far apart as Iceland and Ireland.

A large piece of wreckage, a section of bow, was located in May 2001 off the Irish coast, 50–60 miles west of Donegal Bay. It measured some 6–7m and had the logo 'Let's make things better'.

A day later, a massive section of the port hull was seen some 800 miles away off the coast of the Vestmannaeyar Islands, in south-west Iceland. Along one side was the www.teamphilips.com website address. On the inner side of the hull, poignantly, were the names of the hundreds of people who had made donations to the project. Later, one of the two wingmasts was found on Iceland's south coast.

■ LESSONS LEARNED

With such a leading-edge project, and such an untried, revolutionary craft, perhaps the biggest lesson is that you need to allow plenty of time for sea trials. The sea will always exploit any weakness. Goss was out to test his boat to the limits. The circumstances were exceptional in every way. But sailors should never be pressurised by deadlines which might put them in the wrong place at the wrong time.

Goss realised that he and his crew were drifting away from the shipping lanes and the longer he delayed making a decision, the longer rescue would take. As Mark Orr, Managing Director of Goss Challenges, said of the abandonment: 'It was a difficult decision but we have always underpinned this project with safety and seamanship. It was not a panic decision, but a decision taken in the interests of safety.'

NO ESCAPE AT FÉCAMP

Yacht	*Riot*, a Sadler 45 Barracuda
Skipper	Nigel Porter
Bound from	Brighton, Sussex, to Fécamp, France
Date of loss	May 2000
Position	off the entrance to Fécamp Harbour

Nigel Porter describes the loss of his Sadler Barracuda yacht, Riot, *in a severe storm during the Cross-Channel Great Escape Race to Fécamp.*

THERE WERE 102 YACHTS taking part in the annual Royal Escape Race from Brighton to Fécamp. The event, organised by Sussex Yacht Club, commemorates the escape to France of King Charles II from Cromwell's Republican army in 1651, following the execution of his father. The king's escape vessel was a little coal brig, *The Surprise*. My yacht was a Sadler 45 Barracuda called *Riot*.

Aboard I had what I regarded as a strong cruising crew, rather than a racing crew. But we had a great variety of experience between the six of us. John had sailed from childhood, with three Atlantic crossings to his credit and was a Cape Horner, too. Helen, local chairperson of the Sail Training Association, was also a Cape Horner, having circumnavigated against the elements on one of Chay Blyth's steel yachts, *Nuclear Electric*. She had also sailed for many years in a variety of yachts. Bob, a yachtsman for 18 years, was a keen navigator. Chris was a dingy sailor who had moved up to bigger boats and Jennie had taken to the water about eight years ago and gained much experience. Lastly, there was me. A sailor from my student days, 55 years previously, the last 20 of them as owner/skipper. My crew had sailed many miles together in all sorts of weather.

We split up into three watches of two, with an hour on the helm each. The forecast was discouraging: southerly, backing SE Force 2–3 at first then building to Force 4–5 and eventually veering SW Force 2–3. It was going to be a slowish trip. We had plenty to eat and drink and in view of the forecast didn't expect much excitement.

As a 'cruiser' embarking on my first race in a fleet of over 100 boats, I was pleased we got off to a trouble-free start, crossed the line two minutes after the gun and made up a little distance on some competitors before we reached the first mark.

At this point the fleet split, some going south-east, against an ebbing neap tide. We chose to use the tide and go south-west in the hope that when the tide flooded east it would give a bit of a lift towards Fécamp. The wind was fluky and *Riot* was not surging along in her usual fashion. Even so, we were easing ahead of the nearer boats. The cross-track error on the GPS was building, however. A round of bacon sandwiches helped raise morale. The helmsman changed hourly and the chart plot slowly crawled southward, but not on the course we wanted.

By noon we were not even level with the Meridian light vessel. Then the wind freshened and backed a little so that we could head east more and, with the help of the flood tide, reduce the cross-track error.

By 1500 hours we were just south of the east-bound shipping lane and the plotter showed us bang on course for Fécamp.

'Not so bad. We'll be in by 2200 hours,' I announced confidently.

This was the last time we had any cause for self-congratulation. From then on the wind and the weather played increasingly vile tricks on us.

Back home, severe conditions were forecast and during the day a storm warning had been broadcast. The first boats arrived in Fécamp by 1830. But the bad weather would not appear until after 2000.

The wind shifted further and increased and we had to start tacking to stay anywhere near our course. It was also plain that we would lose the favourable tide and need to get further east.

As the light faded, so the wind shifted and strengthened. Time to put two reefs in the main and roll in a bit of the genoa. We all checked our lifelines were securely hooked on. Matters were not going according to plan or forecast! The boat took all this and was going at her usual rapid pace with Helen at the wheel enjoying some very good sailing. Suddenly the wind whipped round through 180° and we had a crash gybe and were sailing back towards Brighton at 10 knots. With the wisdom of hindsight, I wished we'd kept going.

No damage was done. As we began to sort ourselves out, Chris exclaimed 'My God, Nigel, look behind you!'

Down to the west there was a black wall of threatening cloud which seemed to be roaring towards us. The main was reefed right down and the genoa reduced to a rag, just in time. Then the front hit us with lashing rain and a Force 9 wind. I thought it was a squall, but not a bit of it. This was the weather for the whole night. It just went on and on. At times, gusts reached 48–50 knots and the seas got very rough.

By now we were about 10 miles north-east of Fécamp, tired, wet and hungry. The options were to make for the harbour, run up channel to Dieppe, or even go back to Brighton. We chose Fécamp.

Riot was sailing well with little weather helm and though we were having to work hard we felt confident we could make it. It was tack, tack and tack again. By now I was on the helm, Chris and John on the sheets, assisted by Jennie and Helen tailing lines. Bob, meanwhile, calmly called out the bearing and distance to our target. Reassuringly, we were getting closer. Green seas were pouring over us from time to time, seeking every crevice in our oilies and flooding the cockpit. We were a good team, we knew each other well and as we clawed our way nearer to Fécamp our spirits rose.

Finally, we weathered Cap Fagnet, but needed to put in yet one more tack to make the harbour entrance. As we came round onto port tack we became aware of four boats on starboard tack bearing down on us. I was in an awful dilemma. Did I turn further to the right and risk a collision with the nearest boat, or go back onto starboard and head in again? I chose the latter. We had, however, seemingly made enough ground to lay the harbour entrance. We were going to make it.

But within 150m of our target, I looked to starboard and saw an appalling great wave. The next moment we'd been knocked down on our beam ends. I was under water and washed off the helm. Helen grabbed my leg as I started to go overboard and the whole world was chaos.

Riot was lifted sideways, like a cork, by another great wave and hurled onto the shore with a grinding crash. This must have been about 0130. There was a long, long pause of stunned silence as the sea washed us in towards the rocks east of the harbour, a place known as the Trou au Chien, with an evil reputation for claiming sailors' lives.

Helen recovered first and shouted to Bob to send off a MAYDAY. Helen and Chris found the flares and fired off two, as people on shore were not certain where we were. John got the main down to reduce windage. Jennie was below in the flooded cabin doing 'subaqua salvaging' of wallets and other small and important items. I launched the liferaft. Fortunately, we didn't use it, for amongst the rocks in the huge seas it would have been torn to pieces. Shortly afterwards, it turned over, punctured and sank.

No one panicked. A shocked silence descended on all of us as we waited for rescue. We could see the lights on the shore beneath the towering cliffs about 80m behind us. Suddenly, to our amazement, a swimmer in a wetsuit appeared through the surf among the rocks and came to the stern of the boat. How he managed it, I shall never know. Not only did he do so once, but he came back five more times. Tough, brave, strong? You name it, he deserved all the superlatives I can think of. I'm a Francophile till the day I die.

We were warned to stay put. The currents were too fierce to attempt to swim ashore on our own and the combination of rocks and sea would grind us to mincemeat. One by one, with the aid of a line, we were hauled ashore, helped by our rescuers, members of the Sapeurs Pompiers of Fécamp. First Jennie, then Helen, Chris and Bob were taken off.

One of the Frenchmen came back to tell John and me that it was too dangerous to continue. By this time, about 0400, the tide was well up and the waves were breaking over us. The boat was also breaking up on the rocks. The Frenchman told us a helicopter was on its way, though we didn't understand this last bit. Neither of us thought much of staying on the boat at this stage. By now the sea was up to my chest, the hull under my feet had broken away and every wave washed my feet out horizontally. I was tired and cold. I didn't think I was going to last. The Frenchman realised this and jerked his thumb towards the shore, seized my harness and we pushed off into the sea. He swam strongly. I tried, but my foul weather jacket and boots made it difficult to do more than flounder.

I swallowed plenty of seawater, but suddenly, blessed relief, there was shingle under my feet. Hands grasped me and I was hauled up on the beach, flat on my back. I looked up at a ring of faces. 'I'm all right!' I told them. Two strong men helped me to my feet and supported me on either side for the 200m trudge along the shingle.

Among the helpers on shore were Jonty and Viki Layfield, who had taken part in the race and got there before us. They had raised the alarm when we were wrecked and later helped us all on shore, Jonty heaving us up the steps to the ambulances when our weary legs would no longer support us. Viki got our wet clothes off us and wrapped us in blankets. It was a huge relief when she told me John was safe.

John had a long and very lonely 20 minutes wondering what was going to happen to him, with the waves coming ever higher. Fortunately, he managed to secure himself to the lifelines and grabbed an extra lifejacket, just in case he had to chance his life in the sea and rocks. Suddenly, he was aware of a tremendous noise and thought the adjacent cliff had been brought down in the storm. A bright light appeared from above. The helicopter had arrived. Down came the crewman. John, with his army training, knew just what to do. Up went his arms, down went the strop around his chest and he was airborne. The pilot showed consummate skill in the appalling conditions.

The staff at Fécamp Hospital soon had us warm and comfortable from the effects of hypothermia. That night, the fate of 50 yachts in the race was unknown. MAYDAY calls were received and caused the French Coastguards to impose radio silence. It was not until noon the following day that the whereabouts of all the competitors in various Channel ports had been established. Several yachts were towed into Fécamp and St Valéry by local lifeboats. Six yachts sought refuge in Dieppe.

I and my crew reflected on the fact that you never know how wonderful and generous people can be until some moment of awful and dire need. None of us will ever forget Les Sapeurs Pompiers Fécampoise: Jean-Claude Confourier, David Levasseur, Phillipe Fiquet and Phillipe Duvivier. We also owe a great debt of gratitude to Viki and Jonty Layfield for help, reassurance and kindness. Dany Prevet, a citizen of Fécamp and honorary member of Sussex Yacht Club, visited us, attended to our concerns, arranged the washing and drying of our clothes and devoted her entire weekend to helping us, finally driving three of us to Le Havre to catch the ferry home. Oliver, John's brother, drove the remaining crew, as well as lending clothing and raising morale.

Finally Navigators and General Insurance settled my claim in full, with promptness, and I can buy another boat and get back to sea. The sooner the better! I'm glad to say that we all feel the same.

■ LESSONS LEARNED

No matter how benign the weather forecast, always monitor it. You just never know.

No matter how well your boat sails, go for the safest option and head away from bad weather.

Off a lee shore make sure you have searoom, especially in bad weather.

Don't let thoughts of crossing a race finish line blind you to dangers.

We were asked to monitor VHF channel 72 and not use it as a chat channel. But no weather reports were given on this race channel.

With hindsight, I should have monitored channel 16 as well.

sixteen

PERFECT STORM

Yacht	*Eclipse* (32ft catamaran)
Skipper	Richard Woods
Crew	Jetti Matzke
Bound from	Nicaragua
Date of loss	January 2006
Position	Mexico's Gulf of Tehuantepec

Multihull designer Richard Woods's 10m (32ft) catamaran, Eclipse, *survived 70-knot winds and 20ft seas in the Pacific off the Mexican coast, but which storm tactic worked best – a parachute anchor, running before waves with a drogue, or lying ahull broadside to the waves?*

MY CREW, JETTI MATZKE, and I were well into the Pacific's notorious 'Bay of Biscay' – the Gulf of Tehuantepec in southern Mexico – and keeping very close to shore as the pilot books advised. At dusk the light north-east wind became a strong north-westerly, so the swell, instead of being offshore, started running parallel to the coast, and we were being hit by spray from waves breaking on the beach. There was no moon, and the night was pitch black. The nearest safe harbour was 80 miles away, so we decided to get some sea room.

Less than an hour later the wind picked up to over 30 knots on the nose. As we had been sailing for four days in very changeable weather and had had little sleep, we decided to stop sailing until dawn and deploy our parachute sea anchor. Multihull designer Nigel Irens once told me that he damaged a trimaran's rudder as she was swept backwards when lying to a sea anchor, so I made sure my rudders were centred, properly lashed and the parachute anchor was deployed with a fender to keep it floating near the surface.

Next morning the wind was around 45 knots and the waves 3–4m high. *Eclipse* was being pulled up and over, and indeed right through, the steepest waves. The wind kept increasing, whilst the waves remained short and steep. Most had big breaking crests. By now there were huge loads on the 25mm main warp as well as on the bridles. In the biggest waves, *Eclipse* was being washed backwards, with the front half of the boat clear out of the water. We were also swinging nearly broadside to the waves. Then one bridle broke, followed by the other. I used the main anchor warp to make up new bridles: hard work on a foredeck alternately going underwater and then leaping 3m into the air. Then, our parachute anchor burst. Although 20 years old, it was heavily made, and certainly stronger than others I've looked at. Even so, when I pulled the remnants in I found some of the canopy lines had pulled out and the top had shredded. We were no longer able to stay bows-to the weather, so we now tried running before the waves.

Although *Eclipse* is directionally stable and has regularly surfed at 16 knots, high speeds are only safe when running before a big swell that has long wave lengths. More often, you need to sail slowly. To do this one uses drogues – it doesn't really matter how sophisticated they are, they just need to slow the boat. Fortunately, I had already prepared warps to stream from astern for just this eventuality. I led one to each genoa winch so it would be easy to adjust their lengths. It only took a few minutes to deploy them, and then I added the remains of the parachute and its warp, which slowed us from 6 to 4 knots.

I now found *Eclipse* very heavy to steer and Jetti wasn't strong enough to helm. We couldn't use the autopilot because we needed to avoid the waves ahead. It was obvious that running before these very steep, high waves wasn't safe. Had we gone 'over the edge' it would have been like falling down a waterfall. So we had to sail slower than them, which meant that the breaking waves overtook us.

The first wave splashed into the cockpit, but the second was much bigger and washed over the whole boat filling our dinghy, which we carried in davits, so we had to cut it free and abandon it. Some water got below, too. We decided to lie ahull; broadside to the approaching waves. We cautiously luffed *Eclipse*, lashed the rudders to leeward and streamed warps off the windward stern.

I hoped that when a wave hit, with the daggerboards raised, the bows would be pushed to leeward while the drogues would keep the boat moving in a constant direction. The waves were now averaging 6m in height; however *Eclipse* has a 6m beam so, in theory, we would be safe. Unfortunately, though, statistics show that one in every 1,000 waves is twice the average height. If a wave passes every 30 seconds then that extra high wave occurs about once every eight hours.

The wind was now strong enough to distort my face, and the rig was vibrating in a way that I had only experienced once before, when safely moored in a marina in 70 knots of wind. The sea was covered with spume and looked like those photos in *Heavy Weather Sailing* that give you nightmares. For 28 hours we had been at the mercy of the storm, and so were pushing our luck. Knowing the statistics was a major reason for deciding our lives were in danger from capsize. Despite *Eclipse* being undamaged and upright, we sent out a MAY-DAY, and activated our McMurdo (406 MHz GPS Fastfind) Personal Locator Beacon. I also used my Iridium phone to call Pip Patterson at the UK Multihull Centre in Plymouth. Pip gave me the UK's Falmouth Coastguard phone number, so I called them and then phoned every hour to give a weather and position update. Several countries became involved with our rescue, and eventually we were told the Mexican Navy would be at our position at dawn. However, at 2300 a US Navy helicopter contacted us to say they were 10 miles away. As they flew nearer we set off two flares (the first one didn't work) and made visual contact.

US Navy helicopters carry two SAR (Search And Rescue) swimmers; one who goes in the water while the other acts as winch man. Both are fully trained to do either. Indeed, our team tossed a coin to see who would do which job, and the winner wouldn't stay in the safety of the helicopter – he would be the one who jumped in. The first sight of our rescuers was a man on the end of a wire, suspended 100ft below the helicopter with arms outstretched, directing the pilot to a suitable position off our lee quarter.

Flying at 50 knots to stay in position and going up and down 20ft to stay above the waves was quite a feat.

We tied the grab bags to each other, then Jetti calmly inflated her lifejacket, walked down the transom steps and headed towards the swimmer. Five minutes later, I followed. Getting into the helicopter was a real struggle because the 50-knot flying speed meant that the winch was pulling the lifting strop at an acute angle. We lost one bag containing our log books and diaries when it caught in the helicopter door. Once seated we were startled when the winchman pulled out a long knife, moved towards us and slashed both our lifejackets. He didn't want us trapped inside the helicopter if it had to ditch.

Half an hour later we landed on USS *Ford* where, after a quick debrief, medical check, shower and meal, we were able to get some much-needed rest. Some 36 hours later USS *Ford* berthed in Guatemala. The crew on *Ford* were fantastic. Saving our lives wasn't enough – they also treated us like royalty. So, too, did Colin Gracey of the British Embassy in Guatemala. He met us off the ship and drove us 80 miles back to the embassy, where we phoned home. He even recommended a good hotel and later helped organise the search for *Eclipse*.

■ LESSONS LEARNED

Perhaps 50m of sea-anchor warp wasn't enough, although we had the parachute in the next wave train, but I could not lengthen it in those conditions.

With hindsight, I should have bought a bigger sea anchor: a 5.5m-diameter chute would have been better than a 3.5m one, but of course everything costs money and, even for safety gear, that's always limited.

You can make a sea anchor from a storm jib, but I doubt you could actually rig it up during a storm. Even our 3.5m-diameter parachute had an area of about 12m², much more than our 5m² storm jib.

I was uncertain at the time whether my Personal Locator Beacon had worked or not: I later found out from RAF Kinloss that it transmitted a brief signal. (Editor's note: McMurdo's experts said, 'The PLB worked above and beyond its expected capability, rapidly transmitting an emergency alert signal via

406MHz, despite being operated from within the confines of the catamaran's cabin'). More reassuring was my Motorola 9500 Iridium satellite phone, which I bought for £350. Had we left it on standby when we abandoned *Eclipse*, powered by the boat's solar panels, it would have acted as an indefinite homing device and helped locate the £80,000 yacht, which was not insured, and we could have salvaged her before pirates stripped her. Go out and buy one!

As a multihull expert, I have sat on the International Stability and Buoyancy Committee, which has been defining stability standards, in part for the RCD (Recreational Craft Directive). During the storm, however, it was of little comfort knowing the theory of capsize: that, unless the wave height exceeds the boat's beam, a boat is safe when lying beam-to steep, breaking waves!

When you register your EPIRB/PLB, don't give elderly, non-sailing parents as a contact. Choose someone who can be of practical help. Pip Patterson, of Plymouth's Multihull Centre, has sailed across the Atlantic with me, so I knew he wouldn't panic. Most people don't realise the Coastguard also rely heavily on our CG66 forms, so you should fill one out and keep it updated.

I have been in car crashes and have had a few seconds to think, 'Will I survive?' We had 15 hours of wondering, and that's the real reason we decided to call a MAYDAY. If you haven't been in a similar position, you have no idea what it is like to think that every moment might be your last. I also thought I might survive a capsize, but Jetti, who is an older and less experienced sailor than me, might not have done.

Be warned that the first of our two 'in date' distress flares failed to work.

Don't inflate your lifejacket until you're actually ready to get in the water; they'll just get in your way as you prepare to abandon ship.

Your lifejacket will cope with the extra weight easily, so wear as many clothes as you can get on. Stupidly, we didn't dress up, and arrived in Guatemala wearing just T-shirts and shorts. Shopping for clothes only added to our stress and depleted our emergency funds.

EMERGENCY GRAB BAGS

Grab bags need to be strong and waterproof. I recommend a stowable PVC sack, about 100 litres in size. Make sure the bags have strong ties and that these are long enough to allow you to swim with the bag lashed to your body.

Fill dry bags with passports, money and ship's papers first. Next, put in things that can't be replaced: photographs, logbooks and diaries. Don't worry about cameras or your GPS.

Don't worry too much about weight, as a good dry bag has a lot of buoyancy.

Practise using them before an emergency.

Place items into Ziploc bags before putting them into the grab bag to help keep them dry.

FOOTNOTE

Richard Woods, 51 at the time of this incident, had lived on board *Eclipse* for five years. He has 70,000 miles of offshore sailing experience. The £80,000 yacht was not insured and when she was eventually found by tuna fishermen, 1,000 miles from Acapulco, the salvage fee was too high for her to be worth towing back the 2,200 miles to Ecuador and she was left to drift. She had drifted more than 1,100 miles in 10 weeks. Ocean pirates had already stripped her of electronics, mainsail, and boom.

seventeen

ABANDONED!

Yacht	*Dunlin* (28ft Camper & Nicholsons gaff-cutter)
Skipper	Philip Kerin
Bound from	Antigua, West Indies, to Falmouth, UK
Date of loss	September 2004
Position	345 miles SW of Isles of Scilly

Philip Kerin, from Lymington in Hampshire, tells the dramatic story of his rescue and the loss of his beloved 28ft yacht, Dunlin, *in the tail of Hurricane Frances, 345 miles south-west of the Isles of Scilly.* Dunlin *was designed and built by Camper & Nicholsons in 1890. Philip bought her in 1979, cruised her to France, Belgium and Holland as an open boat and later converted her into a liveaboard cruising yacht, with coach roof and cabin.*

I WAS SAILING SINGLEHANDED from Antigua to Falmouth in the UK and, after a brush with Hurricane Alex, arrived at Horta in the Azores, after 35 days. It had been a slow passage with some minor sail and self-steering damage. I'd owned *Dunlin*, a 28ft wooden gaff-cutter for 25 years. My own sea time includes several years in the Merchant Navy, before becoming a professional skipper in the UK, Mediterranean and Caribbean, with many long passages in all sorts of sailing vessels, including more than a dozen transatlantics.

After two weeks, I set off on 26 August, dogged by light north-easterly winds for the first eight days. *Dunlin*, engineless and gaff-rigged, made slow progress. After two days becalmed, on the afternoon of the 13th day, the barometer started falling and by nightfall the wind increased to 35 knots, from the north-west.

Reefed down, I kept going but by dawn the wind and sea were increasing. I put the last reef in the mainsail and hoisted a storm jib. When the self-steering gear was overwhelmed, I hove-to and remained so all day and the following night. By the following morning, a big 10–12m south-westerly swell set in, across the north-west wind of 40–45 knots. At midday, the wind suddenly went into the south-west and increased to over 60 knots.

Conditions were now almost too much for even the tiny scraps of storm sail I still had up, and it was risky to work on deck with the boat swept by heavy seas. The wind continued to increase (Met reports and maps showed a possible 80 knots). The boat and her gear started to suffer damage. The water tank shifted and ruptured the hose connections; the cooker broke free and smashed itself, puncturing my lifejacket and damaging battery cables. I had no water, no 12-volt power supply for lights, no VHF radio and, although the hull itself wasn't leaking, the hatches and skylight were letting in water.

At the height of the storm, the spreaders on the mast were almost continually in the water. I am still amazed that a 28ft wooden boat could have survived such punishment. During those worst two hours, I was afraid that *Dunlin* was breaking up, as the noise and motion was just awful. When it became clear that I had no rudder, tiller or self-steering, I began to realise that although the hull and rig had survived, the whole situation had radically changed.

The most serious damage wasn't evident until two days later, after the storm had gone into the north-west and I was able to get on deck. The rudder and tiller had been broken, wrenched right off the boat by the slamming, despite being double-lashed when hove-to. The self-steering trim tab had also gone. I had almost no water left and no means of heating food or drinks. I had no steering, no power for lights, instruments or VHF radio and the mainsail was damaged. On the plus side, I had tinned and dried food, a hand-held GPS (with internal batteries) an EPIRB and flares.

My position was 48° 38N–14° 45W, approximately 400 miles WSW of the Scillies. So there were some important decisions to be made. I was still hove-to, in about 40 knots. With a rudder it would have been possible to hand steer and heave-to for rest and food and get somewhere safely, but without steering my course was limited to being hard on the wind. I tried everything possible to rig emergency steering. Even after dropping the mainsail and rigging an oar over the stern with ropes and pulleys and a headsail, she still rounded up hard on the wind. The best course I could make was NNE, or 010°, but the course to the Lizard was 087°. The oar eventually broke and trailing a bucket on either quarter made almost no difference at all.

My options were now to use distress flares to attract the attention of a vessel within sight or activate my EPIRB. At night, without lights and steerageway, I ran a risk with shipping headed for the Western Approaches. Despite a new radar reflector, *Dunlin*, being wooden, presented a poor radar target.

Over the next 24 hours I had one essential question to answer. 'Are you willing to abandon your boat – Yes or No?' By the end of the next day, the painful answer was 'Yes'.

Dunlin had been my home for over 20 years, with all my possessions aboard. How was I to choose what to save? I'd acquired hundreds of sailing books, photos and mementoes, lots of beautiful ship models and paintings. Eventually, after two days of trying and failing to set up a steering system, I reluctantly activated the EPIRB. It was painful, groping in the dark with a torch, and finding the ship's papers, logbooks and passport. I also found letters and gifts of love from the woman in my life, photos, a beautiful Nicola Dixon painting of *Dunlin* and an 1890 print, as well as a lovely wooden carving. It was all I could possibly wrap in waterproof bags and stuff into a bag tied to an empty water container as a float. I felt a traitor abandoning my boat. Tiredness and worry also played their part in my decision. But I knew my options could drastically change. It was also possible that the EPIRB, transmitting on 121MHz and uncoded, might not be detected at all. Without VHF radio contact, my flares would be an essential means of pinpointing my position.

I activated the EPIRB at 1415 on Sunday 12 September as the storm winds were once again increasing. For the first time in more than 48 hours, I ate some dry biscuits and dozed, feeling cold, wet and hungry. At 1615 I thought the EPIRB's signal might be obstructed by the cabin roof, so I fixed it in the cockpit for a clearer signal. The Coastguard's report later stated this coincided with their first strong signal. Coupled with a French report of a good signal,

Falmouth Coastguard was convinced this was not a false alarm.

At 2030 I heard a jet aircraft pass close overhead and saw the lights of several ships on the horizon six to eight miles away. The aircraft was an RAF Nimrod, from Kinloss, Scotland – the listening station that had picked up my EPIRB signal and passed it to Falmouth. I knew they would be trying to call me on VHF Channel 16. Unable to reply, I launched a red parachute rocket flare. It was a pitch black night with no moon and I had no lights. The flare let them know someone was alive, but it was some time before they spotted *Dunlin* with their searchlights. Three ships in the area had been alerted and were also searching for me. One was a Russian Pan Max bulk carrier, another was a car carrier and the third was container ship *Sydney Express*, sent to my updated position. I learned later than even a mile from my position they had no radar or visual contact. I lit three parachute rocket flares and three red hand-held flares, which were seen by the aircraft, but *not* by *Sydney Express*. I activated my personal arm band strobe light when the ship was close and that was their first target. The Nimrod plane illuminated *Dunlin* with their searchlight, which was spotted by *Sydney Express*, who used its searchlight to illuminate me.

Dunlin was still hove-to, drifting 90° to a 40 knot north-west wind with a 5m cross swell from the south-west. The 300m-long ship had to manoeuvre alongside to get me onboard!

I could hear nothing of their shouts to me. With one enormous main engine and no gearbox, the ship had to stop the engine and restart it, in reverse rotation. A more rapid change of engine speed and rotation could seriously damage the engine. Hard over to starboard from hard over to port takes over 30 seconds, I was told. With a freeboard of over 50ft, I was invisible to them on approach.

They lined up for the first of three rescue runs. This almost ended in disaster. The ship's bulk caused a wind deflection and *Dunlin* was in danger of collision as she drifted near the ship's underwater bow bulb, rising and falling 12–15ft in the swell. The top of *Dunlin*'s mast brushed the overhang of the ship's bow as she drifted clear.

It took 30 minutes for the ship to turn for a second attempt. With no communication, I was unsure of what I should do. They tried sending two lines by rocket-launcher, both of which failed to function. A hand-thrown heaving line reached me, but I could not secure it in time.

At the third attempt, the captain performed an extraordinarily brilliant manoeuvre. *Dunlin* was 50m off their starboard midships and the ship activated her bow thrusters' propeller, pushing her bows to port, but sending a powerful current towards *Dunlin's* stern, at the same time as using their main engine propeller half astern, to send another powerful current from the opposite direction, creating a low pressure water-surface suction system. The ship 'sucked' *Dunlin* alongside.

From this point things happened quickly. My lifejacket, punctured by the cooker flying across the cabin, left me with no flotation as *Dunlin* was smashing hard against the side of the ship. It was almost impossible to stand, even holding on. The ship's crew threw lines down from deck, 50ft above, some of which tangled in *Dunlin's* rigging. I managed to pass a light line around the bag I had prepared and a heavy line around my waist and tie a bowline loop under my arms. *Dunlin* was being thrown hard against the ship's side, rising and falling 15ft. I risked being crushed if I fell between the boat and ship, or worse, being smashed by the mast, gaff and boom rigging as I was being hauled up.

I decided to jump clear of *Dunlin* into the sea, and they walked the rope away from *Dunlin* to haul me up the ship's side to safety, with only bruises and scratches. The captain asked what I wanted to do about *Dunlin*. Towing her was impossible, even at 'slow ahead'. The *Sydney Express* would make 10 knots and in those conditions it wasn't practicable to attempt it. Reluctantly I turned away, after watching my yacht suffer a lot of further damage alongside as the ship got underway and resumed course.

The Master, officers and crew of *Sydney Express* were extraordinarily helpful. If the third rescue attempt had failed, they would have launched a lifeboat to pick me up and transfer me to the ship. I am also grateful for the professionalism of Falmouth Coastguard and the RAF Nimrod's crew. It's reassuring to know the brotherhood of the sea still exists. There is one more tribute to make. Despite losing *Dunlin*, she kept me alive in atrocious conditions. She was game to the last – what more can one ask? She was a wonderful little boat.

Having an EPIRB saved my life. If it had been a modern 'coded' version, it would have helped the Coastguard and ship identify my vessel and assess the rescue problems. Make sure it is in a position to transmit a good signal.

Many vessels have an emergency steering system. I made several attempts to get *Dunlin* to steer again, but they all failed. If I'd managed to fix the problem, I wouldn't have activated the EPIRB or abandoned my boat.

The new radar reflector I fitted before leaving the Caribbean simply didn't work. *Dunlin* didn't present any radar target to the ship.

Perhaps I should have dropped my sails for the ship to come alongside.

With my 12 volt batteries disabled, my fixed VHF radio wouldn't function and my small hand-held VHF radio had a flat battery. A hand-held VHF powered by ordinary AA batteries, as well as rechargeable ones, would have been useful.

With no navigation lights, my strobe light arm band was the first and only visible sign of my position. I also carried in my oil-skin pockets a torch, hand-held mini waterproof flares, whistle, mirror and knife.

I didn't have a liferaft and in 80 knot winds and a big sea, it's debatable if I could have launched it and got into it anyway.

The ship had never rescued anyone before. They had a rope/wood pilot's boarding ladder, which they didn't deploy and might have been an asset. The master of the *Sydney Express* has recommended the company's ships should be equipped with a 'boarding net'.

eighteen

MAYDAY FOR *MAY BEE*

Yacht	*May Bee* (Rustler 31)
Skipper	Gordon Stanley
Crew	Barry Thunder, Jenny Warmsley
Bound from	Gosport, Hampshire to northern Spain
Date of loss	June 1994
Position	some 25 miles north-west of Cape Finisterre

Bound for Spain across Biscay, the Rustler 31 May Bee *was rolled over by a freak wave and dismasted. Crewman Barry Thunder recalls the drama and helicopter rescue of the three crew.*

IT HAD BEEN A DREAM to take a two-month cruise visiting new and warm places. The plan was to sail south to Spain and then west to the Azores, returning home via the Isles of Scilly. The crew of three comprised Gordon Stanley (48), skipper and owner of *May Bee*, a Rustler 31, his sister Jenny Warmsley, a teacher, and myself. All old schoolfriends, we had sailed together since our early twenties.

Gordon, an experienced engineer, spent four years fitting out *May Bee* in his engineering shop in Chertsey, Surrey, sometimes helped by me. Wherever possible, the work was done to ensure extra strength and durability.

By 4 June 1994, we had sailed the boat from her home base in Gosport to Falmouth Marina and spent a weekend provisioning. We visited Falmouth Coastguard Station to check weather conditions for Biscay, and two days later said tearful goodbyes to our respective families and cast off for Spain.

The first couple of days were an unpleasant beat, but during the afternoon of the fourth day the wind rose to gale force. In the night it was up to Force 9 and we were down to a scrap of headsail. We estimated the waves were 4m high. Dawn revealed a wild seascape of white-topped waves as seas continued to build, the northeasterly wind gusting from 45–50 knots. The sound was a constant shriek and it was a great relief when it dropped a little to about 35 knots.

Despite the conditions, the boat was handling well, responding fairly quickly to the wheel steering. With the sun low in the sky, you could tell when a big wave was approaching, as it blocked out the sunlight, leaving everything in shadow. Our speed was about 4 knots. We managed to maintain our course, depending on whether we were surfing down a wave or holding the boat up in the big gusts.

Since the weather forecasts sounded no worse, we decided we'd carry on to our preferred port in Bayona, rather than fight our way into La Coruña. Next day, day five, we were well into the shipping lanes off Cape Finisterre and got a weather check via VHF radio from a passing American warship. This confirmed our decision to carry on, since we were only about eight hours away from reportedly calmer conditions on the sheltered side of Cape Finisterre.

Gordon and I were elated with the way *May Bee* was sailing. She took little water over the side and did not feel pressed in any way. Nevertheless, a warp was readied to stream over the stern as a drogue if the yacht's speed increased unacceptably. We each took spells of 30 minutes at the wheel throughout the day. By the afternoon, I was at the wheel, Gordon was off watch, sitting in the cockpit, and Jenny was resting below. Gordon and I were both securely clipped on. *May Bee* was surfing down the face of another wave and as I was correcting the boat near the bottom of the trough, Gordon called, 'Look out, here comes a big one.'

Then I was underwater. There was a sensation of being pulled along in the boat's wake. I have no memory of how I was plucked from the wheel, since I was certainly holding on very tightly. A desperate need for air drove me to fight my way to the surface, and then I saw *May Bee* lying dismasted a few yards away. We later discovered one of the yacht's safety harness fixing points, a U-bolt of 5mm stainless steel, had sheared off as though the 'U' had been hack-sawn away.

My first thought, looking at the mast in the water, was 'how do we get that back up again?' Then logical thought took over as slowly, but surely, I pulled myself along the rigging back to the boat. I had no sensation of fear. I wasn't aware of feeling cold, or of the sea being rough. I wasn't alarmed when I realised how difficult it was to get back on board. Gordon was calm and efficient. He found my harness line, made it fast to the compass binnacle and rolled me safely back on board.

Gordon, who had been looking astern at the time, said that *May Bee* had been hit by a second wave, immediately behind the wave we'd surfed. She had been knocked over to starboard through 180°, the mast snapping off at deck level, with the heel fitting completely shattered. But the boat quickly righted herself.

As *May Bee* was knocked down, Gordon had remained in the cockpit, but as she righted herself, he was sucked into the sea, still clipped to the port side cockpit U-bolt. This was fortunate, as it kept his head above water and, since the guardrail wire had been cut by the shrouds and a stanchion had been swept away, he managed to clamber back aboard.

Jenny, down below, had been thrown around the cabin but emerged from the hatch and was able to collect lifejackets for everyone. A MAYDAY was sent out and the EPIRB switched on. But as there was no mast, and therefore no aerial, the first distress call was never received.

We started to clear up the debris. The main compass had been washed away, but strangely the lifebuoy holder, which was only lashed on with thin line, was still in place, although somewhat bent. A 23 litre (five-gallon) emergency water bottle, securely lashed under the mainsheet fixing point and binnacle stand, had been ripped away, breaking lashings and a 6mm polypropylene rope.

I found the pump handle and began to pump the bilges. During the rollover we reckoned some 320 litres of water had been forced through three ventilators. Waves were still breaking over the boat, but otherwise she remained relatively stable.

The biggest danger was the threat of the mast punching a hole in the hull as it was held against the starboard side by stays and shrouds. One of the port side shrouds had hit the four-man Beaufort liferaft on the coachroof with such force that it had sliced into the hard plastic of the canister like a cheese cutter. Gordon had to use brute force and a hammer to extricate the shroud.

Seeing a tanker quite close and apparently heading towards us, we fired two parachute flares and an orange smoke flare. But the tanker continued on without seeing us. During the next 30 minutes we spotted two or three other tankers, but felt it unwise to waste further flares since they were quite far away. Gordon continued to cut lines to the boom and release more shrouds. We thought about using the mast as a drogue but decided to let it go.

The final stay to be released was the forestay. In such a precarious position, it was difficult and dangerous for Gordon to cut. With the weight of the mast and sails hanging on it, he was conscious of the threat of a whiplash effect when it was finally released. It took a lot of effort to remove the final quarter inch of the clevis pin from the fitting.

With all the rigging gone, the boat was much easier to handle, lying a-hull to the waves. We all sat together in the cockpit deciding what to do about the lack of a VHF aerial. Gordon started to jury rig an aerial, using 3m of wire and the diesel tank dipstick and sent off several MAYDAYs. I continued to pump. We were concerned about Jenny, who was gradually becoming colder. She seemed confused and in a lot of pain. She kept holding the EPIRB and asking if her children were all right. Was it delayed shock? When the yacht had been knocked down, Jenny had hurt her neck and arm. However, what we didn't realise was the full extent of her injuries. (It was later discovered that she had fractured her spine.)

Down below, the cabin was covered in mayonnaise from a broken container. The GPS was still functioning, but despite heroic efforts, Gordon was unable to start the engine.

Fortunately, one of our VHF distress calls had been heard by the tanker that had failed to see our flares. The transmission was very broken, but we believed she was heading back towards us.

We were still very concerned about Jenny. By this time she couldn't move her left arm and was in a lot of pain. We clipped her lifeline to the binnacle stand. I was still pumping and calling out orders, and I remember Gordon shouting at me that if I didn't shut up he would throw me back into the sea again.

The tanker was now only about half a mile away, but despite being given our GPS position, he could not spot us through the breaking seas. It was then that we realised how big the waves were.

Hearing the tanker captain on the VHF telling a helicopter rescue pilot that he couldn't see us, George fired off orange flares and parachute flares. These the tanker eventually spotted. A fishing rod, with a pair of Jenny's red thermal longjohns attached, acted as a flag signal and more flares were set off to pinpoint our position for the helicopter. Some failed to ignite, while the wind strength burnt others like oxyacetylene torches. Gordon burnt his hand and had to throw one flare into the water.

Finally, the helicopter was overhead and we could see how hard it must be to fly in 40 knot winds. A line was dropped, which landed on the bow. Gordon took a flying leap to catch it and then the winchman, complete with flippers, dropped into the sea.

Unfortunately, he came up on the port side of the yacht where the lifelines were still intact and got caught up in the wires. Managing to free himself, he then began to attach Gordon and Jenny into a dual harness. Meanwhile, two tankers took up station to windward, giving us a lee. Large waves made it difficult to stand. Jenny and Gordon began their ascent, but, after moving only a foot or so, they were dropped back on deck.

It was decided that the safest way to lift them was for them to jump into the sea and be winched from there. But when Jenny's life-jacket failed to inflate she disappeared under the waves. Gordon managed to push her up to the surface and they were lifted another few feet before dropping back into the sea. Then they were dragged along the waves before being safely hoisted.

It was my turn next. I not only had the grab bag attached to me, but also had Jenny's handbag round my neck. Summoning all my courage to go overboard again, I jumped with the winchman and felt my lifejacket ride up over my face. I hadn't tied it tight enough. As the lift towards the helicopter began, the air was pushed out of my lungs and I seemed to be swinging into nothingness. Suddenly I was safely inside the helicopter, reunited with Gordon and Jenny. Wrapped in warm blankets, we were still anxious about Jenny's neck.

On landing at La Coruña, Jenny was taken off to hospital in an ambulance, while Gordon and I had warm showers and were given smart new blue flying suits to wear and various forms to fill in. We phoned home to break the news to our wives. Later the helicopter pilot and his wife found us accommodation in the centre of town.

The local Lloyd's agent was notified of our accident and subsequently alerted shipping and the local fishing fleets. *May Bee*'s last position had been some 25 miles north-west of Cape Finisterre. We had been so near the protection of the lee of the cape, yet so far. Lloyd's felt there was a reasonable chance the yacht might be found and salvaged.

Thanks to the grab bag, we had money and credit cards and were able to go shopping for new clothes next day. In hospital, Jenny was laid out flat, encased in a neck brace. Her injuries were serious. She had a fracture to her sixth vertebra, compounded by a crush injury to the radial nerve down the left arm. This in turn caused the loss of sensation to the index and third finger, as well as some reduction in the muscle power of her left arm.

Some days later, Gordon got permission for Jenny to be flown home on a stretcher. With three return tickets (cheaper than singles) we all headed off for Santiago Airport, Jenny in an ambulance. The final hurdle was that the airline insisted on six more seats being paid for (the length of the stretcher was nine seats) before Jenny would be allowed on board. Two hours of argument followed, with Jenny left sweltering in the ambulance in the full glare of the midday sun. The money still had to be paid, despite the fact that the plane was nearly empty.

At Gatwick Airport, staff arranged for a special lift vehicle to take Jenny's stretcher out through the catering loading door and the local ambulance service drove us to East Surrey Hospital, Redhill, where we were reunited with our families.

In Spain we had time to talk, think and reflect. One thing we agreed on was our strong desire to go back to sea and try to do the trip again.

FOOTNOTE

Some days after returning home, Gordon received news from Spain that a fisherman had found *May Bee* 300 miles from where she had been abandoned. She was towed into La Coruña. Gordon flew out with the loss adjuster. The yacht's interior had been stripped, apart from the engine and two anchors. Even the saloon table, cabin heater and stove had been unbolted. The hull was badly damaged and the yacht declared a total loss by the insurers, with no salvage money awarded to the fishermen.

Jenny made a good recovery, but has no feeling in two fingers.

■ **LESSONS LEARNED**

Barry Thunder describes how one of the yacht's safety harness fixing points, a U-bolt of 5mm stainless steel, had sheared off 'as though the U had been hack-sawn away'. U-bolts can have a nasty habit of fracturing. The reason is simple, according to Jeremy Rogers, a well-known boatbuilder. 'A solid looking U-bolt may conceal a narrower gauge threaded end, because the screw thread has been machined out of the original thickness of the bolt. So, for example, a 10mm U-bolt may have a puny 6mm thread below deck. If you're worried about yours, look for U-bolts with the deck-plate welded on rather than a loose fitted one. The welded plates are best.'

Dismasted and with no VHF aerial, the crew found that their first distress call was never received. Fortunately, the skipper was able to jury rig an aerial, using 3m (10ft) of wire and the diesel tank dipstick and sent off several MAYDAYs. An emergency VHF aerial would be advisable in most other cases.

Liferaft stowage is always an important topic. In the case of *May Bee*, one of the port side shrouds hit the four-man Beaufort liferaft on the coachroof with such force that it had sliced into the hard plastic of the canister like a cheese cutter.

Barry Thunder also relates how he jumped into the water with the winchman and felt his lifejacket ride up over his face. He had not tied it tight enough. In these circumstances the use of a crutch strap is shown to be essential.

nineteen

THE SINKING OF
GALWAY BLAZER

Yacht	*Galway Blazer*
Skipper	Peter Crowther
Bound from	Plymouth, England, for Newport, Rhode Island, as a solo competitor in the 1996 Europe 1 Singlehanded Transatlantic Race
Date of loss	24 June 1996
Position	49°41'N 20°33'W

It was 1900 on Monday 24 June 1996, and Peter Crowther was aboard the vast 300m (985ft) container ship Atlantic Compass *heading for Halifax, Nova Scotia. Why? That morning he had been aboard his own yacht* Galway Blazer *competing in the tenth Singlehanded Transatlantic Race, Europe 1-STAR.*

IT HAD BEEN A NORMAL NIGHT ON BOARD — I didn't sleep too well, but it was the first blow. I put two reefs in each sail and the boat was comfortable and going in the right direction. I must have slept a little, for I dreamt of a shallow man-made reservoir next to an old aerodrome and the reservoir workers reprimanded me for putting debris in it from the dinghy; and yet there were hundreds of rats in their control tower and they kept getting into people's clothes.

I got up about 0600, made myself a coffee and noticed that the turbine from Walter the water generator had disappeared and reminded myself to get a new one sent over from Ampair. The solar air vent was letting in water – another reminder to fix it. There was plenty of juice in the batteries and I tried to get Portishead between the chats, but to no avail. I put *Galway Blazer* time back to GMT, ate a banana and planned to have grapefruit later and rice salad for lunch. I read a bit of the post-war history of England. Annie the Aries wind-vane was steering well. I was not in much of a hurry, but at about 0930 it was time for the vitamin pills and cleaning teeth.

I was standing by the chart table when we slid off a wave, hitting the starboard side, aft of the mast, with a horrendous thud. It was as if an invisible shoulder had charged at a door and burst it apart. There, up by the frame which goes under the bed, a torrent of green water poured in. I knew at once there was no way of stopping this miniature tidal wave, given the sheer power behind it.

I fumbled like hell to put out a distress call on the SSB radio. I gave position, name and 'abandoning ship!' The water was almost up to my knees and surging through the boat.

I grabbed a container of water, and a thermal top, which I put on, plus waterproofs. I should have grabbed a bag with passport and money from above the chart table. I should have closed the saloon doors to the cockpit, to stay afloat longer. I should have said goodbye. I should have turned off electrics.

Instead, I grabbed a penknife, always open and by the hatch, plus a portable VHF radio and GPS, and then went up through the hatch aft to get the EPIRB. I wanted the EPIRB in the liferaft and not on the boat. I activated it and carried everything to the Tinker liferaft dinghy, inflated, thank heaven, up forward between the masts.

I cut the restraining ropes, and also the foresail sheet which was in the way. The bows were already down and almost under water, the transom in the air slightly.

I shoved everything under the deflated canopy, and sat on top, soaked and trying to prevent the dinghy from getting caught between the lifelines, knowing I had to get free of *Galway Blazer*. I drifted off the starboard side, avoiding the slapping mainsail. That's how low the boat was in the water.

Then I got under the canopy and bailed with the bucket to get the water out, before inflating the canopy and getting the sea anchor to work. The instructions were still on board *Galway Blazer*, which was a little way away, sails touching the water and transom a little raised, the wind generator and the Aries working. I looked again between surges and only the mast tops above the reefed sails were visible as she chose where finally to head downwards to rest 49°41'N 20°33'W.

Thank you for all those wonderful years of sailing.

I was completely soaked. No socks or seaboots. My waterproofs were lying in the bottom. It was time to take stock. I checked that the EPIRB and the VHF radio were working. The GPS batteries were low. There was plenty of food and water. I tightened the dinghy's bow flaps to stop the waves coming in and also the stern ones, just in case of capsize. I decided to look out every so often but I had no watch and no way of knowing the time.

I put on wet waterproofs. My thermals would dry out. I decided to wrap my feet in a space blanket and stick them inside a waterproof bag when they became cold. The liferaft was very claustrophobic. Enclosed, with no horizon, and bobbing about is a recipe for seasickness, but so far I felt fine. I had some water, a tot of whisky, another recipe for seasickness, and an oatmeal biscuit. Very, very dry, sticking to the top of my mouth.

Between sponging sessions, which took up a lot of time, I decided to lie down with my bum on one canister, my hips on the centre seat, and the top of my body on another canister. I tried to catnap, hood pulled over my head to stop any water going down my neck. With eyes closed the motion got better. I thought I heard a plane, but looked and saw nothing. It was too early anyway. I mentally prepared myself for at least a night afloat.

It must have been the roar of a breaking wave. Later, I heard the same roar again, but saw nothing. I decided to let off a flare anyway. It was a very old flare and didn't work. Most of the new ones were still on *Galway Blazer*. I threw the flare away. The next one was up-to-date and worked. I saw a Nimrod plane and contacted them on my hand-held VHF. I told them who I was. They asked if I was the only person aboard. They told me that a vessel was on its way, 20 miles from me (or was that my imagination?) and stayed in contact between me and the ship's captain, which helped. Then I saw the vessel looming out of the mist straight ahead of me, some 2 1/2 miles away.

The weather was getting worse. Fantastic guidance was shown by the plane as the ship, *Atlantic Compass*, came slowly to windward of me and stopped. I later learned that she used her bow and stern thrusters to get close to me.

A line was thrown and I scraped down the side of the ship and tied it on the thwart. I was pulled to a doorway 3m above the water. It was difficult to get out of the stern of the dinghy. The canopy was rigid. I thought of cutting it, but I was not safe yet and water was slopping over the transom.

A rope ladder was thrown down and a rope with loops. I went for the ladder. Unfortunately, my right leg was behind the ladder against the hull and the other was around the front. It was the wrong way to climb. I swivelled round and moved my feet. Left one first, automatically, like learning to dance as a teenager. And then through the door, thanking faces and climbing up and up through the cargo decks. I arrived at the ship's bridge, dripping water. I thanked the Nimrod crew. My liferaft was still bobbing about far below, EPIRB turned off by me, confirmed. The VHF was still on. It didn't matter. *Atlantic Compass* told me it was not able to pick up the liferaft.

I was taken to a cabin. My clothes, all I had, were taken away to be washed and dried and I was given a pair of overalls. Then I talked to my wife, Alix, and the girls. That was worth surviving for and we shared our grief over the loss of such a happy and beautiful boat.

FOOTNOTE

Peter Crowther (50), Devon pub landlord, arrived home to a hero's welcome at the Green Dragon, Stoke Fleming, near Dartmouth, after landing in Nova Scotia, minus passport and money. It had been his fifth solo transatlantic race, his fourth in *Galway Blazer*, the 12.80m (42ft) whale-backed junk-rigged schooner which he had owned for 23 years. Designed by Angus Primrose, she was built in 1968 for Cmdr Bill King, who circumnavigated in her. Crowther wrote a book on the yacht's chequered history: *Single-handed Sailing in* Galway Blazer, published by Waterline.

■ LESSONS LEARNED

Having a 'grab bag', or 'panic bag', and a well-rehearsed 'abandon ship' routine is essential. So catastrophic was the collision damage to Crowther's boat that, with water already up to his knees, he had only seconds to grab a container of water and thermal top, plus waterproofs, before abandoning ship. On the way out he also managed to grab a penknife, 'always open' by the hatch, plus, more importantly, hand-held VHF, GPS, and EPIRB. He left behind passport and money, as well as seaboots and socks. The instructions for the Tinker dinghy/liferaft were also left aboard the sinking vessel, along with most of his new distress flares.

In an ideal world, we would all rehearse our safety procedures. Deploying equipment, such as liferaft, flares, drogue or parachute anchor, even on a calm day, as a practice run for a real-life disaster scenario, or for heavy weather, ensures a degree of familiarity and confidence.

Crowther found that the batteries for his hand-held GPS were running low. Always carry spare batteries in the 'grab bag'.

The importance of having a hand-held VHF radio is demonstrated by Crowther's ability to talk to the pilot of the Nimrod aircraft who co-ordinated the rescue that saved his life.

A SHORT RACE ACROSS THE ATLANTIC

Yacht	*Ana*, ex *Modi Khola* (a water-ballasted Phil Morrison design)
Skipper	Jason Baggeley
Bound from	Plymouth to Newport Rhode Island
Date of loss	June 2000
Position	Mid-Atlantic

Jason Baggeley had spent the last two years dreaming of, and preparing, for the Europe 1 New Man Star Singlehanded Transatlantic Race from Plymouth to Newport Rhode Island in June 2000. Twelve days out from Plymouth, disaster struck.

THREE WEEKS BEFORE THE START of the race I arrived in Plymouth having bought and refitted the old *Modi Khola* for singlehanded sailing. *Modi* was well known on the short-handed racing scene, having competed in three double-handed Round Britain races. Designed and built in 1989 by Phil Morrison, she was incredibly advanced for her time, with curved decks, improved aerodynamics, and water ballast. No faster 30-footer had been built for offshore racing, as evidenced by her unbeaten record in the 30ft class. This speed came at a price, as Phil had not built in any comforts – she was a very wet boat to sail, and physically demanding.

I had named her *Ana*, after a dear friend who died of cancer aged just 32. I made several changes to the boat, including putting in a saildrive engine, to replace the old outboard, and totally upgraded the electronics with new Raytheon/Raymarine instruments, Yeoman Sport Plotter/Raymarine and SSB radio receiver, as well as installing a deck hatch in place of the normal companionway that had always let in water. I also put in a seat at the chart table – the only seat on the boat, and one I knew I would spend a lot of time in.

I had not raced singlehanded before, and once the buzz of the start had died down and few boats could be seen it was time to relax and settle into a routine. I had made a last minute change to my game plan to follow the rhumb line, instead of the Great Circle route, as I was concerned how far south the icebergs were. I had no radar, and the idea of icebergs and fog over the Grand Banks had little appeal.

Four days into the race we got the first gale. It was expected, but going upwind into a gale in such an extreme 30-footer is not much fun. It was, in fact, the first time I had used my trysail in anger. I quickly developed a routine of catnaps, food, housework (bucket and sponge), navigation and steering. The gentle Atlantic swell and settled winds of fairytales never developed, so I had to change sails, alter water ballast, and tack more often than my body thought appropriate. Generally everything worked well. My early problems concerned the autopilot – the mountings for the tiller drive (I had one each side) both collapsed in the first four days, even though they were epoxied in. I managed to rig a repair, but was surprised at the loads, and often had to re-secure them. Then on day 10 one tiller arm just broke in two.

The weather was very variable with lots of fronts coming through – a general description would be 'miserable'. There was a massive amount of rain, and I didn't see the sun or stars for nine days. The wind continued to be variable – reefs and water ballast in and out, in and out. I spent lots of time at the chart table trying to get weather-faxes etc. I got very lonely and missed friends and family; because I had a limited budget I had no two-way communications, so I didn't know how I was doing. This sometimes made motivation a problem . . . but then that's what singlehanding is about and I'm a stubborn and competitive sailor.

One of the reasons *Ana* had such a good record is that she has been pushed hard by her various owners. But for this race I had to take a different approach – there are no stopovers and 2,900 miles of beating is more than most boats do in several years, let alone 20 days. As a result, I had a golden rule: reef as soon as you think about it; shake it out half an hour after you think about it. My tactical requirement was always to be on the making tack. At times, this meant several tacks in an hour – hard work, as I would transfer all my water and food to the high side each time.

Day 11 was a defining point. I was approaching the halfway mark, and ready to celebrate with a bag of sweets from my sister and a double ration of chocolate from Fortnum & Mason (a present from Mary Falk who held the class record of 19 days). Although I didn't know it at the time, I was leading my class, and in front of many larger yachts. But in the early evening the barometer started to drop fast. We were going downwind with poled-out No. 3 and one reef in 20 knots true wind, and I decided to steer for a while to try and get the best out of the waves. Within half an hour the ride was getting too exciting with the wind increasing and backing. Time for another reef.

The next ten minutes were hectic, I dropped the No. 3 and stowed the pole, put a reef in, got the No. 4 on deck – put it back and got the storm jib, put the third reef in the main, put the storm jib up, dropped the main. I decided that I had enough sail with only the storm jib. The trysail wasn't needed, as I now planned to lie a-hull for the night as the wind had increased to a steady 55 knots plus and was now on the nose. My 2300 log entry shows the pressure at 1001, and falling fast, down from 1014 at 1400. I spent the night in a bunk with a space blanket over my oilies, trying to rest. The noise of wind, rain, hail, and the sea was amazing. A fellow competitor, over 100 miles to the south, saw gusts of 62 knots during the night.

At 0550 the next day I was sitting on the cabin floor mopping the bilges when *Ana* was knocked over by a wave. The floorboard I was sitting on hit me on the head, as did a can of food. As we righted it became clear that the mast had hit the water, but that no major damage had been done. Inside, things were a bit of a mess though. *Ana* had an angle of vanishing stability of 127° – I think we used at least 120 of them.

I went on deck to drop the storm jib. The wind was incredible, blowing steady white streamers off the waves, which were only 12–15ft high but steep and breaking. As I was sorting the lines, I saw a large wave begin to break above us and grabbed the lifelines. Again, we were knocked down. The boat came over me and I was dunked up to my chest – I was rather annoyed as these clothes had been fresh on the day before and still had four days to go.

At this stage I thought things were getting a bit serious. One knockdown could be considered unfortunate, two was a bit much. I wanted to improve the boat's angle to the waves and put out a form of sea anchor – two kites on long lines from the main anchor and line. It made not a jot of difference. While I was below cleaning up, we got hit again.

My memory of this one is a bit vague, linked, I think, to a new bruise on the side of my head. But this knockdown dismasted the yacht. As I started to cut away the rig I realised that maybe I had lived in Scotland long enough to become a native – I was trying to save blocks and lines rather than cut them away. I finally got the rig away, but was on my last hacksaw blade.

Waves continued to hit the boat hard, but no longer capsized her. I went below and started to bail, getting most of the water out before sitting down at the chart table to have one of my sister's flapjacks and some water and to take stock. I was in the middle of the Atlantic, but still had plenty of food and water – so maybe I could get home under jury rig. Whilst thinking about this I realised more water was coming in. That was the deciding factor.

With heavy heart, I set off my EPIRB and rewired my Satcom-D which had come adrift. Almost immediately my radar alarm went off. I set off a rocket flare, which vanished about 10ft above the water, not to be seen. The conditions were still poor and I didn't know how any-one could spot me. When things improved, I planned to rig up the spinnaker pole with a radar reflector and strobe light and to lash my Dayglo orange trysail across the deck.

I soon realised that the radar alarm was reacting to the EPIRB and turned it off. I tried to settle into a routine of bailing every 15 to 20 minutes and resting in between. I was aware that I could have quite a wait and had to be careful not to get dehydrated.

I regularly gave out a MAYDAY on the VHF, but held little hope as I had cut the emergency aerial when I slammed the hatch shut to avoid a breaking wave. In between bailing and sending MAYDAYs, I started to read the history of Shackleton. The first page dealt with the loss of the *Endeavour*; I thought it would give me hope since, in the last gale, reading about Willy Kerr and his latest adventures in his Contessa 32, *Assent*, had been a great source of encouragement. I was on page three, and about to start my next round of bailing, when I thought I heard a voice on the VHF. I was right. I made contact with the tanker NCC *Baha*. Before then I had imagined all sorts of voices, including the sound of RIBs (rigid inflatable boats) coming alongside.

Within two minutes of making contact, the ship had a visual fix on me.

I quietly congratulated their lookout and helm as well as staff at the Marine Rescue Co-ordination Centre (MRCC) Halifax, Nova Scotia, for such an accurate search pattern. Meanwhile, I was still at the chart table desperately trying to do up my Musto survival suit (undone for a call of nature) and get on deck. As I appeared on deck, I saw a bright orange chemical tanker 400 yards away – a wonderful sight indeed; they may not be the most beautiful of ships but they have a fairly low freeboard – during the whole episode my greatest concern was the transfer to the ship as I saw this as the most dangerous part. As the ship manoeuvred I sat in the cockpit crying and patting *Ana*, saying 'I'm sorry, I'm so sorry darling' – it was all I could do.

The master of the ship, Gwyn Armitage (British) brought his vessel alongside to the weather side of me – my engine actually started, although it lacked power, and my rudder was damaged. A line was attached under the guidance of Ivar Glesnes, the Norwegian mate, and Gary Rodaway, the British chief engineer – who grabbed me by the scruff of the neck and hauled me over the handrail from the netting.

Ana had swung away from the ship and was now being towed backwards. The line was cut and she was left to it – I lacked the courage to go and look at her. I was worried that she would be a danger to others, as her five buoyancy tanks would help keep her afloat for a while. But the master did not want to have to turn around again in those conditions – once had been more than enough. I understand, though, that the Inmarsat-D stopped sending a signal fairly shortly afterwards.

My rescue ship was a Norwegian registered chemical tanker on transit to Stockholm, nine days' sail away. The master and engineer were extremely good company, and I feel it important to say how it has changed my view of ships – although I don't think they are converted to the yachties' cause yet.

At no stage was I made to feel that they had lost time because of the rescue – in contrast to many stories of ships being keen to plug straight on.

The first phone calls to my family were very emotional, and followed by a cup of tea and a shower – I had a number of bruises, cuts and strains but nothing serious, although I was worried about the lump on the side of my head.

■ LESSONS LEARNED

It is good to know that when you set off a distress beacon, a well oiled process swings into action. The rescue services sent a Hercules aeroplane to look for Baggeley and made contact with the nearest ship by telex.

Make sure your EPIRB is registered to your yacht. Baggeley's was, although at first it was reported as belonging to another competitor. If it is correctly registered to you it helps people know what they are looking for, and to establish if it is a false alarm or not.

Storm sails should be coloured high-visibility orange.

The deck should be a bright colour – white hull and grey decks are very hard to see from a ship in those conditions. It was Baggeley's storm jib, floating off the bow, that was seen. It might not look good in the marina, but a bright orange foredeck would make all the difference.

If your self-steering has a tiller arm then have more than one point to mount it.

Take lots of hacksaw blades – Baggeley was on his last one.

Two-way communications, such as Inmarsat Satcom-C, would have made a huge difference – 'to know someone was coming and not far away would have been great,' said Jason.

His roving bilge pump was a godsend – especially good for shallow-bilged boats.

A space blanket will only last a maximum of two nights – Baggeley had not used his sleeping bag because of the amount of water taken on board, and slept in oilies or survival suit.

His kettle was secured in a deep baking tray with shock cord – it still flew out. On most boats the gimbals would not hold much – if you are next to a hot kettle it can be very dangerous.

A radar transponder makes it easier for rescuers to home in on you. It bounces a signal off the ship's radar.

Keeping calm is important. At least at first, as you know there is so much to do. It's worthwhile taking a few minutes to think through the job list and what tools you need, and to establish a routine. Make sure you continue to eat and drink – a little often will keep you fitter and better able to cope.

'Many people will say this experience only happened because I was racing an unsuitable boat,' said Baggeley. She weighed only 2,500 kilos and had a big rig and deep fin and bulb etc, but she was very seaworthy. He had sailed her over 5,000 miles in all conditions. 'I believe the only reason I had the difficulties was a rapid change of wind direction as a front went through – the boat changed its aspect to the waves, and I guess their nature had changed with steeper breaking faces. The Master of the *Baha* has said that they experienced steady Force 10-plus winds throughout the night, and the low deepened to 980, having started life the evening before at approximately 1014. I was simply in the wrong place at the wrong time.'

twenty-one

FASTNET RESCUE

Yacht	*Griffin* (Offshore One-Design 34)
Skipper	Neil Graham
Navigator	Stuart Quarrie
Mate	Peter Conway
Crew	Four students from the National Sailing Centre, Cowes
Bound from	Cowes to Plymouth, racing round the Fastnet Rock
Date of loss	14 August 1979
Position	approximately 40 miles south-east of the Fastnet Rock

---

This account of the loss of Griffin *was written by her navigator, Stuart Quarrie. The subsequent rescue of* Griffin's *crew from their liferaft was such a remarkable feat of seamanship, Alain Catherineau's account of how he and the crew of* Lorelei *saved lives is also included.*

WE EXPECTED A GALE DURING THE RACE – the Met office had forecast one – and we just hoped to be going downwind when it arrived. Rounding Land's End in almost calm conditions we discovered a short in a lighting cable which had drained the batteries – 'someone' had turned the isolator to 'both' during the night and this meant we couldn't start the engine and only had minimal electrics. It had been impossible to get all the charts we really wanted, owing to a strike in part of the Hydrographic Department. This meant we were short of large-scale charts of Southern Ireland, and those which we had were mainly metric charts but with no colour – very difficult to interpret, especially with a torch.

By the time we got the 0015 forecast on the night of the storm, we already knew we had a blow on our hands. We had progressively gone down from close reaching under spinnaker through No. 2 and No. 3 jibs and reefing the main as the wind came up from just before dusk. As the forecast time approached we were still racing – with Pete and Neil putting the third reef in while I steered. The mouse, which we had put in for reefing the third deep reef, had come adrift and the operation took about half an hour – we were also down to storm jib.

I asked one of the crew to take the forecast since I was busy, and I could hardly believe it when he said SW/NW 10–11, possibly 12! Unfortunately, he had not taken down the time period for the veer to NW, so we didn't know how long the southwesterly would last.

After that forecast we decided to stop racing and I was asked to decide whether to run for shelter or stay at sea. Not knowing the Irish coast, and being hampered by lack of some charts, I wasn't able to tell that Cork was a possible refuge even in a southwesterly; and, not knowing the timescale for a veer, I didn't want to close the coast. We therefore opted to stay at sea. We reduced sail to storm jib only and found that with a maximum allowed IOR storm jib we surfed and planed in a manner difficult to control, so went to bare poles.

With three crew below and four on deck we then sorted things out and I tried various different helm positions in the hope that we would be able to lash the tiller and all go below. We were quite happy for about 20 to 30 minutes with the helm pushed moderately hard to leeward, until an exceptionally big, unbroken wave rolled the boat. It is worth noting that those waves that had already broken didn't appear to be dangerous as their crests were mainly foam.

At this stage I was thrown from the boat and my harness hook – which had been clipped to a stanchion base – opened out to leave me 'free swimming'. This was at about 0130. I first thought of my life insurance then I miraculously saw a high intensity lifebuoy light 20 or 30m away. I swam to it and found the whole boat upside down with the light still in its clip. Neil Graham swam out of the cockpit air-gap and we talked somewhat inanely on the back of this upturned 'whale', until another wave finally rocked her upright.

After a head count – with everyone OK – we tried to take stock of the situation. It appeared that the boat was awash to the decks with the cabin almost full to the washboard level, and after a brief attempt at pumping, Neil decided – after talking to Pete and me – that it would be prudent to abandon ship in good order, rather than wait for her to start going down.

At this stage I was in shock to some extent; I had been so sure I was dead just minutes earlier and therefore didn't take as full a part in the decisions as I might have done, but I did agree with Neil.

We launched our Avon eight-man raft with no real difficulty and, taking the yacht's flare pack, abandoned ship into the raft. We couldn't find a sea anchor – whether by stupidity or not we will never know. We arranged ourselves around the raft to try to give it stability. We let off just one parachute flare, more as a gesture than anything else, and settled back to wait for daylight. After about 30 minutes a big wave rolled the liferaft upside down, ejecting two crew as it did so. While righting the raft we lost its canopy, and so after that we were like an open dinghy and up to our armpits in water.

At this stage we realised that one crewman, who had been below, hadn't got an oilskin top on and he was semi-comatose with hypothermia within about 15 to 20 minutes. After less than half an hour in the open raft we saw the mast-head light of *Lorelei*, and the rest of the story belongs to Alain Catherineau . . .

We were racing with 50 knots of wind, using the No. 4 jib and with three reefs in the Hood mainsail. Thierry, my first mate, was at the helm, taking great pleasure in the almost effortless sailing; the boat was standing up well and quite stable. Towards 0230 we were 30 or 40 miles from Fastnet and well on course. For about an hour we passed many boats, both windward and leeward of us.

Suddenly we were astonished to see a red parachute flare about half a mile downwind. I donned my harness and rushed forward and, with the help of Marc and Gerard, hauled down the No. 4. I had been prepared for this: the wind was remarkably gusty and our anemometer was recording up to 60 knots. Thierry and I decided to get closer to the red light; with three reefs in the mainsail it was easy for us to steer towards it. After failing on the first try, we finally went about. We were heading roughly south, Thierry still at the helm, when we saw a rocket or a red hand-held flare. We could not see the source of the light, only a red halo that was visible from time to time above the waves. I asked Thierry to stop heading towards the glow and ease off by about 30°; we had no idea what sort of boat we would find.

Some hours earlier we had met *Rochelais*, a rusty French trawler from La Rochelle, a most impressive sight. For some reason I thought that the crew in difficulty now was on a fishing boat.

We were very comfortable below deck; however, on deck, we would have lost two or three crewmen had not our harnesses been well-fitted. We were still heading towards the light when we saw two smaller lights above something dark; these were in the same wave and about 50m downwind. It was a liferaft. Some way farther on we turned and headed towards the liferaft, our mainsail at three reefs. We came 3m upwind of it, the same distance away from it, and at a speed of about three knots. One of my crew threw a rope to the liferaft, but it would not reach. Two of the liferaft's crew hurled themselves towards us in an attempt to catch the hull; instead they fell into the sea and were hauled back by their colleagues.

I decided to take over the helm. I felt it was possible to save these men as long as I was at the helm and an integral part of my boat. I know *Lorelei* (a Sparkman and Stephens-designed She 36) very well and can often demand – and get the impossible. I started the engine and hauled down the mainsail. The engine is a 12hp diesel, but the propeller has automatic variable pitch which gives maximum power very quickly and greater than normal acceleration and deceleration. After seven or eight unsuccessful attempts I finally managed to come about and headed into the wind. During this time we had covered some distance. We were heading south, in total darkness, in search of the red light. Suddenly we saw it. I turned again – an easier job than it had been the first time – and cautiously headed towards the red glow, which lit up the surrounding blackness whenever it became visible. I turned to the north and crossed at about four or five knots. I approached the liferaft and aimed *Lorelei* straight at it when we were about 25m away. I threw the engine into reverse in the last few metres and, thanks to *Lorelei*'s propeller of variable pitch, she drew rapidly to a halt, stopping within a metre of the liferaft.

Thierry and Marc each threw a line to the raft and the crew hauled themselves alongside *Lorelei*. I felt dead. There was some confusion on the liferaft as the crew leaped to catch hold of our ropes or deck. One or two climbed aboard easily; three more remained in our stern on the aluminium toe-rail. I suddenly noticed that the liferaft was drifting away from us with two of the crew still on board. Luckily, one of them managed to grasp a rope that had stayed on board and pulled the raft back alongside. A few moments later the liferaft drifted away, empty. The end of the rope had not been made fast. I stopped the motor for safety and some of my crew helped two men climb aboard and three or four more of us at the stern helped the remaining three. The first few castaways were already in the cabin; there were only two left in the sea.

I sent the fit members of the liferaft crew to help out on deck. I was holding on to one who had been under the counter with only his head above water. He was one of the few to have a harness and I managed to pass a rope through it and then over the pushpit. In this way I lifted him out of the water. However, the harness slipped over his shoulders and I had to release him into the water again. Philippe was holding him by his T-shirt, the only garment he had. Finally, helped by his fellow English crew members, the castaway was rescued from the waves. He was heavy and it took five or six heaves on the ropes to pull him into the cockpit.

In the cockpit his leg became trapped between two ropes, but we soon released him. The most injured member of the English crew was forward but there was still one more in the sea. I can no longer remember how we finally rescued him. I think that *Lorelei*, crossing the waves, heeled on the right side, sometimes very severely, so that we could grip the last castaway and haul him in a few centimetres. He was stiff with cold and could not help us rescue him. Soon he was in the cockpit surrounded by his rescuers. I realised that there was something wrapped around his head; he was being strangled by a cord on his T-shirt. I pulled at it with all my strength and it finally snapped.

It was about 0400 by then. An Englishman came out of the cabin and warmly shook my hand in thanks. All seven of his crew were safe; it was a happy moment. Thierry and I were in the stern. We hugged each other fiercely: we had succeeded.

A crewmember aboard *Griffin* transcribing the radio weather forecast 'unfortunately' failed to note down the time period for the storm force wind veer to NW, so no one knew how long the southwesterly winds would persist. The crew also discovered a short in a lighting cable which had drained the batteries – 'someone' had turned the isolator to 'both' during the night so they couldn't start the engine and had minimal electrics.

Another problem that revealed itself later was that it had been impossible to get all the charts they really wanted, owing to a strike in part of the Hydrographic Department. Thus they were short of large-scale charts of Southern Ireland. When the strong winds came, Quarrie, hampered by this lack of charts, and not knowing the Irish coast, wasn't able to tell that Cork was a possible refuge even in a southwesterly; and, not knowing the time-scale for a veer, he didn't want to close the coast. *Griffin* therefore opted to stay at sea.

When they abandoned the yacht for the liferaft, Quarrie was thrown from the boat and describes how his lifeline harness hook – which had been clipped to a stanchion base – opened out to leave him 'free swimming'. Another crewman, who had been below, and hadn't got an oilskin top on, was semi-comatose with hypothermia within about 15 to 20 minutes. Even when off-watch in extreme conditions it can pay to wear proper clothing. The safety harness of another crewman slipped over his shoulders when the rescuers tried to get him aboard *Lorelei* and he had to be released into the water again. A modern-day harness/lifejacket with a crutch strap solves this problem. The crew of the RORC boat *Griffin* may well owe their lives to the fact that the French yacht *Lorelei* was able to use her engine – a 12hp with variable pitch propeller – to manoeuvre alongside their liferaft. The automatic variable pitch gives maximum power very quickly and greater than normal acceleration and deceleration.

twenty-two

CAPSIZE! HOW I LOST
GULF STREAMER...

Yacht	*Gulf Streamer* (trimaran)
Skipper	Phil Weld
Crew	Bill Stephens
Bound from	America to Plymouth, England
Date of loss	27 April 1976
Position	38° north by 64° west in the Gulf Stream

Grandfathers are normally past the age for spills and thrills in the ocean, but not Phil Weld. In this extract from his book Moxie, *the American Challenge, the 65-year-old adventurer who shattered every previous record with his victory in the 1980 Observer Singlehanded Transatlantic Race, crossing in under 18 days in* Moxie, *his trimaran, describes how he spent five days trapped in his previous trimaran,* Gulf Streamer, *when she capsized on the way to the start of the previous 1976 OSTAR.*

THE IRONY OF LOSING GULF STREAMER in the Gulf Stream still makes me wince. It had been in a mood of celebration racing to Bermuda that I'd chosen the name. To pay tribute to this elemental force had seemed the friendly thing to do.

When planning the voyage to England for the 1976 OSTAR, it never occurred to me to regard the Stream as anything but a beneficent force that would hasten us on our way. It would sweep us past Florida, once we'd made our way from St Petersburg to Key West, at 4 knots. From Cape Canaveral, we'd follow a Great Circle to the Scilly

Isles. This track would cut north-east inside the Stream's curve. We'd rejoin it east of New Jersey, somewhere north of Bermuda, to allow it to keep us warm and boost us on our way to Plymouth.

The low coast of America disappeared in the sunset on the after-noon of Tuesday, 20 April 1976, as *Gulf Streamer* cantered along at 10 knots in a light southeasterly. The stern, relieved of the weight of the diesel engine, had risen two inches to give her a new lightness of foot. In light air, it could mean 8 knots instead of 7. Both the boat and I felt up for the race.

A new antenna rigged from the port spreader captured the Coast Guard's new sequence of voice broadcasts of North American weather. All through Sunday, 25 April, as we ran almost dead before a freshening southwesterly, it warned of a new gale centre over Cape Sable, Nova Scotia. It forecast winds from 25 to 35 knots and waves to 20 feet as far as 450 miles from the centre. Our position midway between Cape Hatteras and Bermuda came within that circle.

Bill Stephens, my 21-year-old shipmate, from Birmingham, Michigan, helped me to tie in a second reef before it got dark. By Monday's dawn, continuous streaks of foam were showing in the wave troughs. Time to drop the main. Under staysail only, it required constant attention at the wheel to hold the course without flogging its 300 square feet in accidental jibes. All through the day, the seas built up. Between wave crests, the surface took on that creamy look that indicates Force 9 – over 47 knots.

'I'm rapidly gaining respect for the power of the Atlantic,' Bill remarked mid-morning. His offshore sailing had heretofore been in the Great Lakes.

Frequent checks on WWV, the government station broadcasting from Fort Collins, Colorado, at eight minutes past the hour, indicated that the gale centre, per the prediction, was moving north-east, as were we, but much faster. As it out-distanced us, conditions would steadily improve.

'Bet on the wind's veering north-west tomorrow,' I said. 'Then look for six days of perfect reaching to England.'

So dawned the fateful morning of Tuesday 27 April. The wind had veered. We'd come over to the port jibe. During my watch from 0500 to 0900, the seas had notably decreased. It seemed prudent to put the helm under the control of the electric autopilot, while I took a sun sight through the patchy clouds and plotted our position.

I was using an old small-scale chart that showed this was the sixth time in two years that *Gulf Streamer* had been within 300 miles or less of this intersection of latitude and longitude, 38° north by 64° west: eastward from Gloucester to England, May 1974; St Martin to Gloucester, April 1975; back and forth on the Bermuda race, June 1975; Gloucester to Puerto Rico, December 1975. Like Old Home Week!

When Bill came on deck to take over the watch, we remarked upon the abating seas and noted that our speed had dropped to 8 knots. 'If we were racing,' I said, 'we'd be putting up the main.' But we agreed in the interest of rest and comfort to postpone this until I came on watch at 1300.

I went below and kicked off my boots for the first time in 36 hours, hung up my harness and oilies, and prepared for a nap. My bare feet tucked into the sleeping bag, my head pillowed in the outer corner of my berth, my knees wedged against the canvas bunk board, I felt utterly content. I munched a RyKrisp.

Bill had impressed me as an alert helmsman more than once in the past ten days. I could see him through the companionway checking the Tillermaster autopilot. I hadn't the slightest worry, only a small guilt that, had I been solo racing, my lot would have been less easy. I took out *Can You Forgive Her?*, the first volume in an Anthony Trollope six-pack that my mother had given me for Christmas, and was in the middle of the first sentence when I heard Bill shout, 'Look out!'

A second to rise up. Another to swing my legs off the bunk. Four seconds. Bill's next agonised cry coincided with the cracking, clapping sound of flat surface slamming water with maximum impact. Cracker boxes, dishes, cups, books, came tumbling over my ears. Water, sunlit and foam-flecked, poured through the companionway.

Even as the mast must have struck the water, and *Streamer* lay like a wing-clipped swan on her side, I still felt confident that the immense strength and buoyancy of her outrigger would be able to heave her upright.

'This just can't be,' I thought.

A second shattering smack. Then gently, as the mast subsided below the surface, the bunk revolved upward above my head. I stood calf-deep in water on the cabin ceiling. All was suddenly quiet except for the water gushing through from the cockpit.

Panic for Bill seized me. The trapped air was being compressed upward against the bilge by the rising water which had yet to reach the level of the cockpit sole. I wanted him clear of the cockpit. He put his head into the rising water to swim down beside me but had to withdraw to unhook his safety harness. Then he swam down inside.

Ten, twelve, fifteen seconds might have passed since his shouted warning, surely less than thirty.

I remember the smell of damp Naugahyde, the plastic fabric sheathing the underside of the bunk cushions. As the outstretched arms of the outriggers assumed their upside-down position, their buoyancy took over part of the support of the main hull, now resting on the flat surface of the main cabin top. The water level had stopped rising at about our belt line. The last temperature reading had shown 68°F. As the sea surged both fore and aft and crosswise inside the hull, the sun shone through the glassfibre, causing the interior wavelets to twinkle merrily.

Bill and I discussed the air supply and agreed it was adequate. We both seemed gripped by the same icy calm. 'Well, I'm sorry if I dumped your boat,' said Bill. 'But I don't feel guilty because I know I did the right thing.'

'I know you did,' I said.

'I'd been looking ahead. I turned around. This wall. Forty feet high. I had two crests just off the stern. I kicked Tilly clear. Grabbed the wheel and pulled her off with all my weight. Three spokes. I thought she'd come back until I saw the mast hit the water. Then the second crest hit us.'

'I could see you hauling on the helm,' I said. And with few more words we got down to the business of survival.

Multihull designer and sailor Jim Brown, who had questioned the survivors of *Meridian*, a trimaran that had capsized off Virginia in June 1975, had told me the key: 'The hulls will float high. Don't rush the vital items into the vulnerable liferaft. Safe your energy to live aboard upside down.'

From the welter of objects surging in the waist-deep water we grabbed first for the three radio beacons. We tucked them with the two sextants, the almanac, the navigation tables, a pair of pilot charts, the first-aid chest, the waterproof metal box of flares, into the shelves and corners most nearly high and dry, in this topsy-turvy world. The crown-jewel safekeeping spots were the underside of the chart table and the two bins for cleaning materials beneath the stove and galley table. Here, safely wedged, we found the two-gallon jerry can of emergency water.

Now came the urge to communicate with fellow men. As I'd planned with Jim Brown, I unscrewed, from what was now 'the overhead', the through-hull fitting for the log propeller, just forward of the mast and of the midships bulkhead. Through the two-inch hole I could see blue sky. I'd punctured the seal of our air cushion. Would the escaping air cause the water to rise? We thought not and it did not. The craft's inherent buoyancy from her Airex sandwich construction, together with the four airtight compartments in each outrigger, provided us with what would prove to be raft status of indefinite duration.

Into the little window on the world, I thrust the rubberised antenna of the oldest of the three beacons and set it to pulsing.

Next we had to cut a hatch through the keel to the outdoors. It took three hours to complete the fourteen-by-eighteen-inch aperture. First a drilled hole. Then enlargement with hammer and chisel to make a slit admitting a hacksaw blade. Then a pruning saw with a curved, coarse blade to lengthen the slit on one side. My talk with Jim had prompted me to tuck these tools for safekeeping beneath the chart table. We repeated the process at three subsequent corners. It was tiring, this reaching overhead to saw. Glassfibre dust got in our eyes. Mounting claustrophobia kept us hard at it until finally we'd hammered the rectangular panel free.

Once again we could look out into the real world, and a sombre sight it presented: grey sky, grey water; squall clouds all about on the horizon, but nary a ship. Here and there bits of Sargasso weed.

'We're in or near the Gulf Stream,' I said.

'The nearest shipping lane?' Bill asked.

'About 30 miles south-west of here the pilot chart shows a

junction point. But I think we shouldn't plan on a quick pick-up. Let's think in weeks. Not hours or days.'

Looking out of our hole in the hull, I saw the big red spinnaker clinging to the aft end of an outrigger. However did it get there? It takes the weight of a man to force it bagged through the forward hatch. Only then did we note how empty the cabin had become of floating debris. Investigating the head, we saw that the hinged hatch cover had opened under the pressure of water on its 'inside' surface. Through that two-foot-square opening the hungry sea had sucked seven-by-three foot cushions, sailbags bulky as barrels, boots, clothing, pillows, bottles, cans, fruit, anything that floated.

We began then to retrieve whatever we could grab and to dive for heavier items lying on the cabin's former ceiling, now its floor, or caught in bunk or locker corners. I dived five times to grope for and find the pistol-grip hacksaw and extra blades that I'd taped inside three waterproof bags and secreted in the aft starboard locker where it could have been reached from outside after capsize. Triumph!

I'd bought three extra sets of these to present as boat-warming presents to the skippers of the three 31ft Newick trimarans fitting out at Vineyard Haven, Massachusetts, before their 500-mile qualifying solos for the OSTAR. All during Monday's gale, I'd worried about them and thanked my stars that I had more boat under me than they. As it turned out, all made uneventful fast passages to England.

Outside, the sea remained too rough for us to want to venture out onto the keel to commence cutting through to the aft cabin where we knew we'd eventually find food aplenty. Both encased raft and deflated dinghy remained beneath the cockpit seat, now upside down.

FIRST NIGHT ADRIFT

Bill waded to the forepeak to fashion us a dry lair on the underside of the bow deck. Though it was dark and narrow, with the one remaining bunk cushion as a base, and the new staysail and light spinnaker to use as coverlets, he made us a bed just clear of the water.

'The first night will be the worst,' I said. We discussed strategy. Protection against cold and wet came first. We calculated that we had a liquid supply for three to four weeks. Juice in cans of fruit and vegetables to be salvaged later would stretch it out.

The underside of the chart table formed a mini quarter berth, more nearly high and dry than any other place inside. I stuck it out there for two hours, then gave up when a cramp knotted my thigh. Sucking wind as I lowered myself into the waist-deep water, I lunged forward to join Bill. Flecks of phosphorescence gave our cabin the eerie glow of a darkened discotheque, 'Davy Jones's Hideaway'. My left leg went down through the hatch to the open sea. I checked my descent by clutching the toilet seat dangling overhead. I muttered an oath.

'You all right?' from Bill, deep back in his den.

'Yes, but I just lost the bottle of bourbon,' I had to confess. My lurch had dumped it from my oilskin pocket. It was a dreary moment.

I crawled inside beside the daggerboard trunk and stretched out on the bunk cushion. As the hulls pitched slowly to the ocean's rhythm, the water ebbed and flowed up my trouser legs. My shoulders, resting against Bill's knees, felt him shivering. 'Tomorrow we make a hammock,' he said.

SECOND DAY ADRIFT

At first light we shared a can of orange juice. Even if we'd had food, I doubt we'd have eaten anything.

From its bag came the never-used staysail, reserved for the race. Neither of us could bear to hack at the pristine Dacron so we gathered it at the corners – as one would knot a handkerchief headdress – and hoped for the best. Every 20 minutes one of us would squirm shoulders through the lookout for a scan. We agreed that the wind and the sea had dropped. From a skein of wires suspended from the chart table's instrument panel, we retrieved the bubble compass from the RDF set and established that the hulls lay on a north-south axis athwart the wind with waves still coming from the west.

Gingerly, I folded back the sodden pages of the Nautical Almanac, noted the declination of the sun for 0400 GMT, Wednesday 28 April, mentally calculated the sextant setting for a meridian crossing of the sun at latitude 38°30', and settled down to pounce on 'noon' like a duck hunter awaiting dawn in his sneak box.

Squall clouds rimmed the north horizon. Sargasso weed floated in the cabin. A Portuguese man-of-war had hung itself up in one of the wing nets. The water felt warmer than the air. The sea was smooth enough to go 'on deck'.

'Time to tackle that hole to the aft cabin,' Bill said. He wriggled out, humped himself aft along the keel to a point we'd agreed on over the engine bed, and set to with a will to saw slots through the inch-thick keel, laid up of layers of solid glassfibre, hard as steel. Bill kept at it for two hours. Two slits athwartship, through the tough spine of the keel down to the foam sandwich, testified to his zeal. Having earned a rest, he took to the hammock and I took his place astride the keel. It was slippery and sloped down toward the stern. I had to grip with my knees, as if riding bareback on a horse that's stopped suddenly to crop grass. At a fraction of an inch a minute, the slit lengthened. I drilled, chiselled, and hacksawed four corners. When it was almost too dark to see, I knocked off. Only one side of the rectangle remained to be cut in the morning.

SECOND NIGHT

I tried to leave the hammock to Bill and stretched out in the forepeak. More water had settled way up in the bow so that it continually rinsed me, first down the collar, then up the crotch. Bill insisted I join him. We lay head to feet. I actually slept fitfully, despite the frequent splashes from below. But at Bill's expense, I fear. The bulk of the sail had bunched up on my side, leaving him slung lower and less protect-ed. He didn't sleep until daybreak, when I returned to my hacksaw.

THIRD DAY ADRIFT

The sea was down. Only a gentle westerly riffled the surface. Pink in the east. Blue sky above. Using a fresh blade, I attacked the last 18 inches with vim. A final hammer-whack broke out the V-shaped segment. Bill heard my gleeful call and stood in the lookout prepared to receive each recovered item. We'd rehearsed the priorities.

Four cases of tins had stacked themselves on the underside of the bunk projection – high and dry as if placed there by a grocery clerk.

Then through the hole to Bill's outstretched arms went a five gallon jerry can of water, three lifejackets, two radar reflectors, a horseshoe life ring, floorboards, strips of batten, the rubber survival suit, a sleeping bag, a tool box. I emerged with a can of chicken stew and a can of corn. We breakfasted astride the hull. The roofs of our mouths were unaccountably tender.

Refreshed, Bill took charge of rehanging the hammock. Working down from the head of the sail to a point where its breadth would then span the gap between the bunks, we measured off a further seven feet, and sliced through the Dacron. We cut more lanyards, drilled more holes. Stretched taut by the bolt rope on one side, by rolled cloth on the other, at last there was a proper litter. A length of anchor warp, pulled tight beneath, provided a fore-and-aft dividing ridge and extra security. So absorbed were we that I missed my noon sight.

We rested in the late afternoon sun, squeezing water from the down in a sleeping bag, scanning the horizon, and planning for the morrow.

'We need a way to get from the hammock to the lookout without getting soaked,' Bill said. 'And tomorrow I'll unscrew the big cabin mirror, break it up and glue pieces with epoxy to the hull. We need more ways to attract attention.'

He had stuck a 6ft aluminium extrusion, a spare for the jib-furling system, into the daggerboard slot and had wired the metal reflector to its peak. But the first of three beeping beacons had exhausted its battery some time the night before. We agreed to husband the expensive unit with the capacity to receive and transmit voice as well as beep, for moments when planes might appear over-head.

'Every helicopter in Vietnam carries one,' the boat show salesman told me. Pilots with whom I'd checked it at both Boston and Beverly airports considered it good. We even had an extra battery for it. The less costly beeper-only beacon would remain in reserve. Its test light failed to blink but because it was brand new, we had a right to think it would work.

THIRD NIGHT

The hammock, though vastly improved, lacked room for two to sleep. Inadvertent jostling kept one or the other awake. Wavelets from below splashed up water that pooled in the hollows. By using my end of the damp, down sleeping bag to cover my nose, and exhaling forcibly, I generated enough heat to forestall shivering.

At dawn we agreed hereafter to split the dark hours into two five-hour shifts, sundown to midnight, midnight to light. Off watch in the hammock, on watch in the survival suit.

FOURTH DAY ADRIFT

I rose first, made a bad guess on an unlabelled can: cold watercress and lentil soup. Bill began to make a 'crawlway' to get from the hammock to the lookout without getting wet.

Soon we'd unscrewed the seven-foot mahogany planks that served as the outer edges of the forward bunks. We cut one into two-foot lengths. Into one end of each we drilled a hole. We screwed down the outboard ends to the hull, then lashed the inboard ends with wire to holes drilled in the reinforcing of the daggerboard trunk. Thus they served as the trestles in a swinging bridge. Twisting the drill chuck a quarter turn at a time by hand (the rusting handle turned hard) had chafed the soaked skin of our fingers so they were painfully raw.

While I took the noon sight, Bill tackled the adhesion of the broken mirror shards to the flanks of the main hull, well forward, and aft by the rudder.

About 1500, basking in the sunshine and holding damp sweaters to the light westerly, Bill spotted a ship's bridge just appearing from north-east.

The flare sequence was an orange, a big parachute rocket, then the small rocket and the cartridges for the signal pistol. Our logic: first an attention-getter, then the big one to mark us by, then the smaller ones for follow-up.

'Perfect angle for visibility.'

'Let's hold back till they're within two miles.'

We each took a sizeable hunk of broken mirror and practised bouncing the focus of the sun in the west toward the approaching vessel whose white bridge and three buff cranes were now visible.

Now the orange flare was stripped of its protecting tapes, the 'scratch-to-light' directions reviewed.

'Two miles? Okay. Now.'

The hot magnesium sputtered. It was plausible that the torch, held high for nearly a minute, could have been seen by an alert lookout.

'I believe they've altered course.'

'Now for a rocket.'

First I tried one dated 1971, expecting a dud, and it was; then one of the five fresh ones.

'Point downwind . . . press the lever firmly.' Up, up, 300ft. High in the sky burst a pinky-orange ember that floated slowly down, in perfect view of any watcher on the bridge, now well within a mile.

'They've slowed down.' We fired the small rocket with the pistol.

'They've got to see this mirror. See it bounce on the bridge.'

We called 'MAYDAY!' on the beacon that had a voice transmitter. There was the odd chance that the ship might monitor its aircraft frequency. We waved orange towels. Now she was broadside.

'She's going to drift down on us.'

'She's going away.' The last of the three cartridge flares in the pistol packet proved a dud. What a fraud.

'They just had to have seen us,' said Bill, momentarily enraged.

'Maybe we only thought they slowed down,' I said. Disappointment engulfed us. We shared an inch of bourbon from the remaining half-bottle and a can of stew.

FOURTH NIGHT

A coin toss gave me first watch. At sunset I pulled on the survival suit over oilskins and sat snug where I could catnap and peer around the horizon every 20 minutes. It was comforting to hear Bill snore. Solo, the hammock worked.

I reviewed our state. My reading had buffered the impact of the ship's failure to see us. Dougal Robertson, the Baileys, *Meridian* – all had shot flares for several ships that didn't stop before, at last, one did. By the law of averages, over a period of weeks in this busy area east of Norfolk and New York, we were sure to be sighted. We had food and water to wait it out for at least five weeks. We could now manage to stay dry and out of the wind. There were no signs of the hull connections weakening. We'd ration our flares, watch for planes on which to use the beacon.

My only haunting worry: my wife, Anne, had a ticket for the plane to England on 16 May. By then we'd be overdue. We just had to be picked up in the next two weeks. But until then, it was comforting to know that no one was worried. When the handle of the Big Dipper stood erect, I swapped places with Bill and slept like a felled ox till dawn.

FIFTH DAY

A half-can of juice, a can of stew. The warming sun had Bill down to bathing trunks and safety harness while he stood barefoot on the underside of the bunks with a screwdriver, scratching 'SOS' in four-foot-high letters into the bottom paint.

We'd agreed on today's goal: rest the hands, dry out the clothes, settle in for a long siege. But the ship-miss had Bill restless.

I tore some pages from the back of a used notebook to make a log. On one sheet I mapped our position showing Bermuda 325 miles south; the Azores, 1700 miles downwind, downstream to the east; Nova Scotia, 300 miles north; Nantucket, 350 miles to the west.

'I'd vote to head for the coast and lots of ships,' said Bill. 'If we had a stretch of good weather, we could make it in nine days rowing in the dinghy.'

We exhausted the possibility of sawing off an outrigger and, with the raft and the dinghy to support the arms, converting it into a proa. At the rate our saw blades and other tools were turning to rust, we'd have lacked the equipment. Besides, to have violated the integrity of our raft would have been an act of desperation.

We agreed to forgo as futile further discussion of leaving the ship for at least another week.

We decided to use up the canned and bottled liquids before calling on the seven gallons of water, our most easily managed drinking supply in case we took to the dinghy.

'Look, jet,' Bill said, grabbing for the transmitter, and pointing to a contrail travelling towards New York.

'And there's another,' I said, pointing south-east at one homing on Washington. Two planes at once after four blank days. Unnerving. We fumbled with the antenna before extending it all the way for a sure transmit. The encounter with fellow man, even 35,000ft away, left me tingling. Petrels dabbling their feet in water, dolphins bounding, small fish swimming about in the cabin, all represented planetary life. None set the pulse pounding like that white trail in the sky saying People.

'Well, now we've had a practice run with a ship and planes,' said Bill, 'maybe we score next time.'

'It'll not be till the seventh ship,' I said.

He retired for a nap while I, in the late afternoon sun, tackled the pulpy wad representing the complete plays of Shakespeare. Whole folios of the least-read chronicle plays remained intact. *The Tempest* had taken a beating. Here was intellectual nourishment for many weeks. Lovingly I pressed pages one by one in the fold of a sun-dried towel. My spirits soared.

'Another jet. Eastbound.' On with the beeper. Then: 'MAYDAY, MAYDAY, MAYDAY! Capsized trimaran *Gulf Streamer*. Estimated position thirty-nine north by sixty-four west. Please report us. Over.'

I paused to listen for a reply and to let the beeper pulse a minute, then repeated the message. There was time for four sequences before the trail vanished on its way to Europe.

At sundown Bill got into the suit and I hit the hammock for four hours' sound sleep.

FIFTH NIGHT

'Ship's lights. Coming from the south,' Bill called. He was astride the keel by the time I'd wormed my way to the lookout. 'What luck. I'd just put my head down for a nap when this big wave smacks me in the face. I sat up again to dry off and there she was.' Bill was jubilant.

Ship's lights they were. Now we could see red and green running lights as well as the white lights bow and stern.

'First we'll give 'em an orange flare.'

It burned hot, glowing much more impressively than in the daytime. Bill held it high in the suit's rubber mitten while I readied the 'chute rocket.

'Now for the big one.' It soared magnificently.

'He's blinking. Let's give him a white one to home on.'

In close succession, we lit two whites and an orange. Each brightly illuminated the three hulls and the blessedly calm sea surrounding us. Now the ship had halted 100 yards upwind. I scrambled forward for two lifejackets hanging from the hammock and urged Bill to get out of the suit, which was too heavy for climbing ladders.

As the ship drifted closer, we could see men readying a cargo net and a figure on the bridge directing a searchlight on our hulls. I had only time to tuck passports, wallet, and letter of credit into a sleeping-bag sack, hang it around my neck, and crawl out.

In big white letters on her lee starboard side, I read *Federal Bermuda*. The rungs of a rope ladder stood out against the mesh of a net as the vessel nestled gently along the outrigger.

'Nip up, lads,' a voice called from the deck.

Hand over hand, first Bill, then I, scrambled up the swaying ladder and swung ourselves over the rail onto the steel deck. Concerned British faces came out of shadows created by the glare of a floodlight.

'The master asks do you want to salvage anything?' asked a big blond-bearded man in a heavy white turtleneck sweater.

'No, thanks. Not a thing,' I replied.

'Pity we're a container ship,' said another voice. 'We have no crane.'

From the living quarters in the superstructure at the stern, a bare white deck stretched 250ft to the stem. We were guided to the bridge, where we shook hands with the skipper standing at the wheel.

Master John 'Tony' Stapleford, Norwich, England, shone a flood-light down on *Gulf Streamer*'s upturned hulls. The letters SOS, the orange flag, the radar reflector, the two holes, the rudder aloft like a mizzen sail . . .

'The poor dear,' I said aloud, and my eyes filled with tears.

■ **LESSONS LEARNED**

Advised by multihull designer Jim Brown, Weld knew that the hulls of a capsized trimaran would float high. 'Don't rush the vital items into the vulnerable liferaft. Save your energy to live aboard upside down,' Brown told Weld. *Gulf Streamer*'s inherent buoyancy from her Airex sandwich construction, together with four airtight compartments in each outrigger, provided 'raft status of indefinite duration'.

As Weld had planned with Jim Brown, he unscrewed the now 'overhead' through-hull fitting for the log impeller, and through the two-inch hole, a 'window on the world', he thrust the antenna of one of the three emergency beacons and set it to pulsing.

Jim Brown had also prompted Weld to tuck emergency tools for safekeeping beneath the chart table with which to cut an access hole through the upside-down hull. 'It took three hours to complete the fourteen-by-eighteen-inch aperture. First a drilled hole. Then enlargement with hammer and chisel to make a slit admitting a hacksaw blade.Then a pruning saw with a curved, coarse blade to lengthen the slit on one side.'

Next, he and his crew, Bill, unscrewed the big cabin mirror, and broke it up and glued pieces with epoxy to the hull as another way to attract the attention of rescuers. Crewman Bill stuck a six-foot aluminium extrusion, a spare for the jib-furling system, into the daggerboard slot and wired the metal reflector to its peak.

Bill also used a screwdriver to scratch 'SOS' in four-foot-high letters into the bottom paint of *Gulf Streamer*'s hull. Sensibly, they both decided to use up the canned and bottled liquids before calling on the seven gallons of water, their most easily managed drinking supply in case they had to take to the dinghy.

twenty-three

'I AM NOT GOING TO DIE!'

Yacht	*Lottie Warren* (27ft Heavenly Twins catamaran)
Skipper	John Passmore
Bound from	singlehanded and non-stop around Britain anticlockwise
Date of loss	June 2000
Position	80 miles north-east of Shetland

These were not the records I was looking for as I set out to sail single-handed and non–stop around Britain and Ireland: The lowest barometer reading for June since records began in 1871 – 966 millibars. The highest recorded windspeed for June, also since records began; gusts up to 96 knots. And finally the third record to turn the whole project into a sort of sick hat trick: the first recorded capsize of a Heavenly Twins catamaran.

IT GOES WITHOUT SAYING that if I had known I would meet these sorts of conditions, I would never have set out. That if I had suspected I was about to be engulfed in Scotland's own version of the 1987 'hurricane', I would have sought shelter in the Shetland Islands. But that is with hindsight.

When I sailed out of the River Deben ten days earlier it was with 'reasonable confidence', as I told the local television reporter. As it happened, anyone who witnessed the start would probably not have put money on me getting out of the river at all: In the euphoria of waving to all my well-wishers, I put *Lottie* aground on the Deben Bar. Like all the best boats she shrugged off the incompetence of her skipper and floated herself off as if to say: 'Let me take care of this. You get on with the PR.'

And for the next week she demonstrated to me why this Pat Patterson design has been such an enduring success for so long. Without the weight of a family of four and all their belongings – without the hundredweight of Lego and 200 books – she flew.

With a northwesterly Force 4–5, we were doing a sustained 6.5 knots with bursts up to 8 knots, and in a 27ft boat designed for maximum accommodation. I sat at the saloon table with my laptop computer in front of me, enthusing about the sensation of sitting on a pebble that some youthful giant has sent skimming across the surface of the water. Then, since all this was taking place on an even keel, I would leave the computer sitting flat on the table and connect it to the mobile phone with the aerial on the top of the mast and fire off reports by e-mail to *The Daily Telegraph*.

It was while I was doing this that, I received an e-mail from Mike Golding, automatically forwarded by his press office as he nursed a damaged *Team Group 4* through a viciously low depression in the Europe 1 New Man Singlehanded Transatlantic Race.

Conditions, said Mike, were atrocious – and this from a man who had sailed three times round Cape Horn the wrong way. The unusual low featured again on the long range forecast after the 0535 shipping bulletin on the Saturday morning. It would bring gales to North West Scotland on Monday or Tuesday. On Monday or Tuesday, I planned to be off the coast of North West Scotland.

It was fortunate that I was not in a race. All I had to do was get back by the beginning of July for the church fete, the cat's kittens and a weekend in Paris. And so, when I reached the top of the Shetlands, I stopped. I sorted out my long warps, re-read Pat Patterson on the management of catamarans in gales and waited to see which quadrant of the west the unpleasantness would be coming from. If there was to be any north in it, I would duck back down the East Coast. Anything else would see me running off towards Norway.

After 24 hours, during which every fishing boat in the Shetland fleet came to see whether I wanted to be salvaged, the Coastguard shipping forecast gave the definitive SW Force 9. Ideal, I could get some westing before it arrived. It was while I was on the way that I heard my last Coastguard broadcast which had now become: 'SW Storm Force 10, soon.'

Suddenly time seemed to stop as the significance of that cheerful Scottish voice came crashing down on top of me. I had never been in a Force 10. What I did know was that I had no business to be in one. I knew that very soon I would be in a survival situation and everything depended on how well I managed my boat. If I had wanted to end my long-distance sailing career with a flourish, then I was certainly getting the opportunity. The storm arrived with unhurried deliberation. When progress to windward started to put a strain on the boat, I hove-to.

This is stage one on the guru Patterson's storm management manual. Since I knew that we would soon reach stage two, I went straight into it while the wind was only 25 knots and I could walk around the deck without being blown off. I organised 100m of 14mm anchor warp in a bight from starboard bow to starboard stern. In the middle of this bight was attached a 25m length of 16mm plaited warp with a car tyre on the end. Then I handed all sail and trussed up the main like a mummy. *Lottie* settled immediately broadside to the seas and began to bob up and down like a little duck. Now monohull sailors may be horrified at the idea of lying beam on to breaking seas but they have deep keels which bite into the still water below the surface and 'trip up' the boat as the moving crest presses on the hull. That is how they get rolled. A catamaran with no keels behaves like a raft and is simply swept sideways but stays upright. As the wind increased that is exactly what happened. We lay like this for 24 hours and it worked.

Every 20 minutes or so I would go on deck to check for chafe and shipping. I wore, next to the skin, a Montane Interact thermal suit and on top of that Helly Hansen's Ackland gear. I cannot praise either highly enough. Best of all, I had Dubarry's Gore-Tex boots which I had been wearing 24 hours a day for over ten days, only needing to change my socks once.

Gradually the windspeed crept up and up. Pat Patterson offers a third and final stage in his book. This is for conditions of Force 10 and above. The point at which to make the change is when the impact of the waves from abeam becomes what he calls 'shock-like'.

Once or twice I suspected we had received such impacts – a loud bang, with small items being thrown across the cabin. Then, in the space of five minutes, it happened three times – culminating in the pot of spare light bulbs being shot across the 14ft cabin as if fired from a catapult. Very carefully, slithering about the deck on my belly to reduce windage, I transferred the bow line to the port stern. Obediently *Lottie* swung to present her stern to the seas. I switched on the autopilot again and she set off NNE at six knots.

It was, of course, the wrong direction and something of a disappointment after the two knots drift I had logged while we lay beam-on. But compared to the sensation of calm now, we were going with the storm, instead of trying to resist it; what did that matter? For half an hour, I watched the seas and the compass. The boat was sailing fast and straight under bare pole. I went below for a biscuit and a glass of pink grapefruit juice. It would have been helpful, at this point, to have had another forecast. The barometer had stopped falling but I was appalled to see it reading 769 – I had never seen it that low before.

If the depression was tracking NE, then presumably the wind must veer at some point. But I was not getting forecasts. When I set out I reasoned that I had four sources of information: Coastguard on VHF – now out of range. Navtex – the aerial connection had shaken loose and the motion was such that four attempts to re-make it had all ended in failure. I had a radio cassette player, but in this kind of weather the two Aerogen wind generators set up such an electronic howl that I couldn't hear a word. Finally I had been presented with a Freeplay wind-up radio. I was thrilled with this. There was something wonderfully wholesome about earning your episode of the *Archers* by grinding a handle for 60 turns. Yet what possesses anyone to manufacture an expensive radio with wonderful tone and AM and FM – not to mention two short-wave bands – and then not include long wave?

I cannot say if things would have been different if I had known that the wind shift was imminent. Certainly I imagined that when it came I would have half an hour before the difference in the wave pattern would be significant. I set the kitchen timer for 20 minutes, backed it up with the loudest alarm clock out of the Casio catalogue, and lay down to sleep. Later the helicopter pilot was to tell me that with windspeeds at this level, the wave pattern would change within five to ten minutes.

All I knew of it was when I awoke to the insistent hiss of rushing water as *Lottie* – still steering the original wind direction – began her broach. I saw the bulkhead start to cartwheel. Small items began to cascade from cave lockers. 'Oh,' I said. 'She's going over.' I was, at the time, extremely calm. I suspect this was because up until now everything had gone according to plan. Somehow I imagined this was just another development and I knew what I had to do. First the EPIRB: It was already flashing as I took it from its bracket in the cockpit and brought it into the starboard hull, tied the line to the toilet pump and pushed it out of the head window. Next the liferaft. This was when I first began to get frightened.

The liferaft was in a valise and stowed in the starboard aft cabin. I had thought about tying off the static line, but worried that if it should shift and fall off the bunk, the thing would inflate. Also, in fog, I might want to keep it in the cockpit. Now I did need it, I looked into the aft cabin and saw the hatch wide open. I hoped that the liferaft had not simply dropped out and gone spiralling down to the seabed, complete with line. I dived under the water and began to search. I found the dingy floating in its bag. I found my beloved sextant, the boards I had made for blocking up smashed windows, the brand new Autohelm, which Raytheon had lent me in case I should need it. But the liferaft? No. In the time I could hold my breath, I just could not find it. And besides, it seemed logical that it had indeed dropped out of the hatch.

This meant the best option was to stay inside the hull. Thinking of Tony Bullimore, I wedged myself clear of the water and tried to think of anything else I could do. I was surrounded by apples. I picked up one and bit into it.

It turned out to be an orange. I have no idea how long I was in there because after a while sensations took a while to register. One of them was that I was now in the water, not because I had moved but because the boat had begun to settle. Then I realised that I was breathing very fast. Of course: I was using up the oxygen in this confined space. I made plans to get out. Now which way should I turn when I got out of the hatch? My befuddled brain just couldn't handle this one at all. In the end I knew I had to go for it while there was still enough good air around to make a deep breath worthwhile.

I think I even told myself 'Go!' and I was out, losing my lovely boots instantly, dropping the flare canister straight away – but popping up next to the rudder. In no time at all I was standing on the bottom of the bridgedeck, holding onto the starboard keel. And there I knew I had to stay. When the first really big wave hit me, swept my feet from under me and left me in the middle of a breaking crest holding on by my fingertips, I knew I was in real trouble.

In all the survival manuals I have ever read it tells you that the single most powerful tool in your possession is your mind. You must never, ever – even for the tiniest moment – remotely consider the smallest possibility . . . of not coming through alive. This was kind of difficult at the time – partly because during that last morning I had been taking photographs in the cockpit and kept wondering why the flash was going off. But it was not the camera flashing. It was the EPIRB. I had sat on it and set it off. Reasoning that it had only been activated for a few seconds, I switched it off again and broadcast a 'false alarm' message on VHF. Now it was transmitting in earnest, I wondered whether there was someone down in Falmouth saying: 'Oh that's just the false alarm, don't worry about that one.' But that, as I say, was not to be considered. Instead I concentrated, wave by wave, second by second on holding on, thinking of Tamsin and the children and shouting at the sky: 'I am not going to die. I am coming home.'

The estimate is that I was in the water – both in the hull and on top of it – for between two and three hours. When the Coastguard helicopter arrived, it took maybe another ten minutes to find a calm enough slot to come down below the 30m maximum wave height to get me off. That seemed like the longest time. But once a magnificent and very brave man called Peter Mesney had swung down on his line and literally plucked me to safety, I was hardly able to speak and shaking uncontrollably.

They flew me to the Murchison oil platform and treated me for hypothermia. It seems almost unreal as I sit here writing this looking out over the garden to a tranquil River Deben while little Theo points to the Montane suit on the line and says: 'Daddy was upside down in that.' Meanwhile, the telephone keeps ringing and the postscript continues to be updated. Premium Liferaft Services say the EPIRB was accurate to within 100m only because the Americans have now unscrambled the GPS signal. Shetland Coastguard ring to say that an anchor handling vessel has located *Lottie Warren* but must remain on station, what do I want to do about this? I call Pantaenius and say I had been planning to sell the boat anyway and would be happy to agree a total loss.

■ LESSONS LEARNED

After talking to the helicopter pilot, Passmore assumed a wind shift had set up an immediate cross-sea which pushed the boat beam-on to a breaking crest – and then acted as a stumbling block to prevent her from surfing sideways. However, Pat Patterson, the designer of the Heavenly Twins catamaran, disagreed. He believed this was a case of the boat surfing before an uncommonly large wave, rounding up when the autopilot failed to correct in time and then capsizing from a combination of kinetic energy caused by the sudden deceleration from 14 knots and the absorbed energy from the wave itself.

His advice was that a multihull must not be allowed to surf in such conditions. Passmore knew this and when he went below, the boat was running steadily at six knots and since she did not normally surf at speeds under 12 knots, he assumed this was a good safety margin. However, he had already seen one very large wave and should have realised this was merely the first rather than the exception.

At any event, he said he should have been at the helm – because he was well-rested from lying beam-on to a warp as the storm reached its crescendo. Meanwhile, in the light of his experience Patterson decided to buy himself a parachute anchor. Passmore had thought about getting one himself but couldn't justify the expense for one last trip at the height of the British summer. 'Don't you just love hindsight?' he said.

'Never forget that the single most powerful survival tool in your possession is your mind. You must never, ever remotely consider the smallest possibility of not coming through alive.'

FAULTY NAVIGATION

twenty-four

SHIPWRECKED ON AN UNMARKED REEF

Yacht	*Fleur de Mer* (Bowman 40)
Skipper	Jacques Demarty
Crew	Catherine Demarty
Bound from	Tobago Cays to Bonaire, Caribbean
Date of loss	26 January 2006
Position	Los Roques archipelago

Sailing in the Caribbean with the 2005–7 Blue Water Round the World Rally, the chart-plotter on French sailor Jacques Demarty's yacht put him three-quarters of a mile off course . . . with disastrous results. Jacques, 63, and his wife Catherine are very experienced sailors, having logged over 100,000 miles, circumnavigating Britain, rounding Ireland twice, cruising Norway's Lofoten Islands, the Azores and completing the Atlantic Rally for Cruisers in 2003. But, as Jacques says, even 45 years' cruising experience isn't proof against shipwreck.

IT WAS MID-AFTERNOON WHEN *Fleur de Mer*, our Bowman 40, sailed from Tobago Cays in the Caribbean Windward Islands, bound for Bonaire, with my wife, myself and four crew. We made a detour to explore the Los Roques archipelago, off the Venezuelan coast, which is famous among the cruising community. Anchoring at El Gran Roque, the main village of the islands, we spent a day sightseeing. It was close to nightfall when we made our departure for Bonaire, 100 miles away. The wind was Force 5–6 and we left with one reef, paying great attention to the difficult channel out of the protected lagoon.

Five miles away we could see a small island, Selesqui, with two wide channels on both sides. At sunset (1835) our course took us to starboard of the island, still visible in the gathering darkness. My wife Catherine twice suggested we gybe, to give a wider berth to the island, but it was 15 minutes before we did so. By then it was too late.

Within another minute, I heard a horrible grinding noise and *Fleur de Mer* heeled over at 30°. We'd hit the coral reef which extends south-east of the island. We were using our electronic chart, even though we had noticed its incredible lack of precision only the day before. This had nothing to do with the 'traditional' correction between WGS 84 and the local co-ordinates. The error between the electronic track and our true course over the ground was more than three-quarters of a mile. We had tried to correct this point on the plotter without success and when we left the archipelago, we simply forgot about it! This meant that instead of being one mile off the island, we were only 400m away.

It was soon clear that we weren't going to get out of the fatal trap into which we'd sailed. Big breaking rollers continually raised the yacht and punched her down onto the reef. Even though the general structure of our strongly built yacht was intact, huge fractures began to appear. Water poured inside and it was obvious we'd have to abandon her. We launched the liferaft and four of the crew got into it.

I then remembered the discussion I'd had with the Blue Water Rally director Peter Seymour during the safety visit in Gibraltar. He had made the point that one should wait until the yacht is really sinking to 'step up' into the liferaft rather than climb down into it. As a result of this short instant of doubt, the four crew quickly climbed back aboard. Jean-Claude, one of our crew who had ignited a red flare, saw that the island was only 75m away. Then we saw the liferaft had been punctured by a coral head and was no longer usable anyway. Jean-Claude suggested he swim a long rope ashore which we could use to get the rest of the crew to safety.

We had with us four long lines for transiting the Panama Canal and used them as our safety line. Thanks to the courage and strength of Jean-Claude, all the crew eventually reached the island safely, soaked and exhausted but alive and unharmed. It was now 2200 and we did our best to protect ourselves from the cool and fresh wind, lying close together and contemplating the wonderful stars in the tropical sky.

Before we abandoned *Fleur de Mer* we sent many distress messages: one using the DSC/VHF; another using the SSB radio. We received no response to either. I also activated the EPIRB but, of course, we had no means of knowing if the signal had been received.

(*Editor's note*: In fact, just three minutes after Jacques activated his EPIRB, the French emergency marine rescue services (CROSS at Gris Nez), the equivalent of MRCC Falmouth for French registered boats, was informed by automatic Telex of two possible positions for the beacon. The position was fixed after the second pass of the satellites. At midnight GMT, Coastguards at CROSS contacted a member of Jacques's family which he had previously nominated, to check the signal was not a false alarm and that *Fleur de Mer* was actually in the vicinity of Venezuela. At 0011 GMT, Coastguards contacted their counterparts in Venezuela, informing them of the distress. Some 3,000 miles away, Blue Water Rally directors Tony Diment and Peter Seymour were woken soon after midnight to hear news of the sinking. They released the names, radio call signs, and contact details (Iridium and Inmarsat sat phone numbers) of rally yachts that could assist.)

It was still dark at 0330 the next morning when we saw the navigation lights of two different boats. With our hand-held VHF radio, which was miraculously still working (it was a waterproof Icom), I made contact with the boats. One was a Venezuelan patrol boat and the other was a fellow French Blue Water Rally yacht, *Paulina 3*, a 42ft catamaran, which had been alerted by CROSS. The Venezuelan patrol boat had been alerted by their local rescue service. Both searches had been initiated by our EPIRB signal.

Paulina 3, sailed by Bernard Rocquemont and his wife Dominique, was on passage from Le Marin, in Martinique, to Bonaire at the time *Fleur de Mer* was lost. They received a call on their satellite phone from the CROSS telling them *Fleur de Mer* had activated her EPIRB. Bernard, just three miles to the north of us, changed course to offer assistance.

As we now knew to our cost, the approaches to Selesqui are dangerous – too dangerous to attempt in the dark – so *Paulina 3* and the patrol boat waited for daylight to assist us. Even then, we had to swim out to a smaller patrol craft manned by rangers of the El Roques National Park.

This stupid accident would have been much more dramatic if the disembarkation on the island had gone badly. Thankfully, with the efficient help of Jean-Claude, everything went well. Back at El Roque we were delighted to meet fellow Blue Water Rallier Niels Jahren and his yacht *Blackbird*. He took care of us all, which was most welcome after the disastrous loss of our beloved *Fleur de Mer*. I would also like to thank all those on El Gran Roque, who helped us organise our flights back to Paris.

If this dramatic story doesn't have a tragic ending it's because a lot of people did the right thing at the right time. I'd like to thank the crew of *Fleur de Mer*, who behaved fantastically. They never went into a panic and lost everything with a smile – happy, simply, to be alive.

FOOTNOTE

Later, Niels Jahren of *Blackbird* paid a visit to the wreck of *Fleur de Mer* and salvaged some personal effects belonging to Jacques Demarty, which he returned to him.

Jacques's insurers, Pantaenius, paid the full claim for the total loss of his yacht. Jacques flew out to visit the rally in the Galapagos Islands and has since bought a new boat to join the 2007–9 Blue Water Round the World Rally.

■ LESSONS LEARNED

Knowing we had an error of three-quarters of a mile on our chart-plotter, we should have checked the distance off with radar and the depth sounder, but everything seemed so easy that we failed to do so.

Our late-running schedule meant we were navigating in dangerous waters as darkness fell. Though the island was visible, it was difficult to appreciate distance, particularly in the case of a low island just two or three metres above sea level.

From the island, the sound of rolling breakers and the noise of the sea crashing on the reef was very loud. But offshore on the yacht, with a following wind, we didn't hear anything, even when we were only 40m away.

I am fully responsible for the absence of clear and precise instructions. To say 'pass the island on starboard or port but avoid it' is not a clear order, but an approximation. I also failed to organise a proper lookout.

We should have immediately used our Inmarsat-C distress messaging capability (on our laptop) because there is a built-in GPS which automatically puts the position in the distress message. When I tried to use it, it was too late because some circuit boards were under water.

We received no answer from our fixed VHF/DSC or SSB radios after sending a MAYDAY on both. Our hand-held VHF radio worked well, even after a 60m 'swim'. I would never put to sea without a hand-held and fixed VHF radio.

Although our liferaft inflated immediately it was quickly punctured by the reef. Had we been miles offshore this would have proved fatal. Take great care when deploying a liferaft in shallow waters.

Make sure you have a grab bag prepared – complete with passports. We did.

Even after 100,000 miles of offshore sailing you can never afford to be complacent. Our experience had made us overconfident.

twenty-five

THE FATAL REEF

Yacht	*Nainjaune* (35ft Super Sovereign ketch)
Skipper	Peter Middleton
Crew	wife Val
Bound from	Caribbean for Mayaguana, at the eastern end of the Bahama chain
Date of loss	23 February 1977
Position	off the coast of Mayaguana, Bahamas

Peter Middleton, a retired airline pilot, had sailed since 1949 on the basic principle that 'a sailing boat is an aeroplane tipped on its side'. Here he recalls the last moments when his blue water cruiser ran hard aground on a coral reef in the Bahamas.

THE HARBOURMASTER STUCK A LABEL, reading 'Welcome to S Caicos', on the coachroof, gave us a sleepy smile and ambled back to his comfortable basket chair on the verandah of the sun-soaked, harbour office. 'Goodbye, Captain, and have a good trip.'

We had come a very long way, just the two of us, five months out from England in our 35ft ketch *Nainjaune*, along the lazy man's route to the West Indies. The longest passage had been the 23 days from Gran Canaria to Barbados. We had wandered from Barbados to Bequia, at the north end of the Grenadine chain, then through the islands, until we fetched Antigua for the traditional English yachtsman's Christmas. We were on our way to Fort Lauderdale in America to enter the Intracoastal Waterway.

Re-orientating ourselves from the high-sided Leeward Islands to the almost totally flat Caicos proved difficult. We had got used to seeing targets from 20 to 30 miles away. If not the actual land, you could nearly always see the cloud cap sitting on top. But Caicos was only a few feet out of the water and had no telltale 'lid' on it.

Our next port of call was to be Mayaguana, right at the eastern end of the Bahama chain. We expected a two-day passage, and we had sufficient stores and water from our previous trip to cover this twice over, so we had no worries on that score. The only doubt that nagged was this change from high land and deep water to flat land and shallow water.

In the pilot books I had read that you need a crewman up the mast to watch ahead for the discoloured water which marks the coral lurking only inches under the surface. And the positions of these reefs are not always marked accurately on the charts.

One up the mast, one on the wheel, and one keeping an eye on the navigation should be the minimum crew for Bahamian waters. We were, therefore, one short. But we had met several American crews on their way east, who told us that on no account should we bypass the delights of the Bahamas. Just one Englishman, who had sailed for many years in the area, had warned us not to try it with such a small crew. We should have listened.

Needless to say, as we prepared to leave Caicos, I had forgotten all about this. I was more concerned with the decision whether to cross the Caicos Bank, in about 12ft of water, or sail outside it, in deeper water. Even when I went forward to get the anchor up I had still not decided. For once, the sky was covered in high cirrus, and looked very flat. The sea lacked colour and the sand bottom was featureless and dead. These things generated a strange feeling of doubt, and I opted for the longer passage in the comfort and safety of deeper water.

At 1030 on 22 February 1977, we sailed clear of South Caicos, towards Mayaguana, on what turned out to be *Nainjaune*'s last voyage.

Taking the outside passage meant leaving South Caicos in a northeasterly direction, supposedly into empty ocean. A glance at the chart, however, will show that you can't sit back and wait for the ETA to come up. There are several extensive reefs unpleasantly close to the track – some of them out of sight of land, all of them unlit. Since the trip will take about 24 hours, clearly some of them will threaten you after dark. I am talking about a time long ago, before satellite navigation, when offshore navigators used sextant, hand-bearing compass, and eyeball.

On this occasion, visibility was good and the islands we were leaving were in full view. In fact, the log shows that we were still taking bearings of identifiable objects seven hours after we left. In this time we had cleared most of the Caicos reefs, and the course had turned northwesterly to miss another offshore reef. Now it got dark, stars were covered, and we proceeded on dead reckoning.

Our extremely rugged windvane gear had taken us right across the Atlantic almost without a human hand on the helm. It was steering us now, through the dark night, leaving my wife free to cook and sleep, and me free to navigate and keep a watch – not that there were any ships in this area to watch for. However, wind changes resulted in course changes, so that a regular look at the compass was essential. We had become so used to this efficient and uncomplaining helmsman that it was easy to forget who was doing all the work.

While we were bowling along at 4–5 knots, I had time to decide on several imaginary turning points, all designed to miss various reefs by a good margin. But one reef remained a threat, and I estimated that we should be on it before dawn, so at 0230, after a lot of calculation, I wrote in the log a memo, for whoever should be on watch at the time. It read: 'Assuming one knot current on to dangers, when log reads 124, STOP, and wait for daylight.'

Duly, at 0430, with the log reading exactly that, we hove-to on port tack, drifting slowly south. I went to my bunk and left Val to stare into space and wait for the first tinge of dawn. It says in the log: 'Stars at 0520' – the time at which you can expect to see the fading stars and the dawn horizon at the same time, enabling you to use the sextant for a three or four star shot. Such a shot takes some time to work out, but gives you a fix, as opposed to a single position line. On this occasion, a fix was what we needed.

By 0645 we were once again under way, having plotted our star fix, and worked out an ETA to sight Mayaguana. All seemed well. The only remaining reef was a few miles off the island, the dark night was over, the worries behind us, and though the sun was not actually shining, the light was improving and the sky clear.

Just after midday, the south-east point of Mayaguana appeared as a very thin line on the horizon; the sort of line which leaves you wondering whether it really is land, or just a bit of haze in the distance. No point in reaching for the hand-bearing compass. It was much too early to identify anything. We would not be there for another three hours.

As the time passed and we approached nearer to the island, some detail began to appear. We knew there was a large American tracking station on it, left over from the moon-landing. It was reported to be inactive and occupied by a caretaker. But its position on the chart was uncertain and the height of its buildings and aerials was unknown. This made such information practically useless in trying to measure our distance-off by horizontal or vertical sextant angle.

About 1430, we were sailing along the south coast of Mayaguana, still seemingly about 10 miles off, for what we could see of the land was very low on the horizon and without any detail. I went to the chart table to look for clues, and as Val was on watch in the cockpit and the vane gear was doing the steering, I called to her to come down and look at the chart to explain what I was hoping to see.

'Before you come below,' I said, 'can you see any white water, discoloured water or anything which looks like coral?'

'No sign,' she replied, and I stuck my head out of the hatch to make sure. The sea was smooth, its colour was deep, dark blue and the sun was shining. No thought of imminent disaster.

About 30 seconds later the boat seemed to hesitate under our feet. It was like the first shake of an earthquake, giving warning of impending disaster. The stunned silence was followed by a noise like a massive tree being felled, a tearing, rending, ripping, splintering noise, which brought our hearts jolting into our mouths. It took a fraction of a second to realise that the ship had juddered to a dead stop.

We bolted for the cockpit and stared in astonishment. How could this happen to us? We, the experienced long-distance sailors, were hard on a reef. We could see the three-feet-long jagged blades of stag-horn coral only one or two feet under the water.

The mast was still standing, and immediately we lowered all sail straight on to the deck. Then to the engine, to see if we could back off. Engine started – into reverse. Clanking noise of bronze on coral – propeller gone. To the wheel – perhaps if we hoisted a genoa she could be turned? Wheel jammed. Looked over the side and saw pieces of rudder floating past, in a slight current – towards the reef. Wind and current behind us – not a hope.

There was no help in sight. No buildings on the shore. No passing ships. No fishing boat to tow us off. And slowly, relentlessly, the hull started to lift on the swell and crunch down on to the reef, port side first, then starboard – heavily, and fatally, the sharp and jagged coral pounded at *Nainjaune*'s teak planking, as she rolled 30° either side on her lead keel. With each little sea breaking she was pushed further up on to the reef. Our hull had seemed so strong – 1½in thick in places, and backed by oversized frames. She was wedged where she had come to rest, after ploughing like an ice-breaker through 50ft of stag-horn coral; the channel she had cut dead straight and very deep. She took some stopping that boat, but stopped she was.

The immediate panic died down, and I got out the portable Callbuoy, set it up on 2182kc, pulled up the retractable aerial – and it broke off. I sent a distress message anyway, but was certain no one had heard it. Next, an orange smoke signal; I lit it on the foredeck, downwind, and the lurid smoke drifted low over the water, parallel to the shore. Watching the land through binoculars for a possible reply, I could see nothing but scrubby bush and a thin strip of sand. No people, no houses, nothing.

It was now about two hours before dark, and a decision was needed: should we spend a night being pounded to splinters on this reef, or should we abandon ship and row ashore? Frankly, it didn't seem safe on board. Already the planking was starting to split, and the shaking of the hull made it difficult to move about without being thrown off. There would certainly be no rest on board, and if she fell apart during the night, we should have trouble reaching an unlit shore.

The beach was more than 2½ miles away, north of us, and the trade wind just north of east, so it would be a cross-wind row; it would take at least an hour, and there was the risk that the wind, plus any current, might take us right round the western end of the island

and out to sea. Then we should indeed be lost. It would be dark soon – better get started.

We inflated the liferaft from the foredeck, where there was some shelter from the breaking seas. The dinghy was also inflated and the two boats tied together. We collected valuables and necessary paperwork, sextant, chronometer, money, alcohol and some food, two water containers, medical box, camera, passports, etc, and secured them in a waterproof holdall. Dragging this load up the perilous sidedeck and dumping it in the boats was extremely risky, for anyone falling over the side would certainly be crushed by the hull on its next roll.

With Val in the liferaft and me in the Avon dinghy, we shipped the oars and cast off. In fear and trepidation we floated across the ugly, sharp coral, in water only a few inches deep, expecting the boats to be ripped to pieces on every swell, but thankfully we reached the deeper waters of the lagoon undamaged. Looking back, we had a dismal view of our lovely ship in dire straits, being savagely smashed to pieces on the reef, her ensign still proudly flying on the stern.

We got to the shore just before dark, hauled the two boats up the narrow strip of beach, and congratulated ourselves on our survival. Then a quick look around disclosed a row of posts, each one numbered, apparently marking an underground power cable. Weary, and not too sure of finding anything, we followed these along the beach. Nothing but scrub and sand in one direction and still nothing. Darkness fell suddenly, as it does in the tropics; we were utterly alone, and a little afraid.

We made our home, as best we could, in the liferaft, and dined off ginger biscuits and a slug of Scotch with the moon and Venus bright in the night sky. Light was provided by putting the liferaft's sea-water batteries into a jug of seawater, but this only served to underline our isolation. Throughout the long night, we both woke every 20 minutes or so, wondering whether this was all a bad dream, and believing that we were still at sea, rolling up the miles towards America. But when daylight came, there we were, still sitting in the liferaft on the beach and our yacht gone.

After breakfast (more ginger biscuits and Scotch) we set out, this time with more determination, to find civilisation. Walking up the beach we discovered a pair of blue plastic fenders which looked vaguely familiar. So they should; they were our own, blown ashore during the night. *Nainjaune* was out of sight over the horizon – out of sight but not out of mind, for we had loved her dearly. It took all of that day and a lot of exhausting walking through the bush to find other human life, and at one time we were convinced that the island was uninhabited. But we did eventually make contact. We spent a week on Mayaguana, where there was one other white man, and Val was the only white woman. That was an experience not to be missed – but that's another story.

Apart from the boat, the worst of our various losses was, surprisingly, our visitors' book. It contained the names of all the people we had met on this voyage, like-minded people engaged on an adventure like ours, with whom we would like to have kept in touch.

The voyage from Hamble to Mayaguana was 5,700 miles, and since then we have owned two more boats and sailed another 11,000 miles. Although you could say that 23 February 1977 was not our day, it did not put us off sailing. But eventually, at the age of 70, after 40 years' cruising, I sold our latest boat and 'swallowed the anchor'.

■ LESSONS LEARNED

The distance-off was wrongly judged as the Middletons were used to high islands. Mayaguana is only a few feet high and he thought they were at least 10 miles off. From sea level, changes in the colour of water are hard to spot. Calm weather meant that there was no white water breaking on the reef, to mark its position, though it was visible from the landward side. Someone should have been up the mast, Middleton concluded.

The timing was wrong. You should approach coral with the sun behind you. It was 1500 and they were heading north-west, almost dead into sun.

'While we were considering how to measure distance-off, we should have disconnected the windvane gear and hove-to.'

The fact that the echo sounder was running at the time was not a lot of help, because the wall of the reef was almost vertical from a depth of about 100ft. For this reason, an anchor put out astern would not have pulled them off.

If there had been a powerful motor-boat waiting when they struck, this might have dragged them off the reef backwards. She might then have been beached inside the lagoon, and since the damage would have been less, she could have been patched up without heavy lifting gear. They might then, hopefully, have sailed her on her own bottom to Miami.

'We had done so much work on *Nainjaune* during the long voyage, that the "Work to be done" notebook contained only one entry – "oil port toe rail". Small comfort that when she sank she had never been in better condition.'

twenty-six

THE LOSS OF *KEELSON II*

Yacht	*Keelson II* (Vancouver 32)
Skipper	Hugh Cownie
Crew	Sue Cownie
Bound from	Trinidad to Tortola in the British Virgin Islands
Date of loss	11 December 1999
Position	off the island of Nevis

A year after the launch of Keelson II, *their Vancouver 32, in 1985, and a month after their retirement, Hugh and Sue Cownie sailed out of the Solent for the Caribbean and ports in between. Nearly 14 years later they swam from their cherished Caribbean home, and left her wrecked on a reef off Nevis.*

WE LEFT TRINIDAD IN LIGHT airs and had to motor towards our destination, Tortola, in the British Virgin Islands, some 500 miles away. Caribbean cruising had persuaded my brother-in-law to ship his yacht from Greece and we were sailing with him and his wife to greet its arrival. After two windless days and nights under engine and with little prospect of wind, we ran short of diesel; it was touch and go whether we had enough to motor to the island of Nevis. Unwisely, in the event, we abandoned our non-stop voyage to buy fuel in Martinique.

Hurricane Lenny had gone the wrong way, travelling eastwards instead of westwards. Lee shores became weather shores. Swells, as high as 30ft off some islands, caused considerable damage to westerly facing harbours and installations from the south of Grenada to St Maarten, where, we were told, several yachtsmen had been lost.

We sailed into Anse Mitan, a popular anchorage opposite Fort de France in Martinique, to find that the recently rebuilt marina and fuel jetty was totally destroyed. The tourist beach, usually decorated with topless ladies, had no sand and was deserted. Its many restaurants and bars were nearly all derelict.

After refuelling in the small marina at Fort de France, we set out to resume our sail northwards to the Virgin Islands but, ironically, were ambushed by a tropical wave with 40 knots of wind and big uncomfortable seas. A night in Portsmouth, in the north of Dominica, seemed preferable to continuing on a night sail in such awful conditions. So we altered course and, in the blackness of early evening, crept into the anchorage for a good night's sleep.

Once again we set sail for Tortola. After passing the Saintes in glorious sailing conditions our guests decided they should fly to Tortola as they were running out of time for the arrival of their yacht. So we diverted to the unaccustomed luxury of the marina in Pointe-à-Pitre in the south of Guadeloupe. Sod's Law ruled that we should be weather-bound there for some ten days, by far the longest time we had spent in a marina since 1986. We endured, and too frequently succumbed to, the temptations of delicious French cooking.

On a beautiful morning we set off, intending to spend a couple of days in the Saintes, one of the loveliest anchorages in the Caribbean. But the weather was so good we decided to carry on northwards, again towards Tortola. Well offshore we lost the protection of Guadeloupe and began to have a pasting from high north-north-easterly winds and sharp seas over a sizeable swell. These conditions were not for us so we altered course to regain the protection of the island to spend the night in Deshaies, a popular anchorage on the north-west coast. In the lee of the island one is normally motoring in calm seas, but not on that evening. We had a strong current against us, a heavy swell and continued strong winds.

Even knowing the entrance quite well, we had a few uneasy moments until we saw the anchor lights of yachts. To our delight, our anchor held at the first attempt and we enjoyed relaxing in the cockpit over a beer, relieved to be safe and comfortable for the night. Our intended one night stay lasted three because of persistent large swells from the north and heavy winds and seas.

David Jones, the Caribbean's omniscient tropical weatherman, forecast a window for the weekend of 11–12 December, with the threat of deteriorating conditions thereafter. So, after George's ham-net forecast had confirmed David's, we left Deshaies on the morning of the 11th and had a superb sail northwards, passing the sad sight of Montserrat with its terrible destruction from the active volcano. Yellow dust from the lava flow whirled over the once picturesque town of Plymouth, where we had anchored a few years before.

Because of an adverse current, it was getting dark when we came under the lee of Nevis. We calculated that, with similar unfavourable currents, a non-stop sail northwards would mean arriving off Tortola in darkness the following evening. A night at anchor off Charlestown or Pinney's Beach would allow us a leisurely meal and a good night's sleep to fortify us for a day and night passage the next day to arrive off Tortola on the Monday morning. And then nature intervened.

On our passage northwards we had seen a bank of cloud ahead. This was lying in ambush for us as we came under the protection of the island. The quarter moon was obscured and it began to rain. We were well offshore when, to our surprise, we saw through the glasses a well-lit dock with a ship alongside. In the poor visibility we wondered whether an unknown current had quickened our progress.

The Garmin GPS showed us to be close to its latitude. We altered course to investigate but, as we closed the coast, saw that this was not the jetty we wanted. Because of the poor conditions and our failure to identify any navigation lights, we decided to stay where we were. I tried to anchor to the north of the jetty, but, unknown to us at the time, the bottom had been recently dredged and was hard; two attempts failed to set the anchor.

Slowly we resumed our way northwards, much closer inshore than we had planned, in search of Charlestown, which we knew must be close. The recently corrected Imray Iolaire chart showed a light to the south of Fort Charles and another marking the Charlestown jetty. We searched hard for the former without success; it was when we were looking for it against the background of shore lights that we struck the bottom.

There was quite a heavy swell running. One minute a wave would lift us clear of the reef only to dash us down again the next. I put our new Yanmar engine full astern each time the swell lifted us, expecting to get free and return to deeper water the way we had come. But as we rose, the swell drove the boat relentlessly shorewards until the seas were breaking over us.

We immediately recognised we were in trouble and put out a PAN PAN. A local radio operator responded and relayed our call to the Coastguard who could not help as their vessel was being refitted in St Kitts. Captain Greene, master of the Nevis–St Kitts ferry, offered help but, when told of our position off Fort Charles, decided that he couldn't hazard his vessel in such shallows, or his crew at night in such surf. We received one radio call from a cruising yachtsman at anchor off Charlestown to tell us that we were going aground, but that was too late. We were already aground.

Nothing else was heard from the anchored yachts, although I am sure that a couple of stiff-bottomed dinghies with moderate sized engines could have saved us if they had responded to our distress call. We were only about half a mile from the Charlestown anchorage.

After some two and a half hours the Coastguard and the police, who were by now above the beach, advised us that, as nothing could be done to help us and with our lovely yacht in danger of being swamped or worse, we should consider abandoning ship.

Sue distinctly recalls the solemn message from the Coastguard: 'We urge you to remember that your priority should be the preservation of life rather than property.'

'You bet,' Sue had hissed under her breath.

With our starboard toe rail underwater, the decision was made and, with heavy hearts we donned our lifejackets, unfastened our lifelines, climbed over the rails and slid backwards into the sea. We swam only a few strokes before feeling the reef under our shoeless feet. As we struggled ashore, the breaking surf and undertow tried to prevent our advance but, by walking sideways on to the swell, we made slow progress, the ship's papers, passports and Sue's credit cards dangling in bags strung around our necks.

Helping hands stretched out to pull us from the surf onto dry land and we were quickly whisked away to the police station. There, with the Caribbean dripping from our sodden clothes and bodies, making pools on the office floor, we had to attend to first things first

– the completion of entry formalities, though our passports were too wet to be stamped. Once all this had been attended to, a kindly policewoman lent Sue a diaphanous dress – many times larger than her usual size – and a pair of large flip-flops. A young policeman lent me underpants, a jazzy shirt and shorts, also with some flip-flops. He wanted me to keep them all when I returned them a couple of days later.

We were lucky and were relatively unharmed physically, although devastated mentally. Sue was bruised from being wedged against the chart table during her time on the radio. She had also been unlucky enough to tread on a sea urchin while wading ashore.

Brian David, the Commissioner of Wrecks, arrived and could not have been kinder. It was a Saturday night and, with the official work completed, I mentioned with some feeling that we could do with a drink. After I had explained that we didn't mean tea, Brian, with Captain Greene, took us to a local watering hole where the lovely owner refused to accept payment for generous tots of Black Label and local rum. Seated at the bar, Mr Walters, a friend of both Captain Greene and Mr David, offered us accommodation at his holiday apartment block on Hilltop. We arrived to find a clean and comfortable bed for the night and a television to help to distract us from our disaster. Captain Greene took our wet clothes for washing.

Early the following morning Captain Greene stood off the reef in his ferry. In a dory three of his crew took us alongside our stricken yacht so that I could recover some cash and basic clothing. But the surf was so heavy the dory was swamped and nearly capsized. I found oily water up to the chart table and this, on my bare feet, caused me to slip, making movement difficult. I just had time to grab some money and a few clothes, but no shoes; I tried to unfasten our new Autohelm autopilot but was urged to get in the dory before it capsized. It was heartbreaking to feel our lovely yacht being dashed on the reef and to abandon all our possessions.

The police later told us that by midday the boat was stripped. Some items were of little worth, but of great sentimental value; even the running rigging and ground tackle had been taken.

An American yachtsman, Steve Macek, who had heard of our plight, came to see us and was almost in tears as we told him our story.

He told us that a Brazilian yacht and later a large new Oyster also found themselves at the same point where we were. They were luckier as they had grounded in daylight and had escaped with relatively minor damage. The following day he went aboard *Keelson II* and managed to retrieve our precious but sodden visitors' book.

On the Monday I asked Mr Walters for my bill for the two nights' stay and good food, but he wouldn't hear of accepting a cent. We moved to a seaside hotel near Charlestown to be close to faxes and shopping. There, the owner volunteered us a highly discounted daily rate. The kindness and friendliness of the Nevis folk has to be experienced to be believed. Admittedly we had lost all our possessions to looters but, sadly, an abandoned yacht would be looted in Devon or Cornwall or indeed, anywhere else in the world.

In Charlestown we received many words of commiseration from shopkeepers and local passers-by but, surprisingly, none from fellow yachtsmen we saw wandering the streets. This touching kindness was not confined to the black population. The American owners of the exclusive Hermitage Inn invited us to a delicious family dinner, accompanied by fine wines.

On the Sunday morning, after our visit to the yacht, Brian David took us to his office to telephone our daughter who was able to contact our insurance brokers the following day. They could not have been more helpful: they arranged for a surveyor to fly in from Antigua and he inspected the wreck two days later. Mr David also drove Sue to the hospital where her painful and now swollen foot was treated.

Thankfully, Sue's credit cards were able to equip us with shoes and other essentials, such as our flight to Antigua, from where we could fly home. And in Antigua those cards were more than essential. We had lost our air tickets with the boat. Although our return booking to London was clearly shown on the airline's computers, both at the airport and at their St John's office, the staff insisted on our paying £800 for tickets home. This has since been refunded.

Now we ask ourselves what comes next? Do we buy *Keelson III* in our seventies? Two days ago we had decided definitely against it, but in the next morning's post came the Ocean Cruising Club's Newsletter. It reminded us of our lovely friends in Trinidad and of happier times; we both doubt whether we want to cut ourselves off yet from the cruising way of life.

FOOTNOTE

Willie Wilson, Managing Director of Imray, said: 'There is always a time lapse between verifying corrected information and updating a chart. Our Caribbean charts, in particular, warn about not relying on lights.'

■ LESSONS LEARNED

Cownie's Imray Iolaire chart (A25), corrected to December 1999, showed three lights that were not functioning. The commercial jetty, shown as being 'under construction', was, in fact, completed. Even Doyle's 1998/1999 *Cruising Guide to the Leewards* referred to the jetty as being 'planned'. It was this jetty that had attracted the Cownies shorewards. Never assume that even a corrected chart will be 100 per cent accurate. Lights fail, things change. Chart errors are known to exist for all the Caribbean islands but it bears repeating that great care has to be used when employing GPS for pilotage.

The Cownies had a 'panic bag' below the companionway, but this was designed for an offshore escape to the liferaft. It was of no use to them in this predicament. Always have your ship's papers, passports, credit cards, any return air-tickets, and some money in a waterproof bag that can be grabbed in an emergency and dangled around your neck when swimming.

The Cownies had been insured with the same Lloyd's underwriters since buying their first yacht in 1981. They settled for the full insured value. Chopping and changing one's insurance company to save a few pounds could prove expensive.

Most important of all, said the skipper: 'Be sure to sail with as competent and as brave a wife as mine.'

twenty-seven

SONG – THE FINAL EPISODE

Yacht	*Song* (26ft hard-chine, twin-keel sloop)
Skipper	George Harrod-Eagles
Bound from	England to Australia
Date of loss	19 January 1982
Position	on Roncador Reef, east coast of Puerto Rico

George Harrod-Eagles set out, singlehanded, from Lowestoft, Suffolk, in the summer of 1981, to sail the 26ft sloop Song *back to his native Australia. She was a smaller version of the Maurice Griffiths-designed 31ft Golden Hind class. Her auxiliary engine was an 8hp two-stroke Stuart Turner. Harrod-Eagles left Santa Cruz, Tenerife on 3 November and reached Barbados in 42 days. After Christmas in Carlisle Bay and a week in Fort de France, Martinique, he left for Fajardo, on the east coast of Puerto Rico on 14 January 1982.*

I LAID COURSE HARD ON THE WIND for St Croix, our first landfall, some 300 miles to the north-west. With no possibility of a sight, beacons not working, and the extremely poor conditions, there was little sleep for me. *Song* was making a fair amount of leeway, being closehauled, so I was unable to point up enough to make St Croix, and that landfall was abandoned in favour of Punta Tuna, the second option, which was now preferable since strong northerly winds would put us on a lee shore if we attempted the passage to windward of the Island of Vieques.

As I was unable to obtain a sight, it was fortunate that the beacon at Punta Tuna was operational, and gave me a bearing down which I could run until I was able to pick up the light. In the early hours of the third morning this light came into view and was positively identified. I had made landfall on the extreme south-east corner of Puerto Rico.

This portion of the Puerto Rican coast lies in a roughly north-east south-west direction, the distance from Punta Tuna to Fajardo, our destination, being 38 miles. The wind, as we neared the coast, was lighter than before and about NNE. A big swell, caused by several days of northerly winds, made more tedious the long tacks needed to traverse this coast. Navigation was complicated by the Island of Vieques, with a long unmarked spit protruding from its south-western extremity, far out into the passage between it and the Puerto Rican coast; and by the dearth of navigational aids in these waters, which abound with natural hazards.

Song crept through the passage de Vieques, progress further slowed by the wind becoming light and uncertain in direction. It was time to make a decision, keeping in mind the golden rule of reef-strewn waters: do not sail at night. I weighed the odds of reaching our destination before darkness. The choice lay between finding a suitable anchorage (hazardous, in view of the uncertain weather, no information as to the holding quality and the horrible consequences if we dragged), turning around and running back until there was enough searoom to stand off (the safest course, but one that would make pointless all the hours spent getting this far), or continuing towards our destination.

It was early afternoon and warmth in the sun shining through great blue rifts in the cloud cover was a scene to grace the cover of a glossy brochure advertising the delights of the Caribbean. But I was about to enter an area with few navigational aids, with islands and unmarked reefs on either side. The mile or two between them was a very small distance, particularly once darkness fell. A decision had to be made, and I chose to go on – a fateful and perhaps imprudent decision in view of the contrary winds and the slowness of our progress, but one prompted by the desire to end this tiresome passage.

To assist progress I started the engine and ran at half throttle. I motor-sailed past Roosevelt Roads, the US Naval Base, and as we cleared Punta Puerca and the Isla Cabeza de Perro, the wind, no longer diverted by the land, and unaffected by the small islands and reefs in its path, reverted to NNE about Force 3. The swell was still with us, and I estimated about a knot of tide against us, a factor which, with no information about the tides and currents hereabouts, had not entered into my calculations. Nevertheless, Fajardo and the Isleta Marina were visible, and slowly becoming clearer, as we continued to tack, heading for Isla de Ramos and the last buoy before Las Croabas, on the north side of the Bahia de Fajardo and some five miles distant from Isla de Rumas. As we passed this rocky island with the most difficult miles of this passage still to be traversed, the sun was already low over the mountains of Puerto Rico, the shadows growing longer, and the outline of Isleta Marina's two islands becoming difficult to distinguish from the darkened hills behind them. I realised I was unlikely to make the anchorage before darkness. I took a bearing of the buoy lying behind us, close to Isla de Ramos, and one on the buoy ahead near Las Croabas. These were the only lit buoys in the area that would be visible and if we could stick to these bearings we ought to be well clear of reefs, particularly the long reef guarding Isleta Marina, named El Roncador, The Snorer.

The difficulty of keeping one light in view among a confusion of unrelated lights and the bright glow from the shore is well known. Not surprisingly, as night descended with tropical swiftness, the light astern became impossible to see, leaving me with no reference except the buoy ahead, the light from which I could see reasonably well. To continue tacking in the Stygian darkness that now surrounded me was plainly foolish. I lowered all sails, and continued under engine, keeping the light from the buoy ahead. The shore lights of Punta Gorda ahead, and those of Isleta Marina to port, were partially obscured, but coming more into view as we plodded on into the blackness for, with the stars obscured by the overcast sky, the only light was from the distant shore.

I was stowing sails and watching for white water with the echo sounder registering 30ft and the lights from the complex on Isleta Marina in plain view off to port. The depth on the echo sounder plunged to 15ft then up to 20ft, the chart indicated a number of relatively shallow spots, and I thought to check to see if I could relate our position to the charted depths when the echo sounder plummeted to 5ft and immediately the boat struck, crunching and bumping half a dozen times before coming to a stop.

There was a horrible, cold, heart-sinking moment of realisation, before I reacted and put her hard astern, hoping that she would come off: a forlorn hope, for the tidal set which had by its invisible and unknown presence put us up on the reef was, aided and abetted by the strong swell, acting on our bows, pushing them round, pivoting the boat on the stern, which (being the deepest part) was stuck hard, forcing the bilge plates against great jagged coral heads, which were crunching and grinding in a horrifying way against the hull.

The swell, now that we were aground, was lifting the boat up and bumping it further on to the reef. Clearly I had to get an anchor out and try to pull us off. The inflatable dinghy was unlashed and inflated, and the anchor got ready, but the tide was falling and what was a swell now became breakers. Great rolling walls of water were roaring down upon us, lifting *Song* and smashing her down, with shuddering impact, onto the cruel coral, amid great clouds of spray and solid water which broke over the boat continually. Obviously *Song* could not take much of this pounding, and I think it was then I knew she was doomed.

I do not think I can describe the sickening despair I felt at that time; the self-recrimination, followed by intense feelings of being terribly alone and forsaken. It is an awful thing, the knowledge that all you have striven for, over so many months, is being destroyed while you are impotent to prevent it. The continued pounding of the hull and the bilge plates against huge coral heads was not long in taking effect. Within what seemed no time at all, but must have been an hour or more, during which, wet through and continually pummelled by the breaking waves, I struggled to get all in readiness so that I could kedge the boat off, she heeled sharply to port and water appeared with a rush inside her. She settled on her side and, as the port bilge plate had broken, it was now just a matter of time.

What difference it would have made I am not sure, but only the shortage of time and the lack of equipment prevented me from cutting off the bilge plates before I left England. Not to offset the effects of striking a reef (I had not envisaged that problem) but because, having read accounts of attacks by killer whales on sailing boats, I thought them an invitation to disaster, should a whale decide to attack head on.

It was time to call for help and the US Coast Guard was contacted on VHF radio (not without some difficulty). Details of the situation and position were given, and an assurance received that assistance was forthcoming. Whilst I waited, I gathered essentials, wading waist-deep inside the boat in the dimming glow of the overhead fluorescent light, transferring books and equipment to the crowded but still dry starboard-side lockers and shelves. I was thrown violently off balance as each wave, striking with thunderous impact, lifted the boat and let it fall back again. The tide, ebbing fast now in the darkness, revealed a foaming expanse of white water informing me, too late, of the implacable El Roncador.

Several hours elapsed as I waited for the Coast Guard. Inside the cabin, the light had winked out some time earlier and I was in total darkness. Incessantly soaked with spray, I remained in the cockpit, with some difficulty because of the acute angle of heel, feeling wet, cold and bedraggled in spite of the relative warmth of the water. The wind had dropped with the outgoing tide, and was now gentle from offshore, conveying the cinnamon scent of the land. I sat in silence, lost in my thoughts.

At last there appeared a fast-moving light searching the area of the reef, but away to the north-west. Concluding it to belong to the Coast Guard, I flashed a MAYDAY with the torch I always kept in the cockpit. This soon brought a response, and the light described a wide circle to the north, flicking from side to side, gradually approaching until I saw it was a large inflatable powered by two outboard motors, and crewed by four men in the uniform of the US Coast Guard. They hailed me, while still a considerable distance away, to ask if I was the originator of the MAYDAY. They would not come closer than about 20 yards, requesting that I use the dinghy to traverse the now smaller, but still formidable, waves that were breaking onto the reef.

Taking with me only my valuables, and a sailbag containing dry clothing, I launched the dinghy on the port side, and clambered aboard. I cast off and rowed around the stern to face the waves, taking great pains to keep head-on to them, for a broach would have tumbled me out into the jagged coral, with terrible injuries. There was now little depth of water covering the reef, giving me great cause for concern, should the fragile bottom of the dinghy be caught and ripped upon the coral.

The dinghy bottomed each time the water receded, but was lifted up once more with each new breaker as it roared in, high upon the crest, enveloped in spray and solid water. I rowed as hard as I could to keep head-on to the waves. Perhaps ten minutes passed between leaving *Song* and reaching the quieter waters clear of the reef, but they seemed endless minutes, calling heavily on my physical and mental reserves. Once aboard the Coast Guard boat, the dinghy was made fast astern, jumping and rearing in the wake as we made for the shore at high speed. I was exhausted and drained, the image of *Song*, as we abandoned her, lonely and forlorn, lying on her side like a seabird with a broken wing, still imprinted on my mind.

A mere half-hour later we were nosing into Puerto Chico, and I was put ashore and taken to the Coast Guard station at Cabo San Juan, where hot showers, coffee, and dry clothing were made available. After going through the usual formalities, I discussed my position with the Coast Guard men, who thought that, with the improving weather, the swell should diminish enough to allow us to approach the boat from the inside of the reef, to salvage what we could. But they advised me to make the attempt at first light, for there were scavengers who knew the reef intimately and would soon take advantage of my misfortune.

I accepted the good sense of this advice, and relied further on the good nature of these kindhearted men; some phone calls and a ride back to Puerto Chico brought from his bed Carlos, who runs the diving shop there, and an agreement that he would run me out to the reef in the morning. A visit to the Water Police who are stationed at Puerto Chico, and an explanation of my circumstances and fears, produced complete indifference to my plight. It was past midnight when I returned to the Coast Guard station, spending the remainder of the night in fitful sleep.

The morning dawned bright and clear, with a light wind from the NE. In Puerto Chico, I found Carlos and his charming wife, June, waiting for my arrival. They made me welcome, with sympathy for my loss and offers of whatever help they could give. Leaving my meagre possessions with June, we boarded the 18ft aluminium open boat used by Carlos in his diving business. He informed me that El Roncador was not a place to which he would take any of his clients. On average five boats were wrecked there each year. This number included several small coasting vessels. It was a dangerous and poorly charted place.

With *Song*'s dinghy in tow we made the half-hour run out to the reef. Our approach was on the lee side, where although we would have to cross the full width of the reef, the waves would have spent most of their energy. We dropped anchor in a few feet of water onto white sand, and prepared to row the dinghy across to where *Song* lay on her side, still shuddering as each wave lifted her; but now the sun was shining and the seas moderate. Progress across the reef was slow and it was not until we were quite close that I saw something was wrong. Where was the boom with the main sail stowed upon it? Where were the genoa and working jib I had left lashed to the pulpit? With a sinking feeling, I scrambled on board to discover the full extent of this second catastrophe to overtake us.

The boat had been stripped of everything easily removed from on deck and below. Sails, anchor, rope were gone, lockers rifled, empty spaces only remained where once had been the VHF radio, tape recorder, short wave radio, camera case with all the lenses and film, clothing and equipment. In their search for valuables, the thieves had swept books from shelves and emptied the contents of containers, all of which had been still quite dry, into the swirling waters, invading the boat, turning them into sodden pulp or shattered pieces. Saddest of all was the loss of my sextant and my log book, with its record of the memories of my grand venture. I think then I reached the depths of bitter despair, looking into the chaos and destruction wrought upon my boat. I pitted myself against the sea and lost, but it would have been better had the boat sunk in deep water and everything been lost, than to have my boat thus defiled by such human dregs.

As George Harrod-Eagles unashamedly admits, his decision to sail in to an area with few navigational aids, with islands and unmarked reefs on either side, and with darkness falling, was 'fateful', in view of contrary winds and slow progress. Lack of information about tides also stacked the odds against him. Finally, the well-known difficulty, even to experienced sailors, of keeping a lit buoy in view among a confusion of unrelated lights, as well as the bright glow from the shore, certainly didn't help. As night descended with tropical swiftness, the light astern was impossible to see.

After *Song* struck the reef, Harrod-Eagles contacted the US Coast Guard on VHF radio, but they still had the problem of locating him in the dark among dangerous reefs. It was his torch, which he always kept in the cockpit, which brought rescue. Once again, a torch, as well as a knife, are essentials to have at hand on your person, or in the cockpit.

twenty-eight

LAST TIME OVER

Yacht	*Northern Light* (45ft Colin Archer type gaff-cutter)
Skipper	Lt Cdr James Griffin RN
Crew	Ann Griffin
Bound from	Horta, Azores to Gibraltar, Spain
Date of loss	10 September 1982
Position	on Spanish coast, 6 miles south of Cadiz

Lt Cdr James Griffin and his wife Ann had lived aboard Northern Light *for 22 of the boat's 52 years. After four years pottering around the Bahamas and the coast of Florida, the Griffins had decided to sail back to Europe. Ann Griffin tells what happened after they left the Azores.*

NORTHERN LIGHT IS A 45FT COLIN ARCHER type gaff-cutter, with 15ft 6in beam and 8ft 6in draft, built of 2½ inch Burma teak, copper sheathed, 52 years old, but good for our lifetime. One of our four daughters, Heather, was itching to push us out and buy her off us, but after living in her for 22 years no way would I give her up.

We were almost at the end of our fourth Atlantic crossing, only 100 miles to our destination – Gibraltar. I looked around at our beautiful ship – we had never had a house or a car – our transport was bicycles and they were lashed to the guardrails. We had survived Force 9, gusting 10, on 28–31 August, during which time we were hove-to and had been carried 60 miles to the south by leeway. No hope now of seeing Cape St Vincent and creeping round the corner to anchor and recover. During the blow a new steel strap holding the crosstrees to the mainmast had snapped seven out of its eight stainless steel bolts and was hanging down swinging back and forth, threatening to fall on our heads at any moment. It had sawn through the topsail and jib halyards, and was now threatening the main. We had fitted rigging screws inside the shroud lanyards and all of them had broken their fittings, making it impossible to climb the ratlines and secure the wretched thing, nicknamed Damocles. We were sailing at one knot under mainsail and staysail; we had lost the mizzen gaff jaws in the blow, and the mizzen and the jib were our main driving sails. Jimmy had spent the day repairing seams on the mainsail – the Terylene had stood up to seven years in the tropics, but the stitching hadn't. Everywhere I looked on deck we needed repairs, but there was nothing wrong with the hull, thank heavens.

The wind was dying, but there was still a heavy swell. It had been north-east or east all the way across from the Azores. Only enough fuel was left to get us in the last four miles to enter harbour. No sign of shipping, but there should have been; another frustrating night ahead.

It had been a hasty crossing to Bermuda from Florida, then a glorious 19 days for the 1,850 miles to the Azores, light favourable winds, fantastic sunrises and sunsets, and starry and moonlit nights we would never forget.

Jimmy and I had taken her across the Atlantic in 1974, having left behind all four daughters, now married, but as we were now aged 62 we thought it prudent to invest in a new autopilot. It left us very low on cash, and one day out from Bermuda it packed in. We were watch and watch about for the rest of the trip. We don't carry a radio or liferaft, or any aids to navigation, apart from a sextant, but had lots of flares and a nine-foot ply and glassfibre dinghy.

It had been so hazy that sights had been unreliable for the last two days, but the log was accurate and we were allowing for a half-knot current carrying us into the Straits – the charts and the pilot book said it was so. Just after sunset we saw a ship, and during the night 21 went past us, heading due east . . . we must be near. The ninth dawned heavily overcast – no sights today. At last the wind went south-east . . . we should go north-east. At midday we were suddenly over green water with a fishing boat visible a mile away. A check with the chart revealed where we should have been, on the Banco de Trafalgar, but no sight of land eight miles away. The wind pulled round and went west at last – and we were able to sail direct towards Gibraltar. At 1930 we saw a lighthouse flashing twice every six seconds and went wild with delight . . . we had done it, after 20 days at sea. We celebrated with a cup of tea! We'd be in Gibraltar before dawn, God willing. We got to the lighthouse, but where the heck was Tarifa light? We looked at the lights on the shore – far too many of them, unless Tarifa town had changed a lot in nine years. Feeling very uneasy we put on the engine and hauled off. Shortly after we struck rock and stuck.

The rudder broke off with the first impact, and jammed the propeller. For the next three hours we crashed up and down on the rocks every five seconds. For the first two hours she held, during which time we sent up 20 flares, and signalled with the Aldis lamp to every car that stopped to have a look. Then the water crept over the floorboards and started to beat the pump. I sat on deck in a state of frozen shock, trying to stop three terrified cats from jumping over the side, watching and waiting with the signalling lamp to shine on our sails when help arrived. Nobody came.

Jimmy collected ship's papers and passports; we launched the dinghy, and then he said: 'I'm sorry, darling; it's time to go; if we wait she might fall on the dinghy.' I couldn't believe it; we had been on coral reefs in the Caribbean and always got off, but they were soft by comparison. We put the cats in a sack, and rowed clear, then let them out.

Jimmy rowed two miles inshore, then two miles along through breakers trying to find a beach. We saw a lit one . . . how I got through the surf I'll never know . . . I slipped on rock, but held on; we got the dinghy ashore and tried to capture three soaking wet and petrified cats.

We had landed on a top-security Naval beach. We had left the engine and bilge pump running, cabin and deck lights on. The navy hadn't any English, we hadn't much Spanish, but found we were in Cadiz. We found out later there had been Force 6 and 7 easterlies in the Straits of Gibraltar which had stopped the south-going current. The bank had been the entrance of the Guadalquivir River and the lighthouse had been the Santa Caterina, flashing twice every seven seconds. The Spanish Navy was very kind, gave us cognac and coffee at six in the morning . . . water was running all over the floor from our soaking wet clothes. They offered showers and breakfast, but we were anxious to contact Lloyd's and help.

Jimmy himself is a marine surveyor for Lloyd's, and for the last four years had been working as such for the Bahamas Government. We got to town (two cats in a box, the other one on my lap), and spent three hours trying to get things organised, but as there wasn't a British Consul in Cadiz, went on to Algeciras. After a little difficulty we found a pension that would take us and the cats; sent cables to the girls, and collapsed into bed, cuddling cats.

We were lucky . . . we had each other, and the clothes we stood up in, but oh! the heartache of leaving behind 40 years' diaries and photographs, to say nothing of all the letters the children and grand-children had written us. The tears came in the middle of the night when the shock wore off. Next morning, down to the ferry to go to Gibraltar – but they wouldn't take the cats. Over the next day *Northern Light* came off the reef and drove herself onto an army firing range: a salvage team went down . . . they could get her off with-out any difficulty when we could get the army to stop firing.

We were only insured for total loss, but we would have used our life's savings to get her back. It took five days to get permission, by which time vandals had been aboard, stripped her and taken the bronze strips off our 32 decklights. The water inside pushed them out and she was held down.

The weather deteriorated on 19 September – my birthday – and the answer came that salvage was impossible. At this time both Jimmy and I broke down, but fortunately our eldest daughter, Geraldine, had come over with her fourth child, and that helped. Next day Jimmy went over to see *Northern Light* for himself, and said his own farewell.

Now the tears have stopped; it's only material things we have lost – we must find another boat, and get the cats back . . . they are in a kennel in Spain. We are in Gibraltar with our daughter. We'll never get another boat as beautiful, but nothing will ever take away the memories and we were lucky to own her for 22 years.

■ LESSONS LEARNED

The Griffins' autopilot failed one day out from Bermuda, so they had stood watch and watch about for the rest of their voyage across the Atlantic, and must have been very tired when within 100 miles of Gibraltar.

They didn't carry a radio or liferaft, or any aids to navigation, apart from a sextant, but sights had been unreliable for the last two days. The log was accurate and they were allowing for half a knot of current carrying them into the Straits – the charts and the pilot book said it was so. The classic error was to make the evidence before your eyes fit your assumptions. 'At 1930 we saw a lighthouse flashing twice every six seconds and went wild with delight . . . we had done it after 20 days at sea. We got to the lighthouse, but where was Tarifa light? Shortly after we struck rock and stuck.'

The error was entirely understandable, since only the difference of a second lay between the light characteristics.

They found out later that there had been Force 6 and 7 easterlies in the Straits of Gibraltar, which had stopped the southgoing current. The bank had been the entrance of the Guadalquivir River and the lighthouse had been the Santa Caterina, flashing twice every seven seconds.

twenty-nine

CHARTREUSE ON THE ROCKS

Yacht	*Chartreuse* (31ft cold-moulded half-ton sloop)
Skipper	Paul Newell
Bound from	Cowes in a singlehanded race around the Isle of Wight
Date of loss	26 June 1993
Position	the inside passage between the celebrated wreck of the *Varvassi* and the Needles.

The perils of over familiarity and accidents close to home are illustrated when skipper Paul Newell confronts the awful truth that he sank his boat whilst trying to perform a manoeuvre that he had done many times before.

THE FIRST MISTAKE OF THE DAY was not to switch off the ignition after stopping the engine prior to what promised to be an exciting single-handed Round the Island Race. I settled down to a crisp beat with a flattened mainsail and No. 3 genoa. The Needles were round-ed at 0710. I didn't get any further. Mistake number two had just manifested itself with the biggest collision bang I have ever heard. The boat stopped. I didn't. I hit the companionway bulkhead, via the mainsheet track and runner winch, shoulder first. This is what comes from taking the inside passage between the celebrated wreck of the *Varvassi* and the Needles.

A loud rush of water behind me suggested that I should have seen whatever I had just hit, but it was Richard Burnett in *Albatross*, two boat lengths back and making an impressive U-turn, after seeing that there appeared to be no gap. A cursory glance below was more than enough to tell me that water above the floorboards within 10 seconds meant swimming lessons in the near future. Sinking on the spot was not going to happen straightaway and I reckoned I had half an hour to save the situation.

A beach, preferably with sand and no tide, was needed. Scratchell's Bay was too rocky and Freshwater Bay too far. Alum Bay was not too far (at least in a homeward direction), had a sandy bottom and no tide. I had to tack the boat. I didn't know what I'd hit, but I hoped I didn't hit it on the way back.

The spinnaker pole was in the water, but I couldn't leave the helm as other competitors were turning the corner. I was asked if I was okay and shouted: 'NO, I'M SINKING!' and bore away round the inside of the Needles. The boat already felt heavy, but speed was still good at 6+ knots.

I grabbed a red rocket flare. Caps off. Operate pin. Pin comes away in hand. Useless. Grab another. Caps off. Rocket canister slides out of plastic casing and falls into cockpit. This is really useless. Grab red hand flare. Bet this doesn't work either! It did and it was hot. 'Hold at arm's length,' said the instructions. They were not kidding.

A small fishing boat arrived. I could see it was too small really to help, but might take some gear. They were not interested in saving equipment but told me to 'abandon ship'. I told them 'No chance!' A big fishing boat, *Diana C*, turned up, offering a big tow rope, which I gladly took and tied to the stemhead as boat speed was down to 4 knots and the point of the bow was now at water level. I was only halfway there and I wasn't going to get much further without outside help. The stern was now too far out of the water to steer and the mainsail was making the boat trip over herself by driving the bow down. I lowered the sail and tied it to the boom, and then secured the boom to stop it disappearing when the boat sank. This was now inevitable as the beach was still too far away and progress was getting slower.

I couldn't get the No. 3 down as the bow was 4ft under water. I went below and grabbed a bag of dry clothing. There was so much to save and no time to do it. I threw a bag into the cockpit and climbed out. It was a climb, too, as the boat now took a big surge forward in a downward direction and I could see water at the windows.

I grabbed my car keys and wallet from the companionway locker on the way out and put them in my zip-up jacket pocket. A second big fishing boat turned up full of day-trip fishermen. I passed them a bag of clothes and a bag of food and drink. I tied the tiller off amidships, fitted the washboard and pulled the hatch shut. I coiled down a few ropes that had got their tails overboard, picked up the self-steering gear, climbed over the pushpit and walked along what was now a horizontal transom, then climbed on board the fishing boat just as water started to flood the cockpit.

I was transferred almost immediately to the Yarmouth Lifeboat, where I had a first class view of *Chartreuse* as her transom disappeared underwater. And that was that.

I've written it fast because it happened fast, or at least that was the way it seemed to me. The whole thing took just over 35 minutes. I know that some boats go down in seconds and others take for ever, but those 35 minutes for me went all too fast. I couldn't get enough done.

Some boats go down with no one else around, which must be horrendous, but I was lucky to have boats around me at the time and they were able to help me. I am very grateful for that, but the feeling of helplessness was almost too much to bear. I knew she was going to sink right from the start and nothing I could do was going to stop her, and yet I worked harder to try and save her than I have ever worked before. I hadn't managed to get right in to the beach but 200 yards off wasn't too bad. The water was only 12ft deep and the bottom was mostly sand. This was my worst nightmare come true.

From the lifeboat, I was transferred to *Diana C. Chartreuse's* transom was just under the water so we manoeuvred alongside where I was able to re-board, taking one of his anchor lines, and making it fast to a stern cleat. The anchor was then streamed offshore for about 300ft to stop *Chartreuse* from moving about too much, as the wind had got up to a good Force 5. The No. 3 was still set and showing. The boat had settled on the bottom in an almost upright position, although with only the bow and keel actually on the bottom. It was then decided to go to Yarmouth and get help from Bembridge salvage expert Martin Woodward. The tide was too low to get out of Bembridge that evening and he was already committed to another job, so he left first thing on Sunday morning.

In Alum Bay next morning, strops were put round *Chartreuse*, air bags attached and inflated and at 0910 she was on the surface once again. The tow to Yarmouth was slow, which allowed two big pumps to be put aboard. There was a large hole in the bow below the water-line. It was too big for the pumps to keep up with the flood of water. So we found the cockpit cover as it passed us in the swirling water below decks and fitted it over the hole from the outside, tying it tight to the stemhead and stanchion bases. This made it an easier job for the pumps to win the battle. As the water went down, I disconnected the electronics and passed them to Martin to put into fresh water straightaway with the hope of salvaging them, but it soon became obvious this was a waste of time, as mistake number one reared its head. With power going through them at the time of sinking all the circuits had burnt out; this included all of the engine electrics as well. The terminals and most of the wiring just fell to bits as soon as they were touched. The insides of all of the 'magic boxes' were in a similar state.

By the time we reached Yarmouth, the boat could be kept afloat as long as the pumps were kept going. The tide by this stage was on the flood and the men at Harold Hayles's yard were put on standby to get her out at the top of the tide. Meanwhile, she was berthed along-side the Harbourmaster's office, where I started unloading sails, anchors, sheets, bunk boards, floorboards and anything else that had been washing about down below. They were taken home and rinsed with fresh water. The more gear that I took out, the more damage I found. The hole in the bow was caused by the boat nose-diving into the seabed all night, but at some stage she had heeled well over to port and had taken a severe bashing on her port side right back as far as amidships. This could be seen from the inside with planking burst inward between the stringers. An immense amount of sand that had come aboard through the bow hole was sucked out via the pumps and a rupture in the hog could be seen. The keel had been driven back-wards and the aft end upwards had burst the hog and broken three of the six keel-bearing frames.

Chartreuse was fitted on to a cradle at Hayles and lifted out of the water. I could see the damage to the keel. The leading edge, about halfway up, had been the point of impact; as a result the steel casing had buckled to about 1ft back and the leading edge itself was off centre by about 1½in over a distance of 2ft. A rough guide as to how so much damage was caused by such a light boat is the pinpoint impact load formula of Mass x Velocity (squared). *Chartreuse* weighs about 2.75 tons. Therefore 2.75 tons x 7.25 knots = 19.94 x 19.94: 397 tons. I know that this is not a truly scientific way to work it out, but it does give a guide as to the sort of load that a boat has to put up with when grounding at speed. The insurance company declared *Chartreuse* a 'constructive total loss' and made a reduced offer if I wanted to keep the boat.

This was accepted, and not long after I towed the whole lot by road to A A Coombes's yard in Bembridge where restoration work began.

■ LESSONS LEARNED

Don't go for the inside gap round the Needles as it is exceptionally difficult to judge the distance (as one yacht demonstrated in a later fully crewed Round the Island Race).

Don't forget to switch off the engine ignition; if there's time, isolate the batteries by switching them off too.

Try not to panic because you won't get anything done.

The importance of a grab bag, even on short trips, is driven home graphically.

Newell says he should have used the time before *Chartreuse* sank more constructively. 'The No. 3 genoa should have been taken down at the earliest opportunity. It would have meant a lot less damage to the topsides. I could have removed the electronic navigation boxes so I only had to buy the connecting wires and not the whole system. I'm glad that I tied the mainsail and boom down and tidied the boat up a bit, as they would have got in the way of the salvage team underwater.'

FIRE or EXPLOSION

FIRE AND ICE

Yacht	*Dodo's Delight* (33ft Westerly Discus)
Skipper	Bob Shepton
Date of loss	January 2005
Position	Upernavik, Greenland

Bob Shepton has completed six Atlantic crossings and a circumnavigation via Cape Horn. His awards include the Blue Water Medal (Cruising Club of America), the Royal Cruising Club Tilman Medal and the Ocean Cruising Club Barton Cup. After sailing 93,000 miles over 25 years in his 33ft Westerly Discus, Dodo's Delight, the 70-year-old adventurer lost her to a fire on board in Greenland in 2005.

I SET SAIL FROM THE WEST COAST of Scotland in late June. Over the next six months I'd be joined by different crew, including three mountaineering instructors and six ski instructors. We crawled westwards across a spider's web of isobars as a huge depression lay stationary to the south of Iceland. Our passage took us through the eye of the depression, with confused seas and a radical change in wind directions. It was all a bit of a shock for those on their first ocean passage. Some showed signs of stress but all stood their watches.

We were 18 days on the wind, including 26 hours hove-to on try-sail. After a nasty windswept night motor-sailing past big icebergs to round Cape Desolation, we broke out into a cloudless day motoring past more icebergs in flat calm, blue seas and sunshine, with a whale sleeping on the surface. We reached Nuuk the following morning and headed next for Kangerdluarssugssuq, a 15-mile-long fjord. We sailed up the only line of soundings on the Danish chart and over a reef with 2m showing on the depth sounder, before anchoring in the glacial silt at the head of the fjord. We'd come to Greenland to climb mountains but the weather wasn't kind. We managed three ascents before making our way north to the Akuliarusinguaq peninsula, at the top of Uummannaq fjord.

One day, whilst alone on *Dodo's Delight*, I experienced a mini-tsunami. I'd anchored close to the gravel beach to make it easier to land the climbers. Suddenly, a huge wave picked the boat up and threw her up the beach. She heeled in the swell and rolled violently from side to side on her keel. Fortunately, I got the engine started quickly, watched for the next huge swell, gunned the engine and slid off into deep water. Only then did I have time to be frightened. I imagine a massive berg must have calved from a glacier some 10km away and the tidal wave had made its way down the fjord.

We had a successful expedition to the far north. Finally, we got up to 78° 32' N by Cairn Point, an unforgettable scene: primeval, pristine; with ice, absolute stillness and silence, and narwhals swimming nearby. We believe this was further north than a yacht had ever been in Greenland, but as the sea showed signs of freezing over, I thought it was time to turn round.

I planned to winter in the boat in the Arctic on my own. I was blown out of my first choice of winter quarters and struggled to get the inflatable dinghy aboard in gale-force winds. Then came the day I fell into the water. Not a good thing to do in the Arctic. Falling in is one thing; getting out again, with seven layers of waterlogged clothing and big boots, is quite another. I couldn't pull myself into the dinghy, or up a line from the boat to grasp a stanchion and heave myself over the topsides. I lay on my back with my feet in the dinghy holding the line and occasionally struggling, and wondered how long it would be before they found my body. In desperation, I let go of the dinghy and the line, and swam to the stern. After a monumental struggle, I managed to clamber up what was left of the self-steering gear on the stern, and so back on board. It was then that I began to shiver, not from cold with all those clothes on, but from delayed shock.

Pack ice and north winds later sent me scurrying to Upernavik, to spend an unpleasant night in what I dubbed 'the worst harbour in the world'. I eventually solved the dilemma of ice floes invading my otherwise protected mooring by stretching a huge borrowed warp across the entrance.

In early November, the sun disappeared below the horizon for three months. There was still some daylight around midday, decreasing in length and light as the days shortened. It did begin to get to me as we approached the longest night of 21 December, with very little light remaining. Finding oneself alone in the Arctic is a frightening experience. The underlying feeling was that any mistake could be fatal. But there was the incredible beauty of the Arctic in winter: clear, starlit nights and intense moonlight. When the ice came, life took on different dimensions. I found it difficult to get from the sea ice, across the tidal fracture line and onto the shore ice, to fetch water from a stream, especially in big Spring tides. On one occasion I had another ducking when an ice floe I stepped on sank. But I was only up to my hips.

As the ice thickened, my quality of life improved. The boat was safe from the scourge of floating ice, daylight was lengthening, and re-supply was possible by trekking over the ice to Upernavik. It was intriguing to walk across a fjord you had sailed through a month or two previously.

I began to relax and enjoy it. And then it happened. One afternoon I returned to the boat from a ski trek and decided to charge the batteries with the portable generator in the cockpit. I thought I must fill the Taylor's diesel heater. I took the container and funnel along the deck to the small hole in the deckhead. The heater was gravity fed, so the tank was high up under the deckhead. My usual method of filling was to start down below, unscrew the cap to the fuel tank and insert a funnel. But I had started the process on deck. Pouring diesel, I suddenly saw red flames through the hole. I instantly realised that I'd forgotten to unscrew the cap to the tank and diesel had poured onto the heater below and ignited.

I rushed round to the main hatch but already the noxious fumes and smoke were such that after one breath I knew that I mustn't go down there. I was determined to put the blaze out, but all I could do was try to douse the flames with handfuls of snow off the ice. It was futile. The local fire service, alerted by someone from the airport on the hill above Upernavik, arrived on snowmobiles across 5km of ice, but nothing could be done. The boat burned and eventually sank in 7–8m of water. I had lost everything and was virtually left only with what I was wearing. The police, who were splendid, gave me an official covering letter explaining the loss of my passport, and my wife, Kate, was able to transfer money for my airfare home. My insurers (Yachtsure) were extremely professional and supportive, and enabled me to purchase a replacement boat.

There was still a tremendous sense of loss. Not just for the boat herself, but more that a focal point of life – the thing I did – had been removed at a stroke. There were also feelings of guilt, and shame – that I now had to tell everybody that the 'glorious' expedition had ended so ignominiously. I was left trying to echo those incredible words of Job, 'The Lord gave, the Lord has taken away, blessed be the name of the Lord'.

■ LESSONS LEARNED

This was a simple error where a routine job, which has been performed many times, goes horribly wrong because we either forget a vital element of the routine, are in a hurry, or simply a victim of over-familiarity and confidence. In these situations, it always pays to pause, double check and go over your plan step-by-step before taking action.

FOOTNOTE

Not long after this accident, Bob bought another Westerly Discus and called her *Dodo's Delight*.

thirty-one

LPG – A DISASTER WAITING TO HAPPEN

Yacht	*Lord Trenchard* (55ft Nicholson yawl)
Skipper	Colin Rouse
Date of loss	30 June 1999
Position	Poole Harbour

On 30 June 1999, the 55ft Nicholson yawl, Lord Trenchard, *owned by the Armed Forces and used for adventure training for servicemen and women, was destroyed by a gas explosion whilst alongside Poole town quay. Two people were injured, one very seriously. This first-hand account of the accident, by Gavin McLaren who was Mate aboard at the time, makes sobering reading for anyone with a gas system aboard their yacht.*

THE SOUND OF PEOPLE MOVING around the cabin and quiet conversation wakes me. It is broad daylight and I glance at my watch. Five to seven – I can doze in the quarter berth for a few more minutes. I pull the bunk curtain aside just in time to see two of the crew disappear up the companionway with their shower gear. The skipper, Colin Rouse, is up and about. 'What's the weather like?' I ask.

'Fine,' he answers. 'Looks good for Cherbourg. The kettle is on.'

I lie back and think about the plan for the day. Seven new crew members will be joining us after breakfast and in my mind I run through the briefing that they will need before we can sail. I hear the generator, fitted below the cockpit, turn over as Colin tries to start it from the control panel by the saloon steps. It doesn't start the first time and then I hear it turn over again.

Chaos. I am conscious of the most excruciating pain. The whole of my right leg feels as though it is being electrocuted. The agony goes on and on and on. I can't see, I'm covered in something white and translucent. There is no noise, and then I hear screaming. Deep male cries of agony; it takes a finite time for me to realise that the screaming is coming from me. Illogically, I think that something must have happened to the generator and live cables have dropped across my leg. After what seems like an age the pain starts to ease. Faintly I hear a voice. 'He's lost his leg'. I turn my head to the right and see a severed leg lying beside my bunk where the chart table seat should be. For one dreadful, heart-stopping moment I think that it's mine. Then I realise that the leg is deeply tanned and wearing a shoe and sock – it can't be me.

I think I lose consciousness at this point and the next thing I am aware of is someone dragging me from the remnants of the quarter berth. They are pulling shattered sheets of glassfibre off me. I am lying on the bare hull, the bunk has disappeared from under me. My rescuers drag me through the gaping hole where the coachroof had been. There is a stink of glassfibre, as though I was in a moulding shop. My face and eyes are covered in blood and something seems to have happened to my right foot – it's bleeding and won't take my weight. I look back into the wreckage of what had been the saloon. Colin is lying there with people working on him. The stump of his leg is pointing straight towards me. The cabin is devastated – I cannot conceive what has happened. There is blood everywhere.

I recall nothing else until I step onto the jetty from TS *Royalist*, alongside which *Lord Trenchard* had been berthed. There are police cars and ambulances all over the quay and more are arriving. I only hear their sirens faintly. There is a lot of broken glass and a crowd is beginning to form, held back by the police. A sergeant is talking to me, but I can't really absorb what he is saying. He shakes my shoulders. 'How many people were on board. How many?' I try to pull myself together. 'Four!' I answer.

I look back at *Lord Trenchard*. The whole of the cockpit and after deck has disappeared, leaving a gaping hole some 20ft long. The mizzen mast has fallen forward and the aft end of the coachroof has been torn off. I can see a deep split running down the hull from the coaming to the waterline. The whole deck has been lifted and all the windows blown out. Only at this moment does my mind register what has happened – explosion. I want to go back to the boat to help Colin but, sensibly, I'm not allowed to. 'He's all right – he's being looked after,' I am told. Still dripping blood I am put into an ambulance and driven away.

That is the reality of a gas explosion. The violence of the event is beyond belief. The blast was heard over four miles away and windows blown out on the quay, despite being shielded by the bulk of *Royalist* inboard of *Lord Trenchard*. The other two crew members on board, who had, like me, been lying in their bunks, were miraculously uninjured, but very shocked. The two crewmen who had just stepped onto the jetty probably saved Colin's life. They recall looking round to see parts of the boat – including the complete wheel and binnacle – flying high in the air. They came back on board and administered first aid, helped by officers from *Royalist*, until medical help arrived.

The emergency services deserve every praise. Poole lifeboat came alongside and together with *Royalist* supported *Lord Trenchard* to keep her afloat; she was making a lot of water from the splits in the hull and damaged seawater systems. After Colin had been taken ashore she was towed to the other side of the harbour to be lifted out. I spent some time in casualty, together with members of *Royalist's* crew, who had suffered cuts and bruises. I had the gashes in my foot stitched up – the cuts to my face were only superficial – and discovered that both my eardrums had been burst. The initial pain in my leg, which had been only a few inches from the seat of the blast, was explained to me; the shock of the explosion had stimulated all the nerves in it at once, a common blast effect.

Whilst being treated I heard that Colin's left leg had been amputated above the knee. His other leg was badly damaged but had mercifully been saved. He also had injuries to his hand and neck and, although critically ill, was out of immediate danger.

Later that day I went back down to *Lord Trenchard* to try to retrieve some of my personal kit. She was still being kept afloat, but was half full of water and diesel fuel. The interior was almost unrecognisable with virtually nothing left intact. The explosion had obviously happened under the cockpit and the blast had torn forward through the boat, ripping out the joinery, bulkheads and cabin sole. The forehatch, which had been secured with a massive wooden strongback, had been torn off. The chart table had been blown forward through the saloon, together with the radar and all the instruments. It seemed impossible that four people could have survived. Mixed in with the shattered fragments of glassfibre and plywood were the pathetic remains of personal possessions – shredded clothing and sleeping bags, books, toilet gear, Colin's battered flute. It was a very shocking sight, made worse by the evidence of Colin's injuries – splashes of blood and blood-soaked clothing.

How could such an accident happen? The Joint Services Adventurous Sail Training centre in Gosport has been running a fleet of 24 boats, including nine Nicholson 55s, for nearly 30 years. The boats are deployed world-wide – three of them were racing across the Indian Ocean when this accident happened. They have a regular programme of refits and maintenance and, because many of the service personnel who sail in them are novices, safety procedures and routines are paramount. The Marine Accident Investigation Board carried out a very thorough enquiry into the explosion on behalf of the Health and Safety Executive.

Like the other service Nicholson 55s, *Lord Trenchard*'s gas system consisted of two 3.9kg propane cylinders, mounted in a gas locker sunk into the deck abreast the cockpit. Both cylinders were connected by flexible hoses to the regulator via a wall block and from there a single continuous gas pipe ran to an isolating valve by the cooker. A retaining plate secured the cylinders in the locker with just their shut off valves exposed. One cylinder was turned on whilst the other, shut off, was a standby, available when the in-use cylinder ran out. Whenever the cooker was not in use the isolating valve beside it was kept shut. A gas alarm was fitted, with two sensors, one beneath the cooker and one below the cockpit.

The evening before the accident the in-use gas bottle ran out whilst supper was being cooked. It was turned off, the standby cylinder was turned on and a note made to change the empty cylinder next day.

The accident report identified three failures that caused the explosion. First, the standby cylinder, which had been turned on the previous evening, had not been properly connected to its flexible pipe. The cylinder was recovered after the event and the connection was loose. It had been attached during a previous cruise made by *Lord Trenchard* a fortnight earlier and had been the 'standby' cylinder since then. Thus, when, twelve hours before the explosion, this cylinder was turned on, high-pressure gas leaked undetected directly from the bottle into the gas locker.

This gas should have drained overboard. However, examination of the gas locker, which was also recovered, revealed that it was not completely gas tight. So an unknown proportion of the escaping gas leaked into the watertight compartment below the cockpit.

The final cause of the disaster was that the gas alarm failed to operate. The reason for this could not be determined – the alarm system was so badly damaged in the explosion that testing it was impossible. The report concluded that the generator starter motor supplied the spark that ignited the gas.

■ **LESSONS LEARNED**

So three failures, one human and two material, caused this catastrophe. The most obvious lesson is that gas cylinders should always be turned off AT THE BOTTLE when gas is not being used. But in many boats this is inconvenient – the gas locker is outside in the cold and wet and it is often difficult to get at. It is worth noting that a solenoid shut off valve, often fitted to overcome this inconvenience, would not have prevented this accident, as it would have been 'downstream' of the loose connection.

But there are other lessons too. Gas on boats is inherently dangerous and to keep it safe we have to actively do things. We must turn the gas on and off at the bottle every time the cooker is used and test our gas alarms by injecting butane into the sensors at regular intervals. We must periodically check that our gas lockers are indeed gas tight and that the drains from them are not blocked. We must check pipework and replace flexible hoses, test flame failure devices. Human nature is such that not all of these things will unfailingly get done.

We should all consider whether we really do need gas on our boats. Nowadays there are more alternatives available than the old-fashioned traditional Primus stoves. There are user friendly diesel cookers on the market, now with ovens. Larger yachts with modern, quiet inboard generators might use electricity for their cooking.

On a happier note, Colin made the most remarkable recovery, due largely to his amazing cheerfulness and fortitude, together with the unstinting support of his partner Janis. Within a week he was terrorising the nurses in hospital and within a fortnight he was home. He now gets around well on an artificial leg and still enjoys sailing.

Accidents involving gas are more horrible than most. The crew of *Lord Trenchard* were fortunate that no one was killed. Had the explosion happened the previous day, with the yacht at sea and everyone on board in the cockpit, or had they all been sitting round the saloon table, undoubtedly lives would have been lost, quite possibly the whole crew. To prevent such a disaster happening to you, if you must have gas on your yacht, always, always turn it off at the bottle.

thirty—two

A BLAZING YACHT
IN THE IONIAN

Yacht	Charter yacht
Skipper	unknown
Bound from	Mourtos in the Northern Ionian to Parga
Date of loss	1997
Position	Sivota Islands, Ionian Sea, Greece

Derek and Carol Asquith's charter holiday got off to a hair-raising start when they were called to rescue the crew of a burning yacht.

IT WAS THE SECOND DAY of our flotilla sailing holiday in the Northern Ionian. The winds were light, the sea was flat and the sun was shining as we left Mourtos for Parga. The fleet was a mix of 9.7m (32ft) Jeanneau and 11m (36ft) Beneteau yachts and my wife Carol and I, who sail a 7.3m (24ft) Snapdragon at home in North Wales, had looked forward to the comfort of a larger boat for the holiday.

We sailed between the Sivota Islands and the mainland, cruising slowly down the coast. After a couple of hours the wind died completely so we started the engine. The sea was calm as we motored at a comfortable 4 knots towards the next headland in the distance. We noticed the lead boat close inshore three or four miles ahead of us, with only one or two boats of the flotilla in sight.

Suddenly the radio came to life with one of our group calling the lead boat in a fairly calm way, saying they had a fire. We turned the volume up and scanned the horizon but could see no signs of smoke anywhere. Our lead boat responded on the VHF channel that the flotilla was using, asking if they had found the source of the fire and made any effort to extinguish it. They replied that the fire was in the engine compartment and one extinguisher had made no difference.

The lead skipper then asked their position and from their reply we realised they were perhaps half-a-mile ahead of us with no one else around. The flotilla lead skipper then told them not, on any account, to open up the engine compartment, but to try to use the second extinguisher through the hole in the companionway steps panel. After some tense moments they came back to say that their efforts with the second extinguisher had proved unsuccessful.

At this stage, I called the lead skipper to tell him we were closing with the boat. We increased speed towards the, now visible, smoking yacht and saw four men waving frantically and more smoke pouring from the cabin. When we were within about 25m (80ft) we could hear them shouting.

'Hurry up, it's going to blow!'

Carol turned to me and quietly asked if I thought it would really explode. I crossed my fingers and replied confidently: 'Diesel won't explode, it will only burn.'

Pulling alongside the stricken yacht, we found three crew amidships and one standing in the pulpit, as far from the smoke and burning as possible. Carol held a fender over the side to prevent the stanchions and guardrails becoming entangled as we came alongside in the swell. We did not want to be trapped against a burning yacht.

The three men amidships scrambled aboard, calling for the fourth in the pulpit. In his panic, the fourth man jumped overboard into the sea. We veered slowly away and Carol threw a fender to the man in the water who could not swim as fast as the boat. She then took a mooring warp from the cockpit locker and we reversed very slowly until she could throw him the line. With the engine in neutral we pulled him towards the bathing platform and after a successful recovery motored clear to take stock of the situation.

The crew of the blazing vessel had only two lifejackets between them as the others were stowed below in cabin lockers which were impossible to reach because of the fire.

The lead boat arrived a short while later, but by now the fire had really got hold and no one could have safely gone back aboard. As we watched, the shrouds gave way and the mast collapsed and fell into the sea. Soon the gas bottles exploded in the cockpit and that was the beginning of the end. The lead boat later tried to tow the hull but, when it became obvious she was sinking, they took her back to deep water where she soon went down.

As we returned the four crew to Mourtos, they told us that, as with all the flotilla boats, they had a liferaft and inflatable dinghy; but since no one had been given instructions in launching the liferaft, they had failed to inflate it. They had tried to pump up the dinghy, but felt it was taking too long and had given up. No doubt the proximity of our boat had led them to feel they had more chance of escape with us. Luckily, all survived unharmed.

■ LESSONS LEARNED

We instantly moved our lifejackets from the cabin into the cockpit lockers and made sure we knew everything we needed to know about how to launch the liferaft.

It was our first real man-overboard and, although the stern bathing platform is considered the wrong place from which to recover a person, on an almost flat calm day the platform with a ladder made it easy.

Should you be unfortunate enough to have an engine fire aboard, throw the gas bottles and any spare fuel cans overboard to prevent them exploding.

A longer lead on the VHF radio microphone and a hand-held set in the cockpit would have helped. Apparently, the cabin of the blazing yacht filled with black smoke so quickly that it was soon impossible to go below.

I intend to fit bigger extinguishers on our Snapdragon, including one in a cockpit locker. And make sure that anyone who comes aboard has a thorough safety briefing and knows where everything is stowed and how it is operated.

thirty-three

LIGHTNING STRIKE

Yacht	*Freedom To* (34ft motor-sailer)
Skipper	C Binnings
Crew	J Warrington
Bound from	Hamble, Hampshire to Newport, South Wales
Date of loss	20 May 1981
Position	Five miles south of Eddystone Lighthouse

Freedom To, a Westerly Vulcan, was brand-new and on her way from the Solent to Newport, South Wales, which was to be her home port when she was struck by lightning.

WE LEFT HAMBLE AT 1100 ON TUESDAY, motored down to the Solent and took our departure from the Needles. As we came on to 260°, the wind came up dead astern and with the roller headsail full out and the revs down to 2,200 we made 6 1/2 knots – pleasant sailing.

A week previously I had sent form CG66 to Swansea Coastguard and informed Solent Coastguard of our departure, as well as Portland and Brixham as we passed. We had planned for Dartmouth, but changed our plans when the afternoon brought a blue sky and the evening a good moon. We decided to make for Penzance.

At 0100 we saw flashes of lightning way to the south. By 0400 it was raining and the flashes were getting nearer. Visibility was by now down to about two to three miles. We continued to run under full headsail and 2,200 revs.

Jim had the 0200–0600 watch and at 0530 he joined me below in the main cabin, saying that he would steer from the inside position for a while. He had done more than his fair share of helming on the previous day.

Feeling sufficiently awake, I said I would take over and settled myself into the helmsman's seat with a glance at the compass.

The noise was like a television tube exploding. Our first thoughts were 'the engine', but it appeared to be running normally enough. We raced to the cockpit to look for visible damage and as I looked I noticed the aerial had gone. Jim switched off the engine and gas bottle in the nearby locker. A thick, tanny brown smoke was rolling up the companionway to be straightened and carried away by the wind. It's still raining, I thought, I'm going to get wet out here without oilskins. I quite believed that it was only a matter of waiting for the smoke to clear. I had other thoughts. If the situation deteriorated further, sending a MAYDAY was impossible now with the aerial gone. Top priority was the dinghy, flares and lifejackets.

I took a deep breath and leapt down the companionway. Visibility nil. The lifejackets were in the hanging wardrobe and the flares under the settee berths, but access was still a stranger and familiarity not yet an ally. The attempt was aborted, but I did manage to grab a fire extinguisher which was clipped under the saloon table.

By now Jim was in the cockpit with a full bucket of water, but with smoke issuing from every quarter it was difficult to know where to start the attack. We lifted the cockpit locker to get at the dinghy – more dense smoke. This is a big 7ft-deep locker with the dinghy at the bottom under a mound of carefully stowed warps and fenders, the outboard motor and five gallons of spare diesel. I came out gasping for air. The dinghy was firmly lodged. We climbed to the weather side to avoid the toxic fumes, while *Freedom To* continued to turn. As we came up on to the starboard side we saw the first lick of flame from the main hatch. It was impossible to believe, the possible avenues of retreat were rapidly being whittled away: we had no VHF, flares or lifejackets. A stuck dinghy and two horseshoe buoys were all that was left.

With Jim making a last ditch effort to free the inflatable, I grabbed at the horseshoes, freeing one. Still no flames in the cockpit locker as the dinghy finally freed. We yanked it clear, the rubber warm and sticky. By now the flames were at Jim's seaboots as we hauled the dinghy down the weather side outside the lifelines. The cabin roof was melting, with flames breaking through to leeward. We stood in the pulpit together, desperately trying to inflate the dinghy by mouth. The heat on our backs was appalling, as all deck features folded in before taking on a mantle of flame.

Flame and heat accelerated our departure from the deck and with the dinghy only perhaps 20 per cent inflated we followed it into the water.

We searched with our mouths for the inflation holes which were some way underwater. The dinghy by now was alongside the starboard beam, although I have no idea why. We continued to inflate – it was taking shape, holding air. Then down came the mast immediately above us. Six or seven feet from the hull and it would have hit us, but we were close enough to the side for safety as it lay at right angles into the sea. Seconds later the boom came tumbling into the water alongside the dinghy. It was still, however, attached to the gooseneck and lolled, burning, inches from the rubber. The mainsail which had been left wrapped on to the boom had burned and the metal was molten with heat.

Jim was still busy blowing air. I thumped him for his attention and four hands sent water flying to douse this, our latest hazard. This was followed by our next concern, the danger of explosion from the 40 gallons of diesel on board and the two gas cylinders. Using our hands as paddles we made some distance from the wreck. Ten, fifteen, twenty feet and I looked astern.

She lay in the water, her superstructure gone, a floating cauldron with her spars dangling. We could still make out her lines. We paddled further and as I lifted my head on the next crest I saw the coaster, maybe 700 yards off. You're not safe yet, I thought, she's probably on autopilot. As she neared we could see figures on deck and heard the sounds of reversing engines. Through salt drenched eyes I could read the name on her bows. I will never forget that name *Moray Firth*.

As we were helped up the side and up on to the bridge, the first of two explosions wracked *Freedom To*. She was last reported burnt to the waterline. We informed the Coastguard of our safety.

Flares must be kept dry and to hand – not under the settee berths, as they were on *Freedom To* when she was struck by lightning. Manufacturers go a long way towards ensuring that their flares are kept dry, by packaging them in waterproof plastic containers, but it will always be for the skipper to decide where they are stowed. Any container used for storing distress flares must not only be instantly accessible but also be easily opened on the roughest, blackest night, so that the correct flare or rocket can be found without fumbling or delay. Flares are marked with an expiry date, so don't count on them to work successfully after that time.

When a boat is on fire and the fire is out of control, there is no time to be wasted. But if the inflatable dinghy has been stowed in a locker and is inaccessible the situation can be frightening as the crew of *Freedom To* discovered.

The 'big 7ft-deep locker' had the dinghy at the bottom under a mound of carefully stowed warps and fenders, the outboard motor and five gallons of spare diesel! The skipper came out gasping for air. 'The dinghy was firmly lodged . . . we had no VHF, flares or lifejackets. A stuck dinghy and two horseshoe buoys were all that was left.' When they did eventually manage to yank the dinghy clear it was warm and sticky, so it must have been a very close thing. Then they had to inflate it without a pump, using their mouths instead. When they could stand the heat no longer they tossed the partially inflated dinghy into the water and followed it. Having no oars, they had to paddle with their hands to get clear of the yacht, which, with its tanks of diesel fuel and gas bottles, was likely to blow up at any moment. Somehow they managed to get more air into the dinghy to keep her afloat until they were rescued by a passing coaster. They were extraordinarily lucky and their experience should warn against stowing a dinghy in a locker while underway.

FAILURE of GROUND TACKLE or MOORING LINES

thirty-four

GIRL STELLA'S GOING

Yacht	*Girl Stella* (40ft gaff-rigged ketch)
Skipper	Frank Mulville
Crew	Richard Morris (mate), Celia Mulville, Patrick Mulville, Andrew Mulville
Bound from	Bermuda to England
Date of loss	24 April 1969
Position	Porto Piqueran, one mile north of Santa Cruz, Flores

On 1 August 1968, Girl Stella left Heybridge Basin in Essex, on a voyage to Cuba. On board were Frank Mulville, his wife Celia, their two sons Andrew and Patrick, and a friend, Dick Morris. The 24-ton Girl Stella was an ex-Cornish lugger, built in 1896, but completely rebuilt and fitted with a diesel engine by the Drake brothers at Tollesbury.

ON THE WAY TO CUBA, *Girl Stella* stopped for a while in Spain, the Canaries and the West Indies, before spending Christmas in Kingston, Jamaica. They arrived in Santiago de Cuba on 28 December, and spent several weeks cruising along the south coast and around the western end of the island, including 24 hours aground on a reef in the approaches to Santa Lucia. For the last month of the ten-week stay, *Girl Stella* lay in the harbour of Havana, finally leaving Cuba on 15 March 1969. After calling at the Bahamas and Bermuda, the Atlantic crossing began on 9 April.

Being to the southward of our course had put the Azores almost in line between us and home. 'Of course we'll go in,' Patrick said, 'it will be nice to get a run ashore in a brand new island.' I was doubtful. 'Wouldn't it be better to go straight on home?' Celia and Adrian agreed. 'Let's go home,' Adrian said, 'we'll be late for school – and anyway I want to see the dog.'

Dick, if anything, seemed to be in favour of seeing the Azores. 'I must say I'd like to see the whaling boats,' he said. The argument kept us amused for days. 'Look here, Daddy,' Patrick said, 'you can't go right past these lovely islands and not go in.'

In the end I compromised. If we just went in to Flores, the most northerly of the islands, and stayed for a short time, two days at the outside, it wouldn't waste much time or take us far out of our way. We studied the pilot book. Flores had a harbour of sorts, although it didn't say much about it. It was a whaling island – the last place in the world, I believe, where whales are still hunted with pulling boats using hand harpoons. If the whaling boats used the island there was no reason why we should not, and the port of Santa Cruz was on the lee side and should be well sheltered. 'After all,' Patrick said, 'Sir Richard Grenville lay in Flores off the Azores, why shouldn't we?' 'All right – we'll go into Flores. But two days only,' I decided. 'We'll fill up with water,' Celia said, 'and get some fresh vegetables.'

It was a bad decision. I knew it was a bad decision because a little voice inside me told me so – a decision dictated not by considerations of careful seamanship and what the pilot book would call 'A proper regard for the safety of the vessel', but by nothing more tangible than a passing fancy – a set of frail desires. It was trusting to luck instead of careful planning. Once embarked on, it led inexorably on to other decisions, taken one by one and in themselves innocent enough, which built themselves up to produce a misfortune which, to our small world, was a disaster.

The wind worked its way round to the south-west as we got closer to Flores and the glass went down slightly – nothing to worry about, but if it was going to blow a gale from the south-west it would be just as well to be safely tucked away in the lee of a high island. There is no radio beacon on Flores and, unlike any other of our major landfalls of the voyage, I would have to rely completely on my sextant. Flores is not a big island, perhaps half as long as the Isle of Wight, and there was no other island within 130 miles of it, except Corvo – a very small island immediately to the north-east. I supplemented my sun observations with star sights in the morning and confidently pronounced an ETA. 'You'll see it at half past two this afternoon, lying on the port bow, and there's ten shillings for the first boy to sight land.' It was Tuesday 22 April and we had covered 1,700 miles in 13 days – an average speed of over five knots. At two o'clock Adrian sighted the island pushing its bulk out of low cloud fine on the port bow.

It took a long time to come up with the southern cape of Flores and it was evening by the time we rounded it and came along the east side of the island towards Santa Cruz – close under great cliffs and mountains that dropped sheer into the Atlantic. White houses high up on the mountainside blinked their lights at us – we could see the gulls wheeling in tight spirals against the sheer rock face, and ahead of us the small town of Santa Cruz could just be seen before the sun went behind the mountain and everything was suddenly submerged in darkness. 'What a pity. I thought we'd just get in before dark,' I said to Celia. 'We'll have to hang off till morning – how disappointing,' she said.

We took the sails down off Santa Cruz and just as we were making a neat stow of the mains'l, two bright red leading lights suddenly showed up, one behind the other, showing the way into the harbour. 'Well, what do you think of that?' I said to Dick. 'Do you think they switched on the lights specially for us?' 'Perhaps they did. Anyway it must be quite OK to go in at night otherwise the leading lights wouldn't be there.' I went below where Celia was. 'They've switched on two beautiful leading lights,' I said. 'I think we'll go in rather than flog about here all night.' 'I think we ought to wait till we can see where we're going,' she said. I consulted Dick again and we overruled her. 'Is everything squared up? Get the ropes and fenders up and we'll go in,' I said. I knew, deep inside myself, that it was a silly thing to do. The little voice told me so again. 'You're a bloody idiot, Mulville,' it said. 'Oh shut your blather – I'm tired – I want a night's sleep.'

When everything was ready to go alongside – the mooring ropes ready, fenders out, side lights lit, boathooks handy, anchor cleared away ready to let go if needed – I put the engine slow ahead and went straight for the leading lights and straight for the black cliff which was all we could see behind them. Soon we could hear the surf pounding against the rocks. 'I don't like it, Frank,' Celia said, 'I'm going below.'

'It's not too late to turn back,' the voice said. 'Don't be such a bloody fool.'

'Can you see anything, Dick?' I shouted to the foredeck. 'Yes – there's a gap right ahead – starboard a little.' 'Starboard she is.' 'Steady as you go.' 'Steady.' Suddenly we were between the rocks – close on either side. There was no turning now. A swell took us and swept us forward. 'Hard to starboard,' Dick shouted. I spun the wheel, my mouth dry as the bottom of a bird cage. 'There it is – right ahead – put her astern,' Dick shouted.

There was a small stone quay right beside us – a dozen men on it, all shouting at us in Portuguese. The swell was terrific. *GS* was rearing up and down alarmingly. Dick threw a rope, it was made fast and *GS* was pulled in towards the quay. 'We can't lie here,' I shouted to Dick, 'we'll have to get out again.' Just then *GS* grounded on a hard stone bottom. She only touched once, not hard, and I put the engine astern and brought her a few feet along the quay – but it was enough to be unpleasant. 'Anyone speak English?' I shouted. A big man came forward. 'I pilot,' he shouted. 'This harbour no good for you – tide go down – no enough water.' He and two of his friends jumped on board. 'Full astern,' he said. I put the engine astern and opened the throttle. The pilot took the wheel from me. 'Neutral – slow ahead,' he said. We seemed to be surrounded by rocks on all sides and the swell was playing round them, leaping into the air, and crashing down with a noise like a steam train pulling out of a station. The pilot manoeuvred us back and forth – turning *GS* round with great skill as if he had known her ways all his life. 'I don't know how you get in here,' he said, 'no one come in here at night.' 'Then what in Christ's name are the leading lights for?' I asked. 'Fishermen,' he said.

It was like the middle of Hampton Court Maze, but somehow the pilot got us out, backing and filling and turning until *GS* was clear in the open sea again. The saliva slowly came back to my mouth. 'Give me a drink of water,' I asked Celia whose white face was looking anxiously out of the hatch. 'We take you Porto Piqueran. One mile up coast,' the pilot said. 'You OK there.' We motored for a quarter of an hour to the north and then the pilot put *GS*'s head straight for the rocks. 'Don't let him do it,' a voice said. 'Shut up for Christ's sake. I can't tell him his job.'

There were no leading lights here at all – only the black face of the rock. 'No worry,' the pilot said, sensing my apprehension, 'you OK here. Quite safe – no swell – I know way.' '*Ca va bien*,' one of the other men said, thinking for some reason that I was French and wishing to air his grasp of that language. '*Le Monsieur Pilot – il le connait bien ici.*' The pilot was as good as his reputation. He took us straight towards a tower of rock, looming sullenly in the weak light of the stars, then hard to port for a few yards, then to starboard and to port again until suddenly we were in a small cove – a cleft in the rocks no more than 60ft across but calm and still. 'Let go anchor. Now we tie you up.'

The pilot and his helpers climbed into our dinghy and ran out ropes to the rocks. They jumped nimbly ashore and fastened every long rope we had in the ship – three on each side. 'Best ropes forward,' the pilot said, 'bad ropes aft. Wind come from west,' he said pointing to the sky where the clouds were racing towards England. 'Always strong wind from west here.' I thought for a moment while they were working on the ropes. 'Pilot,' I said, 'suppose we have to go out quickly. Would it not be better to turn her round, so she's facing the sea?' 'No,' he said, 'strong wind from west – always face strong wind – best ropes forward.' The little person inside me said 'Make him turn her round, you weak idiot – this may be a trap.' 'Stop your bloody nagging.'

They tied us up thoroughly, made sure that everything was fast and strong and then they came down to the cabin and we gave them a drink. 'By God – you lucky get out Santa Cruz,' the pilot laughed. 'No ship ever come there at night before. You fine here – you sleep sound.' We put them ashore in the dinghy to a stone quay with a flight of steps hewn out of the rock face and they went off home. 'See you in the morning. You sleep OK.'

We did sleep soundly. *GS* lay as quiet as if she were in Bradwell Creek. The glass was dropping again and it was already blowing a gale from the southwest but Porto Piqueran was quite detached from the gale – the only evidence of wind was the racing clouds far up above and an occasional down draught which would sometimes break away from the body of the gale and find its way like some spent outrider round the mountain and down towards Porto Piqueran where it would hurl the last of its dissipated energy at the top of *GS*'s mast, stirring the burgee 40ft up, making a faint moaning sound and then dissolving into the night. Dick laughed, 'This is a hurricane hole all right – there isn't enough wind in here to lift a tart's skirt.'

'Don't laugh too soon,' the little voice said to me as I went to sleep.

Next day, Mulville met with some difficulty when customs officials accompanied him into Santa Cruz to the office of the International Police, who wanted to retain all the passports. After much argument Mulville managed successfully to plead with them. 'The wind might change in the night,' I said. 'We might want to go out at a moment's notice. We must have our passports.'

Before spending a second night in Porto Piqueran, they carefully checked all the warps before they went to bed and found nothing amiss.

'The two strongest warps we had were out over the bow, each made fast to a rock. On the starboard side there was a rope from aft to a ring bolt let into the rock by the steps and another to a stone bollard at the corner of the quay. On the port side the longest rope led from aft to a big rock on the south side of the cove and yet another from amidships. It was something of a work of art.

'If you got out your crochet needles you could make us a Balaclava out of this lot,' I had remarked to Celia. In addition to her ropes the anchor was down, although I doubted whether it was doing any good, as the bottom was hard and it had not been let go far enough out to be effective. Dick had been round in the day checking that the ropes were not chafing against the rocks and had served a couple of them with rope-yarns. 'I reckon she'll do,' I said to Dick and we went to bed.

A boat is always there – you never stop worrying about her whether you are aboard or ashore – she is always a presence in the mind and you're conscious of her at all times. She may be laid up in some safe berth for the winter or hauled out of the water in a yard, but wherever you may be – at home in your virtuous bed or roistering in some gay spot, a chorus girl on each knee and the air thick with flying champagne corks – a part of your consciousness is always reserved. When the wind moans round the eaves of the house it has a special significance, and you check off in your mind, one by one, the possible sources of danger. Men lie awake worrying about their bank balances, their waistlines, their wives, their mistresses actual or potential; but sailors worry about boats.

A boat is something more than an ingenious arrangement of wood and copper and iron – it has a soul, a personality, eccentricities of behaviour that are endearing. It becomes part of a person, colouring his whole life with a romance that is unknown to those who do not understand a way of life connected with boats. The older a boat becomes, the stronger the power. It gains in stature with each new experience – people look at boats with wonder and say 'She's been to the South Seas', or 'She's just back from the North Cape', and the boat takes on a reputation in excess of that of its owner. *Girl Stella* had become a very real part of our lives – we each of us loved her with a deep respect.

I slept badly, frequently waking and listening. At 2am it began to rain, softly at first and then more heavily so that I could hear the drips coursing off the furled mains'l and drumming on the cabin top. At 4am I heard a slight bump and wondered what it was – then I heard it again and I knew what it was. It was the dinghy bumping against the stern. I froze in a cold sweat. If the dinghy was bumping against the stern, the wind must have changed. I got up, put oilskins on over my pyjamas and went on deck. It was cold – the temperature had dropped three or four degrees – it was pelting with rain and a light breeze was blowing from east by north – straight into the cove of Porto Piqueran.

I undid the dinghy, took the painter round the side deck and fastened it off the bow where it streamed out clear. I went back to the cabin, got dressed and called Dick. I tapped the glass and it gave a small convulsion downwards. 'Dick – the wind's changed. We'll have to get out of here quick. The glass is dropping. We can't stay here in an easterly wind.' Dick got up and put his head out of the hatch. The rain was pouring down and it was as black as a cow's inside. I believe he thought I was over-nervous – exaggerating.

'We can't do much in this,' he said. 'If we did manage to get her untied and turned round, we'd never get her out through that channel in this blackness. All we can do is wait till morning and then have another look at it.' He went back to bed and was soon snoring peacefully.

The little voice said 'Get him up – start work – now.' 'Shut up – he's right – you can't see your hand in front of you – how the hell can we go to sea in this?' I walked round the deck. There was more swell now, and *GS* was beginning to buck up and down – snatching at her ropes so that sometimes the after ones came right out of the water. The forward ropes – the strong nylon warps – were quite slack.

I went down to the cabin, sat at the table and tried to read. I made myself a cup of coffee and sat with the mug warming my hands and the steam wreathing round my face.

Then I went on deck again. The wind was beginning to increase, a heavy swell was now running and small white waves were beginning to overlay it. The rain had increased and was now slanting with the wind and driving into the cove. *Girl Stella* was beginning to pitch and jerk at the two stern ropes with alarming force. Very slowly and reluctantly it was beginning to get light. I went below and shook Dick. 'Come on – not a minute to waste – it's beginning to get light.' I tapped the glass again and again it dropped.

It seemed an age before Dick was dressed in his oilskins and on deck. 'First we'll get the anchor up. It's doing no good there and it will only hamper us. Then we'll let go the head lines – leave them in the water, they'll drift to leeward and we'll come back for them later. Then we'll go astern on the engine and let her swing round on one of the stern lines.' We set to work. It was a relief to have ended the dreadful inactivity of the last two hours. As the anchor began to come up, Celia woke and put her head out through the hatch. 'What's happening?' 'We're going to get out of here – look at the weather – we're turning her round. Better get the boys up.' In minutes the boys were up on deck in their oilskins and Celia was dressed.

The anchor came home easily and I started the engine. We cast off the head lines and prepared another line which would take the strain after we had turned, passing it round the bow so that we could fasten it to the stern line to starboard, which would then become the head line to port. Now the wind was howling with real ferocity – increasing every minute. The swell had become dangerous and was slapping against *GS*'s blunt stern and sending little columns of spray into the mizzen shrouds. I moved the dinghy painter from the bow to the stern and the boat lay alongside, leaping up and down and banging against the topsides.

We were almost ready when there was a twang like someone plucking a violin string. I looked up and saw that the stern line on which we were relying had received one jerk too many. It had snapped in the middle and the inboard end was flying back towards the boat like a piece of elastic. *GS* immediately began to move towards the rocks on her port side. I jumped into the cockpit, slammed the engine into reverse, gave her full throttle, and put the rudder hard to starboard. She began to pick up. 'Let go the port stern line,' I yelled to Dick. He began to throw the rope off the cleat. 'Throw it well clear – she'll come.' The engine vibrated and thundered – the spray over the stern drove in our faces – the wind battered our senses but she was coming astern. 'Good old girl,' I muttered, 'we'll get you out.'

Then the engine stopped – suddenly and irrevocably – the bare end of the broken line wound a dozen times round the propeller. 'Now you're in trouble,' the little voice said.

GS began to drift inexorably towards the rocks – there was nothing to stop her – no ropes on the starboard side and no engine. 'Fenders, over here, quick,' I shouted to the boys and Celia. 'Fend her off as best you can. I'll go over with another rope,' I shouted to Dick. There was one more rope long enough to reach the shore, still in the fo'c's'le locker. The top of the locker was covered with toys and books belonging to the boys and with Patrick's accordion. I threw them off in a pile on the floor and brought the bare end up through the fo'c's'le hatch. 'Celia,' I shouted, 'pay it out to me as I go in the dinghy.' As I got over the side into the Starling I felt *GS* strike the rocks – surprisingly gently, I thought. Perhaps it was a smooth ledge and they would be able to cushion her with fenders until we got another rope out. I rowed desperately towards the shore, the end of the rope wound round the after thwart of the dinghy. The swell was washing violently against the stone steps. I could see the ring bolt but I couldn't reach it – as soon as the dinghy got in close it would surge up on a swell, strike the slippery surface of the steps and plunge back. I took my trousers and my shirt off, plunged into the sea with the end of the rope, upsetting the dinghy as I jumped out of it, and tried to clamber up the steps. But there was nothing to grasp and three times the weight of the rope pulled me back. With a last effort I managed to roll myself over onto the steps, reach up and keep my balance until I was able to grasp the ring. 'All fast!' I shouted to Celia. I swam back on board and clambered up over the bobstay. It was bitterly cold.

Dick and I took the rope to the winch and began to heave. The strain came on the rope and her head began to come round clear of the rocks, but she had moved ahead slightly and the rocks under her stern had shifted their position to right aft, under the turn of the bilge, and begun to do real damage. They were too far below the waterline for the fenders to be of any use. Then she stopped coming. The rope was tight but something was preventing her from moving forward. Dick went aft to look. 'She's all tied up aft,' he reported. 'Every bloody rope in the place is tied up round the propeller and they're all bar tight.' I looked over the stern. It was daylight now and I could see a tangle of ropes bunched up round the propeller. 'I'll cut them free.'

Dick gave me his razor-sharp knife and I jumped over the side again. I dived and saw that at least two ropes had somehow got themselves into the tangle – I managed to cut one and came up for breath. GS's stern was just above me, the swells lifting it and allowing it to settle back on the rock with all the force of her great weight. I could hear the rock cutting into her skin – the unmistakable cracking sound of timbers shattering under blows of irresistible force. I knew then that she was done for.

I dived and cut the other rope, swam round to the bobstay with difficulty in the heavy swell and dragged myself on board. Dick and I wound furiously on the winch – she moved a little further, and then, as the swells came more on her beam, she lifted and crashed down with an awe-inspiring crunch. She would move no more. As I went aft Celia was working the hand pump and Patrick jumped into the engine room and switched on the electric pump. Adrian came up out of the saloon and I heard him say to Celia in a quiet voice, 'Mummy, I don't wish to alarm you but the cabin's full of water.'

'It's all over,' I said to Celia, 'everybody get into lifejackets. We'll have to swim for it.'

Celia and I went below. The water was knee-deep on the cabin floor and was rising as we watched. *Girl Stella* was still bumping, and every time she hit the rock we could hear the heavy frames splitting, the timbers crumbling. I looked at Celia. Her face was grey, her hair hanging in rat tails, and she had an expression of unimpeded sadness. We stood for a moment among the ruin. The ingredients of our lives were swilling backwards and forwards across the cabin floor, soon to be swallowed by the sea. Books given to us by the Cubans, their pages open and eager, as if they would convert the ocean to revolution, Adrian's recorder, clothes, an orange, the cribbage board, the kettle, a pair of chart rulers, rolls of film, my hat, Celia's glasses-case – objects which had somehow jumped out of their context to give mocking offence. The ordered symmetry of our lives was torn apart and scattered – haphazard and suddenly meaningless.

I could see in Celia's face that she had reached the end of a long journey. *Girl Stella* was a precious thing to her – something that was being thrown away in front of her eyes. The years of struggle with the sea were coming to an end – the pinnacles of achievement, the harrowing crises, the lighthearted joys and the endless discomforts had slowly spiralled upwards as we had progressed from adventure to adventure. Now they had reached an explosive zenith and for her there could be no going on. I knew in that moment she would never come sailing with me again. I had at last betrayed her trust – forfeited her confidence in me. Before, we had always come through – snatched victory out of disaster – but now she was facing a fundamental confrontation of truth. I put my hand in hers – pleading for a glance of sympathy.

Celia passed the lifejackets up the hatch to Dick, and then she gathered a plastic bag and put in it the log books – the ship's, the children's and her own – and a few oddments. I found myself unable to think – I was almost insensible with cold. I grabbed my wallet and a book of travellers' cheques, the last of our money, and stuffed them into the bag. I took one last look at the clock and the barometer shining on the bulkhead, the cabin stove, its doors swung open and the water ebbing and flowing through the grate, the lamp swinging unevenly with a stunted motion, and floating lazily across the floor, GS's document box, '*Girl Stella* – Penzance' scrolled on the lid.

On deck the boys were calmly putting on their lifejackets. I bent down to help Patrick with the lacings. 'This is the end, Daddy,' he said quietly, 'the end of *Girl Stella* – poor, poor *GS*.'

Now she had settled deep in the water and her motion had suddenly become sickening. She had lost her liveliness and when she rolled to the swell it was with a slow, tired lurch. Her stability, the quick sense of recovery, the responsiveness that she always had, was gone. 'Quick. She may turn turtle – we must get off. I'll go first, then boys, then you, Celia, and Dick last. Grab the rope and pull yourselves along it. I'll help you up the steps.'

I jumped into the sea, found the rope and shouted back, 'Come on, Pad, jump.' Patrick hesitated for a moment and then his body came flying through the air and he bobbed up, gasping with cold beside me – then Adrian, then Celia. We pulled ourselves hand over hand along the rope. Now the swell was much heavier and there were vicious seas breaking in the cove. It was much more difficult to get on to the steps. The ring bolt was high up out of the water and it was necessary to let go of the rope and swim the last few yards to the steps. My puny strength was of no consequence in the swell – like a piece of floating stick I was swept back and forth across the rock face, the small aperture of the steps flashing past as I was carried first one way and then the other. Then, more by some quirk of the swell than by my own efforts, I was dumped heavily on the bottom step and was able to scramble to my feet. I grabbed Patrick by one arm and heaved him up, then Adrian came surging past and I was able to grasp the back of his life-jacket and pull him on the bottom step. Celia was more difficult. She was all but paralysed by the cold – she was heavy and slippery and there seemed to be nothing of her that I could grip. Then she managed to get her body half on to the step, and with Patrick helping me we pulled and rolled and tugged until she finally got herself clear and struggled to her feet. 'Up you go – quick before the sea snatches you back again.'

Dick had not come. I looked up and saw that *GS* had moved ahead and was now lying athwart a towering rock pillar. I saw that he had been below and had brought up the two sextants and placed them on a narrow ledge of rock which he could reach. *GS* was now low in the water and sinking fast. 'Dick,' I shouted, 'come out of it – now.'

If she sank before he came he would be denied the rope and I doubted whether he would be able to swim through the broken water without its help. He took a last and reluctant look round and then he jumped and we watched him working his way along the rope, hand over hand, until I was able to grasp his arm and he scrambled up the steps.

We stood in a dejected, shivering group on the little stone quay and watched *GS* work out this last moment of her span of life. A thing of grace and beauty – agile, sure-footed, tender in her responses to our demands – at the same time she was a block of solid assurance. We had always felt safe in her – we always knew that she would do whatever was asked of her. She was our home – she gave us a dignity which we would otherwise have been without.

She had come to her end not by any misdeed of hers – not through any wilfulness or delinquency – but by misuse – a sheer disregard of the elements of seamanship. I felt the dead weight of my responsibility settle heavily on my shoulders. It was a score against me that could never be wiped clean – nothing that I could ever do would relieve me of the knowledge that I had destroyed a thing of beauty.

■ LESSONS LEARNED

Frank Mulville had a premonition that trouble would befall *GS* and never forgave himself for ignoring the 'little voice' that told him it was a bad decision that night to moor *Girl Stella* in Porto Piqueran, on the Island of Flores. It was a decision 'trusting to luck instead of careful planning'.

thirty-five

BAD LUCK
IN BOULOGNE

Yacht	*Mary Williams* (Silhouette)
Skipper	Clementina Gordon
Bound from	Etaples (river Canche) to St Valery sur Somme, France
Date of loss	7 August 1962
Position	outer harbour, Boulogne

Many people began their cruising careers in Silhouettes, those small hard-chine bilge keel plywood boats designed by Robert Tucker; but not so many of them were women, and surely the Revd Clementina Gordon was the only ordained woman minister amongst them. In 1961, she won the Suzanne Trophy for her log of a remarkable cruise in appalling weather from the east coast of England to Zeebrugge in Belgium, and in 1962 she set out alone to cruise along the Normandy and Brittany coasts, but ran into trouble, as she relates in this graphic account.

I **WAS TRYING TO CRUISE** on the difficult north coast between Boulogne and Cherbourg, exercising great care, as the anchorages are dangerous with vile bars and ripping tides, also drying out 20ft and more. On Monday 6 August, I left Le Canche river about 0345, nego-tiating the bar with a terrible ebb, and then the SW tide for St Valery sur Somme. At 0645 the forecast was a westerly gale coming from the Plymouth area, so as I hadn't a hope of making Dieppe, I ran back over a foul tide to Boulogne. (The Somme estuary is murder in onshore winds.) I came into Boulogne in pouring rain, and brought up just by the inner pier head, clear of traffic, and of course behind the big west breakwater. There I rested clear of the miseries of that inner basin and all ready to slip in when I had sorted myself out. I must have dozed off, thinking myself perfectly secure. When I came to, the wind had flown round, from offshore, to put me on the lee of the inner pier, about Force 7. I thought it a risk to get under way, and placidly waited for a lull or a pluck in from a passing tug. My signals, even red rocket flares, were unnoticed, so I had to hang on with very heavy ground tackle, two anchors and vast new warps and chain.

By midnight, the wind settled in the SW and increased to force 8, but another report said much more. I now had the far side of the harbour in my lee, down Cape Griz Nez direction, all rocks and old blockhouses, with heavy surf. She held till just before HW 0300, when the west breakwater ceased to function, and a heavy swell came in almost unimpeded. I sent off the remainder of the rocket flares (after I learnt that the inner pier-head, 80 yards away, was manned all night and the lifeboat station was 150 yards away!).

I then took the situation seriously and inflated my good rubber dinghy, as it was obvious that if the anchoring bitts were not torn out of her something would have to go. The surf and the rocks were so nasty that I had a drink of port to steady my poor nerves and stop being sick all the time and therefore inefficient. Just after that there was a bigger heave than usual, and with a roar I found myself trapped under the cockpit with the boat on top of me. (Afterwards, examining the wreckage, I found that the new 2½ inch bow warp had parted about 15ft from the bow, so I presume she was caught underneath by a steep wave and turned bow over stern.) Luckily, I held my breath, extracted my leg wedged under the boom, and got out, with the dinghy, which my safety belt was attached to. Then a gulp of air, before a monster of a wave crashed me down and down. Eventually I came up, and was rushed ahead for 250 yards or so, nearly torn away from the rubber dinghy. A pause, then crashed down again and pushed violently forward. This was repeated while I weakened physically.

Luckily, I missed the rocks sticking out, and after ¼ or ½ mile had slacker water, but a sheer cement wall with an overhang and railings right on top. It was just daylight, and a Frenchman fishing with a rod was there, so I yelled and he slithered down a drainpipe to help. I was too weak to keep hold of the rocks as the dinghy acted like a sea anchor and pulled me back by the safety line. He could not approach to pull me out, as he had a new pair of suede shoes, and leaped back for fear of wetting them. Even then I could see how funny it was! Eventually, I had the wits to pull the release of the belt, and was able to hang onto a rock.

I was hauled out. A baker's delivery man had now appeared to join in the fun, and then manhandled me into a pub where Madame had hysterics and tipped filthy French 'whisky' down me, such as the fishermen use. As I would insist on subsiding on to the floor in a pool of my own private sea, they sent for the ambulance and tucked me up in a nuns' hospital. There I stayed for a couple of days, as I had only a nightshirt lent by a nun, and it stopped short 1¹/₂ft above my knees; so I was a prisoner of modesty.

The unfortunate boat broke up a quarter of a mile offshore. The local yacht club picked up the bits at low water and most of my gear was salvaged. Obviously the whole silly accident was quite unnecessary, I could easily have gone right inside before supper.

■ LESSONS LEARNED

This was a sobering lesson on how dangerous a harbour can become in a gale – and how useful an inflatable dinghy can be – no other dinghy would have had the buoyancy to bring Clementina Gordon through the conditions to shore. It's also a lesson on how distress signals can fail to be seen and how one ought to carry a good number, instead of three of each and some whites, as this skipper had. The two anchors, one on a warp and the other on chain, held until just before 0300, until the west breakwater ceased to function and a heavy swell came in. Then a bigger sea than the others capsized the little Silhouette bow over stern.

BEING TOWED

thirty-six

TYPHOON BRENDA
AND THE TOW

Yacht	*East Wind of the Orient* (Contessa 38)
Skipper	Major Philip Banbury
Bound from	Hong Kong to the Philippines
Date of loss	May 1989
Position	less than 100 miles south-south-west of Hong Kong

Major Philip Banbury describes the dramatic sinking of a Contessa 38, which was being towed away from the path of a typhoon in the South China Sea.

FOR A NUMBER OF YEARS, HM Forces stationed in Hong Kong ran an adventure training exercise in the Philippines, sailing their Contessa 38 *East Wind of the Orient*. It usually took place between January and May, enabling eight crews of eight servicemen and servicewomen to spend a fortnight sailing in one of the most attractive cruising areas of the world. Lest the taxpayer should question the value of such 'exotic' training, I should point out that during those months the prevailing wind is the northeasterly monsoon and often provides fast, exhilarating sailing which can be more testing than adventurous.

The last leg of the exercise was from 5–20 May 1989. A week would be spent cruising the local waters of the Philippines and the last week sailing *East Wind* back to Hong Kong. The skipper, who had assembled and briefed the crew and done the initial passage planning, had to drop out at the last minute, so I flew to Manila and joined the yacht two days after the other seven crew members.

After a few days' local sailing, enjoying sun and swimming, we sailed 300 miles north to San Fernando, the little port which provides the jumping off point for the shortest distance from the Philippines to Hong Kong, 480nm.

On Tuesday morning, 16 May, we had been in San Fernando 36 hours. I returned to the yacht having cleared with immigration and customs. Major Bruce Denton, our doctor, heard that a tropical depression was forming to the south of us. A motor-yacht in the harbour with a weatherfax promised to give us an update at 1700. Meanwhile, I telephoned our exercise control in Hong Kong to see if they had any weather information. As a result of information provided, I decided to set sail as soon as I got the weatherfax from the motor-yacht.

I cannot now remember the precise location of the depression. The dominating feature was a high pressure area over mainland China, which I thought might provide us with north-east winds. We set off immediately for Hong Kong under engine, as there was very little wind.

Throughout Tuesday night and most of Wednesday we motored, because I wanted to keep ahead of the depression and make best speed for Hong Kong. During Wednesday the wind started to pick up and because it was blowing from dead ahead we continued under engine. We listened to the weather report on Rowdy's net (an amateur radio net) at 0800 and also got a weather update at 0900. Both confirmed the depression was moving north and gave predictions for 24, 48 and 72 hours ahead, which I plotted on the chart.

At this stage, there was no knowing the precise path the depression would take, though it was clearly going to enter the South China Sea. It had been given the name Brenda and was classed as a tropical storm.

By Wednesday evening the wind was blowing 25 knots from NNE and the sea was getting up. Thinking that the wind would get stronger during the night, and because it was still on the nose, we set storm jib and trysail, as much to steady the yacht as to make headway under sail. By Thursday morning the wind had increased and veered a bit. We were able to sail on a course of about 315°. At some stage that day we switched off the engine to save fuel. I wanted to conserve enough to meet a real emergency and to charge batteries, so we could maintain radio communications. Throughout Thursday, 18 satnav fixes confirmed we were making a lot of leeway because of both wind and waves. By nightfall the wind was Force 7 gusting 8. I decided that of the four men on watch only two should be on deck at a time to avoid crew getting unnecessarily cold and wet and to conserve as much energy as possible.

On Friday morning we were about 100 miles SSW of Hong Kong. The wind was blowing a constant 35–40 knots and gusts would occasionally take it off the windspeed indicator at 50 knots. During our morning radio schedule with Hong Kong we were told the storm had now been classed as typhoon. Its path could still not be predicted, so we continued to sail as close to the wind as the sailplan allowed in the direction of Hong Kong.

During the morning we tried to start our engine to charge the batteries, but despite the fuel tank being between a half and a third full, the engine would not start; for some reason the fuel was not getting through to the engine. Our engineer tried to bleed the system without success. We think the fuel tank was probably a bad design and the positioning of the outlet pipe meant that all the fuel could not be utilised.

We got a satnav fix at 0810 on Friday. The course continued to be plotted by DR/EP on the chart. I estimated that we were making good a course of 310°.

At around midday, our contact in Hong Kong, having received the latest information on Typhoon Brenda, said he would be asking if HMS *Plover*, one of the Royal Navy's patrol craft, could be sent down to 'stand by' us.

We established communications with *Plover* on our HF set and she arrived in our general area at about 1700. The first flares fired were not seen and it was clear that our estimated position was not sufficiently accurate to avoid her having to search for us. It was now getting dark. At 1818 one of the crew on deck reported sighting a merchant vessel several miles astern. This information was passed to *Plover*, which saw the vessel on their radar and were then able to establish our location. A few minutes later we also got a satnav fix and passed it to *Plover*. By the time they sighted us just after 1930 the wind was Force 9 or 10 and the waves 8–9m high.

Because we were directly in the path of the typhoon, *Plover* informed us that they proposed to take *East Wind* under tow and were preparing a line to be passed to us. I agreed to accept this and they gradually manoeuvred to come abreast of us. After requesting we lower the trysail, they fired a heaving line. This was unsuccessful, as was the second attempt. Eventually, we picked up a line floated astern of HMS *Plover* and the tow was secured just after 2200.

Having been taken under tow, HMS *Plover* started to pull us clear of the predicted track of the typhoon. Up to now, I had spent most of my time at the VHF radio in contact with *Plover*, and the chart table, whilst yelling instructions through the companionway hatch to the crew on deck.

Because the remainder of the crew had been on deck while the tow was being secured, I now took the helm and Major Jonathon Swann kept me company in the cockpit. Under tow the yacht behaved well but had to be steered. She would surf down the front of the waves, which were following us at great speed, seeming at times to be in great danger of catching up with the stern of *Plover*. When this happened, the tow rope obviously went slack.

At midnight, I handed over to Captain Simon Pashley and Major Bruce Dunlop, the first two crew of the other watch. Jonathon and I went down below to rest. The next thing I knew, someone on deck was shouting that the tow must be stopped. I radioed *Plover*. Down below we were taking in water fast. The area by the companionway was immediately affected. I roused the crew and told them to get on deck. It was clear from the speed that water was coming in that we would have to abandon ship.

Everyone, except two of us (including me), was wearing a life-jacket. The liferaft was launched. There had been some difficulty getting it out of the storage locker. Once it was in the water, we saw that the canopy entry door was facing away from the yacht, so we jumped on to the canopy itself, which collapsed, leaving us exposed to the elements. But before anyone even jumped on to it there was an explosion and one of the inflated rings burst. Simon was also having difficulty untying the painter from the yacht. No one had a knife and he patiently untied the knot while someone held in the slack.

We tried to move the liferaft to the bows of *East Wind*, believing that the original orange line, by which we had collected the towing warp, was still attached to both *East Wind* and *Plover*. This would have enabled us to pull the liferaft towards *Plover*. It wasn't, and we concentrated, instead, on trying to push ourselves from the rapidly sinking *East Wind*. We were just a few yards from her when she went down at the bows, up at the stern, and disappeared under the sea, a mass of air bubbles marking the spot.

It was just four minutes since I had radioed *Plover* to stop the tow.

To watch our yacht plunge to the bottom, like some scene from the sinking of the *Titanic,* is something I would not wish to experience again.

We shouted towards HMS *Plover*, which had spotted our plight. For me, cold and without a lifejacket, this was the only moment that I ever felt frightened. I wondered what would happen if our partially inflated liferaft capsized or sank. *Plover* was turning around and, beam-on to the sea, coming back to pick us up. Scrambling nets were lowered over the side and, after some nasty moments, during which we seemed to be inspecting the underside of her hull, we all clambered up and were hauled over the ship's rail by the waiting crew.

Down below in the wardroom, Simon explained what had happened while he was at the wheel. He had been experiencing the same problems with *East Wind* surfing towards the stern of *Plover*. One moment all was well, the next the stern of *East Wind* was pulled around and the yacht was being dragged backwards through the water. There was no response from the helm.

The only explanation seems to be that the slack in the towing warp had got caught around the rudder and skeg and the tremendous force exerted had ripped them off, creating a large hole in the aft section of the hull which so rapidly filled with water.

■ LESSONS LEARNED

If you are towing, or being towed, you need a tow rope that covers at least the distance between two waves in the sea conditions prevailing. A good tip for the yacht being towed is to shackle the end of the tow rope to the shank of the anchor and then deploy the anchor and a considerable amount of anchor chain. This avoids the problems of chafe and the weight of the chain also acts as a shock absorber, hopefully, avoiding the problem of over-running the tow rope and getting a bight of rope caught around the keel or rudder and skeg, as seems to have happened with *East Wind*.

An alternative, but less bullet-proof, method is to lash weights, like anchors or water-filled fuel cans, to the middle of the tow rope. There must be enough weight on the rope to prevent all of it from coming out of the water at once and snatching.

The vessel being towed should also trail a drogue or warps which will help to prevent over-running the tow rope as she surfs down a wave.

Using bridles connected to the primary winches makes any adjustments easier.

Perhaps the first lesson when passage-planning during the period when typhoons are even remotely possible is that every depression should be treated as a potential typhoon and one should remain within a few hours of a good bolt hole to see how things will develop before making a lengthy passage.

The engine would not start, despite the fuel tank being one third or half full. In rough seas it is common for sediment in the bottom of the tank to be shaken up and cause a blockage.

In any situation which is potentially dangerous, the whole crew should be ordered to wear lifejackets and safety harnesses (which they were wearing). Off watch and under tow they should also sleep in their lifejackets.

The two horseshoe lifebuoys mounted on the pushpit, were securely tied to a stanchion and the skipper didn't have his knife, nor did anyone else. A knife is always an essential item for any yachtsman to have at hand at all times. 'This could have cost me my life,' said Major Banbury.

The liferaft had been serviced and tested a few months earlier, but still a part of it exploded and deflated. Close against the side of a vessel it only needs a barnacle to cause a puncture.

thirty-seven

THE LOSS OF *JESTER*

Yacht	*Jester*
Skipper	Michael Richey
Bound from	Plymouth to Newport, Rhode Island
Date of loss	15 July 1988
Position	470 miles south-east of Halifax, Nova Scotia

Both Michael Richey and Jester *had crossed the Atlantic many times and the 1988 Carlsberg Singlehanded Transatlantic Race, from Plymouth to Newport, Rhode Island, was to be their last. But when he left Plymouth on 5 June, Richey could not have anticipated what lay ahead. On 15 July 1988, in position 39°08'N, 58°43'W, some 470 miles south-east of Halifax, Nova Scotia,* Jester *was abandoned and her skipper taken off by the MV* Nilam, *a 60,000-ton bulk carrier bound for New York. It was* Jester's *eighth OSTAR and her 14th transatlantic passage. The incident, a knockdown, occurred some 40 days out.*

BEYOND THE FACT THAT *Jester* had participated in every Singlehanded Transatlantic Race since the event's inception in 1960 and that her entry would thus be widely welcomed, there was, I suppose, little point in doing the race. *Jester* was unlikely to distinguish herself. However, it would almost certainly be my last opportunity to participate and so I entered with the prime intention of enjoying the sail, probably along a route that would neither be too demanding nor stretch the nominal distance too far.

Jester had attempted most of the accepted routes over the years, from the far northern passage with Blondie Hasler in 1960 and 1964 to the trade wind route in 1968, with varying degrees of success. The path one follows in practice is largely determined by what the wind does in the first few days of the race. Nevertheless, for the small vessels, so vulnerable to the effects of current and whose windward ability may well be limited, some overall strategy seems to be called for. On this occasion my intention had been to head south-west to a position sufficiently west of the Azores to avoid the calms associated with the archipelago, cross the ocean south of the core of the Gulf Stream in about 37°N, and then come up to cross the Stream at a broad angle in about 65°W. The route approximates in its early part to the low-powered steamer route shown on the US pilot charts, but the difficulty under sail is the tendency for the wind to head when west of about 50°W, forcing the boat into the Stream prematurely.

When *Jester* emerged from Mayflower Marina on the morning of the race, there was some excitement among the spectator fleet and we were applauded by many of those on board the ferries. Four years earlier, she had been similarly received by the competitors as she sailed into Millbay Dock. The start itself was unmemorable, but for a while *Jester*, *Suhaili* and *Galway Blazer* kept company – a distinguished fleet indeed.

The early part of the passage was uneventful, the first few days inevitably a period of settling down, for I had not sailed the boat that year, fighting lethargy and a tendency to hibernate. By the end of the first week we had covered over 700 miles in a direction 250°T – a highly satisfactory state of affairs.

Jester effectively sailed herself and, although one could reef or put on more sail from time to time, and occasionally adjust the self-steering gear, there was no deckwork and life on board became a matter of eating, sleeping, cooking, navigating and, much of the time, reading.

Navigation, as always, was by sextant and chronometer, the latter being one of the handsome quartz clocks once manufactured for Brookes & Gatehouse. Nowadays, of course, quartz crystal wristwatches, even quite cheap ones, are so accurate and reliable that the problem of time at sea has virtually disappeared. On ocean voyages I found it convenient to keep the digital display, which was less liable to reading error, set to GMT for sights and the analogue display to the zone time. All calculations in *Jester* had for some years been made by hand-held calculator, not so much for speed or accuracy but rather for convenience. However, I have found, particularly with astro-navigation, that it becomes even more necessary than with tables and plotting to know what you are doing because mistakes will not be so readily apparent.

One of the great pleasures of navigation for me has always been using the tools of the trade and in *Jester* I have been able to ensure that they were of the finest. Many of them, too, have particular associations. The sextant, for example, a lovely Plath dated 1939, its mirrors as clear as the day they were made, was acquired from a U-boat towards the end of the war; with its maker's name there was a swastika emblazoned on the index arm. Its box was bolted to the shelf on the starboard side just below the sidehatch and in cloudy weather I would keep it open to avoid delay if the sun showed itself for a fleeting second. *Jester* was the ideal boat for taking sights since, supported firmly in the control hatch, both hands can be used without fear of falling overboard. I used to rejoice in the art and, when my eyes were somewhat sharper, would often take morning and evening star sights in mid-ocean when the results would have little navigational significance.

The dividers were made of solid silver with stainless steel points and a nylon bush in the joint to prevent slippage. They were the most beautiful pair I have ever used, the gift, suitably inscribed, of the talented silversmith who made them. The Walker's Excelsior log which has trailed behind for so many thousands of miles was presented to the boat by the author of that remarkable work *The Principles of Navigation*. The Brookes & Gatehouse sounder, which has seen the boat over the Nantucket and many another shoal, came out of Richard Gatehouse's own yacht *Electron*. And so on. Alas, it was destined to be the last time I would use any of them.

By 15 June the generally northerly airstream gave way to a period of unsettled weather with intermittent calms and fog. The Azores Current was setting us fast to the south-east and I began to wonder whether we should weather Corvo. At times the current could be seen on the surface of the water, creating steep wavelets in a wind of no more than Force 2. North-west of the Azores there was very little wind, and on several days of complete calm on 26 and 27 June we only logged 2¹/₂ miles in 36 hours and set some 20 miles north-east.

Apart from the periods of flat calm, the weather during this time, west of the Azores, was unbelievably pleasant and I spent long hours looking at the waters, admiring in particular a pair of dolphins that stayed with the boat for days, with their extraordinary turn of speed. On one occasion, thousands of sardines broke surface, fluttering like butterflies; occasionally great schools of dolphin would pass by, usually in the evening, as though some migration was under way. One evening later in the voyage I saw two large fins about 20 yards ahead of the boat and had, at the last moment, to put the helm over, to avoid collision with two whales on the surface, apparently oblivious of our presence. I scraped past them a few feet away; one of them started to follow the boat and then gave it up. It shook me slightly, even though they probably live on shrimp.

The sixth of July was my birthday, a dry day as it happened because I had finished the wine, but celebrated nevertheless by a remarkable run (over 25 hours, for the clocks had been retarded) of 161 miles, 35 of which could be attributed to a lift from a Gulf Stream eddy.

The following day the wind backed south-westerly and by 9 July we were being pushed up towards the 40th parallel into the foul current. At noon on 9 July I took the losing tack south and by noon the next day we were some 48 miles further away from Newport. The wind piped up to about Force 6 or 7 for a few hours during the afternoon and backed westerly. 'After an infernal afternoon,' I wrote in the log, 'virtually hove-to under a single panel of sail in appallingly confused seas bursting all over the place in quite alarming peaks. The gale quite suddenly ceased and we proceeded northward under two and later three panels of sail.'

Whether the confused seas we were to meet from now on were entirely due to the Gulf Stream, or were due to some other factor, I am not certain. The Stream was certainly running much faster than the mean speed given on the pilot charts (0.7 knots) and when the MV *Nilam* was standing by with her engines stopped she recorded 3 knots made good over the ground. On the other hand, there was an occluded front to the westward and I later remembered a letter I received in May 1968 from C J Verploegh of the Royal Netherlands Meteorological Office on the general subject of weather in the North Atlantic.

'There is,' he wrote, 'one situation you should be warned of because it is seldom detected on weather charts. Sometimes a wavelike disturbance will develop on an occlusion which is moving slowly eastward between two well developed cells of high pressure. Gale force winds may occur, southerly on the eastern side and northerly on the western side, over an area no more than about 40 miles on both sides of the front. Within this small area, waves may be as high as five metres and west of the front a heavy southerly swell will be running against northerly gale force winds. I have had reports from routed vessels [Verploegh was in charge of weather routeing] and it seems that as the ship approaches the front the wind suddenly increases to gale force with correspondingly steep seas.'

The extent to which my own situation corresponded to that described is perhaps irrelevant, but certainly whatever local conditions prevailed, superimposed on a strong-flowing Gulf Stream, created conditions that not only made progress on either tack difficult but were at times alarming. In addition, I was concerned about a slight movement at the heel of the mast much aggravated by pitching in confused seas. I had used metal shims several times at the adjacent floors and twice taken up the soft-wood wedges at the partners but had been unable to stop the movement, which on occasions sounded as though it was tearing the boat to bits.

In these somewhat disturbed conditions, where much of the boat's movement must be accounted for by a current of unknown velocity, there was generally some ambiguity in the observed position based on a run between sights.

On the morning of 13 July, a merchant vessel, bound north-westward, crossed two or three miles ahead of us. I swallowed my pride and asked him for a position. He gave it, in a Scandinavian voice, as 39°32'N, 58°41'W, which surprised me a little. He then said he could not see me but presumed that the vessel I had in sight was one he could detect on his radar some 12 miles to the south. I found this a bit perplexing but decided to bear all the possibilities in mind until I got some kind of noonday sight (which indeed confirmed that I was well south of my estimate).

We had a sharp blow, up to about Force 7, around noon, although I was able to get the information I wanted from a series of shaky sights. I went down to bare pole for a while because I thought we would make little progress and it would save breaking the boat up. By 1600 we were under way again with two panels up, heading for Labrador.

'Extreme discomfort aboard,' I noted in the log. 'For the past three days every stitch of clothing has been soaked, every towel is dripping, the matches won't strike and so on.'

It is extraordinary how, even in a boat with full enclosure like *Jester*, living so close to the surface in hard weather the water seems to permeate everything, like an atmosphere. 'If only,' I wrote, 'we could have a fine day to dry everything out.'

Morale seems to have been sagging. By the evening, the wind had got up again and by midnight it was blowing a full gale from the south-west. I went down to a single panel and hove the boat to under the self-steering gear. In the early hours I went down to bare pole. The centre of the system must have gone through my position, for at about 0500 the wind dropped completely and a downpour of tropical dimensions went on for about an hour and a half; it ceased as suddenly as it had started, as though a tap had been turned off.

At about 0800 the wind came in again, rising quickly to gale force and getting up a steep and confused sea. 'Some of the breakers quite frighten me,' I wrote in the log. 'They come at you hissing, generally just across the wave train, and carrying you along for a while, generally on your beam ends.' By 1000, it was blowing perhaps Force 9 with visibility affected, but the seas flecked rather than covered with spume. There was not much I could do but wait hopefully for the storm to pass. At about 1030, surveying the scene from the control hatch with as much equanimity as I could muster, I saw a plunging breaker coming at us from the port side and said out loud, 'Oh hell, here's a knockdown,' as indeed it proved to be.

The boat was smashed down to starboard and carried along with her mast below the horizontal until the wave had passed and the weight of the ballast keel brought her upright again. She was full of water, with floorboards, cushions, books, charts, sleeping bags and food all floating free. More important, the starboard sidehatch had been stove in, totally demolished with only its bronze hinges hanging loose. The boat was now open to the sea.

The first thing was to get the water out and I started bailing with the plastic bucket but it seemed a losing game as more water poured in through the open hatch. Eventually, I suppose, as the gale subsided and my efforts had more effect, I was able to reduce the water to a level where the bilge pump would be able to deal with it. But whilst in the throes of the storm, and obsessed with the idea that the boat was open to the seas, I became convinced that I should need assistance to sail on. I activated the EPIRB. A few hours later I thought I must have gone mad.

It is difficult to recall precisely one's motives in a moment of crisis. I was later to regret not having waited until the gale had blown itself out before activating the EPIRB, or indeed in retrospect having activated it at all. But in the throes of the gale I thought the boat, open to the seas, could well founder. Once switched on, of course, the EPIRB should not be switched off until rescue.

By nightfall I had pumped the boat more or less dry, but I was too exhausted to attempt any kind of clear-up. Earlier, when I had thought the boat might founder, I had launched the liferaft and thrown into it a few stores such as a barricoe of water, some flares and a panic bag of sorts. I now transferred them all back. I spent the night on the bunk aft, a wet sleeping bag draped over my knees and my head on some protrusion, wondering between snatches of sleep what action I should take when help came. Having summoned it, I should be prepared to take it. But I earnestly wished the course now lay open to me to reconsider the whole situation.

In the morning, I was able to get one burner going on the cooker to make a cup of tea. Clearing up seemed too large a task and I concentrated on getting the boat operational, seeing how much of the navigational gear was still functional, what, if any, charts survived, what state the instruments were in and so on.

It was a pleasant enough day, the storm now through. I had little idea where we were and took the sextant from its box. The telescope had misted up from the inside but I took a series of shots without it.

The reduction tables, like the charts, were effectively pulped and the calculator, predictably, had packed up. *Macmillan's Nautical Almanac*, however, had been on a higher shelf and was virtually untouched. Unfortunately, after many attempts I failed to extract a sensible quantity for hour angle and declination, for the good reason I was to discover later that I had somehow contrived to drop a day from the date.

Shortly after 1000, an aircraft flew low over the boat with her lights on and I switched on the hand-held VHF on channel 16. The pilot identified the plane by number from the US Coast Guard Rescue Services and enquired, with great politeness, addressing me as 'Sir' all the while, as to the nature of the emergency.

I reported the damage and wondered whether any ship in the vicinity would be able to render assistance, perhaps a tow or hoisting the boat inboard. I should in any case require water if I were to sail on, for two of the barricoes had managed to empty themselves as a result of the upset. The pilot undertook to find out what shipping was in the area and meanwhile instructed me to switch off the EPIRB. He attempted to drop me an SSB (with, for some reason, some apple juice), but unfortunately I was unable to pick up the drop, hindered in my manoeuvring ability by towing the liferaft. The pilot then announced that the MV *Nilam*, a bulk carrier, some 20 miles away, was prepared to help and was closing. He had to refuel but a new aircraft was on its way.

When the new aircraft arrived, we went through the extent of the damage again and I emphasised that, whilst it was of little consequence in good weather, the boat could well founder in a gale. I suggested that the ship, when she arrived, should provide me with some water, if possible some tins of food and some stout canvas with which to effect a temporary repair. This information was passed to the MV *Nilam* and in due course, when she came up with us, she dropped over the stern three barricoes of water, some tins in a large plastic bag and the canvas. I told the pilot there was no chance of picking up the drop without getting rid of the liferaft and then cast it off, manoeuvring astern of the ship to recover the stores.

At this stage the possibility of abandoning *Jester* had neither been raised nor contemplated. I asked the aircraft for a position. My nearest landfall, he volunteered, would be Halifax, Nova Scotia, some 470 miles north-west. How long, he asked, would that take me? I thought about a week and he then undertook to get me a weather forecast for each of the seven days. Meanwhile, the ship stood by with her engines stopped.

After about half an hour the pilot came back and said he now had the forecast. Before reading it, however, he had to make clear that in view of the deteriorating weather situation both the Canadian Coast Guard in Halifax and the US Coast Guard Co-Ordination Center in New York strongly urged me to terminate the voyage now. He then read me the forecasts. Without a chart before me I found it difficult to envisage any kind of weather pattern. I picked up one wind forecast of 34 knots and asked what that was on the Beaufort scale (I still think in sea states); I was told Force 7–8.

The advice to abandon the yacht came as a blow. I asked for a few minutes to consider the matter but I found it very difficult to think. With a plane circling overhead and a 60,000-ton ship standing by, and after 40 days on one's own at sea, a balanced judgement was almost impossible.

Would that I had a friend with whom to discuss the issue. The response I felt must be quick, positive and decisive. I agreed to accept the Coast Guard's advice.

It would be impossible for me to approach the ship's accommodation ladder on the lee side without being blanketed (*Jester* has no engine), so we agreed that I should sail *Jester* two or three hundred yards ahead of the ship's lee bow and she would then steam gently ahead and drift down on me. I got the boat under way, one reef down, the boat sailing as prettily as she can and then suddenly felt I could not go through with it.

I contacted the aircraft again and, now emotionally fraught, said, 'Do you think the captain would be very annoyed if I decided to go on?'

The question must have sounded as silly as it was rhetorical and I don't remember the reply. I then asked if I could talk to the pilot man to man, irrespective of what the authorities had said.

What, I wondered, would he do in my circumstances?

'I don't know,' he said, 'I have never sailed the Atlantic singlehanded. It must be your decision, but I think you ought to accept the Coast Guard's advice.'

He could scarcely, I imagine, have said anything else.

The transfer was effected, the master manoeuvring his ship with great skill with so little way. I had furled the sail and lashed it neatly, put up the canvas dodger, disengaged the windvane, handed the log and (lest it be damaged going alongside!) brought the recorder inboard. As soon as I was on board the ship, I was called to the bridge where the pilot of the aircraft wanted to sign off. I thanked him profusely and before we had finished the master asked me to tell him he would attempt a tow, although he had little hope of success.

It was a quixotic gesture, for at that speed a boat of *Jester*'s size could but be towed under.

In due course I was given a cabin facing aft and some dry clothes. After a shower I watched *Jester* through the scuttle at the end of her long tow. I suddenly realised she was getting smaller. I had taken a quick turn on the king post with a hawser far too large whilst getting aboard, and I suppose it had jumped. 'That's that,' I said out loud, without emotion, for there could be no going back. But as I watched her recede into the distance, looking as trim and pretty as ever, I realised how much I had loved her. Men personalise their boats as no other artefact. I felt I had failed her, that I should have stayed with the boat. It was one of the unhappiest moments of my life and a passage occurred to me from the sad soliloquy at the end of Joyce's story *The Dead*: 'Better pass boldly into that other world in the full glory of some passion than fade and wither dismally with age.'

Jester had been if anything a passion.

■ LESSONS LEARNED

It is not always easy to envisage the forces that can be unleashed in an ocean storm. For safety, as Blondie Hasler would maintain, 'a boat's upperworks and hatches should be as strong as her bottom'. Richey thought the side hatches were not strong enough. After the boat's capsize on the way back from Nova

Scotia in 1986, he had them remade and thinks they could have done with an extra lamination or two.

Jester had been knocked down or capsized three times in three successive years. On each occasion she had been under bare pole; 'but looking back on each I would not have handled her differently,' said Richey.

Somewhere, many years ago, that great cruising seaman Eric Hiscock wrote that in the (to him improbable) event that he were asked to organise a race across the oceans, his first rule would be that there should be no radio transmissions. 'We do not', he went on, referring to yachtsmen, 'have to go to sea and we have no right to call on anyone for help.'

It sounds a bleak attitude, but there is much to be said for it. Emergency beacons such as the EPIRB are made compulsory in such races as the Singlehanded Transatlantic, as much to protect the organisers as the competitors. For the latter they are perhaps a mixed blessing.

It is an idle speculation but there is a sense in which an umbilical cord compromises the responsibility of the skipper for his own vessel.

NOTE FROM MICHAEL RICHEY

There was, of course, a faint hope that *Jester* would still be afloat, drifting in the North Atlantic like the *Marie Celeste*. For initiating steps to locate her I am particularly grateful to Rear Admiral Sir David Haslam of the International Hydrographic Bureau and to Vice Admiral Sir John Webster, C-in-C Plymouth and a member of the Royal Cruising Club. I must also thank Senator Clayborne C Pell of Rhode Island for his efforts to get something going in the States.

My principal thanks are of course due to the United States Coast Guard Rescue Co-Ordination Center in New York and in particular the pilots of the HU 25A Falcon Jet from Cape Cod and the HC 130 from Elizabeth City which took part in the rescue. To Captain Pecunia of the MV *Nilam* of the Ultramar Company, I am grateful for delivering me to New York in such a friendly way, and in such comfort.

thirty-eight

MISCHIEF'S LAST VOYAGE

Yacht	*Mischief* (45ft Bristol Channel pilot-cutter)
Skipper	Major H W Tilman
Crew	Charles Marriott, Simon Beckett, Kenneth Winterschladen, Ian Duckworth
Bound from	Jan Mayen Island to Norway (under tow)
Date of loss	4 August 1968
Position	off east coast of Jan Mayen Island

Between 1954 and 1968, when he lost her off Jan Mayan Island, Bill Tilman sailed Mischief *some 110,000 miles. Sea Breeze, her successor (also a Bristol Channel pilot-cutter and even older than* Mischief*), was lost in 1972 off the south coast of Greenland.*

TILMAN SAILED MOSTLY TO PLACES where there was snow, ice, mountains and very few people. In 1968 he chose Iceland and Jan Mayen Island as his goals and *Mischief* left Lymington on 31 May, after the crew had subscribed for the hire of a liferaft. Having called at Thorshavn in the Faeroes, they were in Akuryri on the north coast of Iceland by 26 June, where they stayed for a few days, leaving on 7 July, bound for Jan Mayen, some 300 miles to the north. The long axis of Jan Mayen Island runs from south-west to north-east, the middle of the island being barely two miles wide. Almost the whole of the north-eastern half is filled by Beerenberg's massive bulk. This 7,000ft peak was of course Tilman's climbing goal. Because the chart agent had mistakenly told him that there was no Admiralty chart of Jan Mayen, Tilman was using a chart on which the 30-mile-long island occupied little more than one inch.

'Variable winds and too much fog marked our passage to Jan Mayen. On 17 July we luckily got sights which put us some 10 miles from the island, so we steered, once more in fog, to clear South Cape by five miles. In fact, that afternoon some very impressive rocks suddenly loomed up only two cables away. These we identified as Sjuskjæram: a group of seven rocks a mile off the cape. Next day we anchored off the old Norwegian weather station at Mary Musbukta on the west coast.

'What few anchorages there are on either the east or west coast of Jan Mayen are wide open, but the west coast is preferable as it is free from dangers. Nor was there any ice in the vicinity of Mary Musbukta, though three miles to the north we could see pack-ice extending westwards. However, I thought we ought to let the Norwegians know that we were there, with designs on Beerenberg, so after anchoring I went in search of their new base. On the east coast, south of Eggøya, where the beach is very wide, and thick with driftwood, originating probably in Siberia, I found a party at work. We had no common language and, except that I had no beard, they must have thought I had been left behind, possibly under a stone, by some earlier expedition. I got a lift in a truck five miles to the present Norwegian station where we were just in time for supper. It is a large installation comprising some 50 men, mostly technicians. The Commandant was surprised to see me, for a Norwegian naval vessel, approaching by the east coast, had been turned back by ice. He showed me a small bay close by which they used for landing stores and suggested that we lie there. We were, so to speak, uninvited guests, so I thought it best to comply, though the bay was more than half covered with ice floes. From this mistake all our troubles stemmed.

'We started round on Saturday 20 July, a brilliant morning on which we enjoyed the only view we ever had of the ice slopes of Beerenberg, the mountain we hoped to climb. The brilliance soon faded, and once more we rounded South Cape in thick fog, having to tack twice to weather it. The wind died at night, and having steered east for two miles to get an offing, we handed sails and let her drift, waiting for the fog to clear. The coast runs SW–NE so that by steering east we had not gained that much offing, and although the ship had no way on, it was a mistake to think she was not moving. I had the midnight to 0200 watch and on the false assumption that we were not moving I sat below, taking a look round on deck every 15 minutes. It was, of course, fully light, but miserably cold and damp, visibility less than a quarter mile. Accordingly, I told my relief Ian that he need not remain on deck all the time, provided he went up at frequent intervals. He interpreted this liberally and must have remained below most of his watch.

'At about 0350 a terrible crash roused me. We were almost alongside a lone rock pinnacle lying about half a mile off the coast – I could have touched it with a boathook – the slight swell bumping us heavily on its plinth. This result of his neglect seemed to have unnerved Ian, who had already pulled the cord of the liferaft without troubling to launch it, so that a huge yellow balloon now filled most of the starboard deck. To make doubly sure of getting off he had also cut the dinghy lashings. Once the engine had started she slid off easily, but not before having struck hard at least six times. She proved to be leaking a lot but the Whale pump and deck pump together kept it under control. To hit this rock we must have drifted in the course of the night some three miles to the north at a rate of nearly half a knot.

'Owing to fog and a lot of ice close inshore, we had trouble in finding the bay. About 0700 we anchored off it while I went ashore to tell the Norwegians what had happened. They said, and I agreed, that the only thing to do was to beach her to get at the leaks. So we brought her in through the floes until she grounded on a beach of black sand. We started taking out the ballast (some 5 tons of pig iron), drained the water tanks, to float her further up, and put ashore the anchor and cable. The rise and fall of the tide was only 3ft (*Mischief* draws 7ft) and the beach shelved quickly towards her stern, so that we could not get at the garboard strake or the planks above it, except at the forefoot. On heaving her down with a bulldozer and examining what we could of the port side at low water, we saw no sprung or started planks; in places the caulking had spewed out, and aft about 10ft of the false keel had broken away.

'With the help of the Norwegians, who generously supplied anything needed, we covered the likeliest leak sources with tar, felt, and copper. Then we turned her round and hove down to get at the starboard side where, too, there were no obvious signs of damage. The leaks had been reduced though not cured, but I thought that we could easily sail her back to Iceland or even home. Ian thought otherwise and had already arranged a passage to Norway in *Brandal*, a sealing vessel chartered to bring stores. Charles, I knew, would stay with *Mischief*, while the two younger crew, though apprehensive, were willing to try.

'Meantime the ice, which the day after our arrival had moved in almost to fill the bay (thus helping us by damping any swell) began to move out. Before refloating her we put back the ballast, all but a ton – no doubt, another mistake. By Saturday 27 July, there remained only an unbroken line of massive floes close to the beach, most of them probably aground. The Norwegian who had been helping me realised better than I did that *Mischief* was now in peril. By means of a wire led from the stern to a block slung on an adjacent rock and thence to a bulldozer we tried to haul her off. She moved a foot or two, but anyway there was no forcing a passage between the floes and no means of hauling them away.

'Next day, Sunday 28 July, the Commandant came down and managed to break up with dynamite a floe threateningly close to our rudder. A floe lying only a yard or so from our port side was too big and a series of underwater explosions close aboard might have damaged the ship. That morning it began blowing hard from the south, causing the ice to surge forward, bumping *Mischief* heavily on the beach, and edging her higher up. I rallied the crew for a last effort to get her off by means of a warp to the anchor winch and the engine. She would not budge. With a couple of bulldozers we might have succeeded, but when I ran to the base for help there was no one about. By the time I got back the ice had battered a hole in her hull below the engine water intake and started several planks. That evening, in despair, I wrote her off.

'She was one-third full of water so we took ashore the gear below deck. Charles, who had not been well, now collapsed and retired to a bed in the base sick-room. On first beaching *Mischief* we had all lived in a small hut close to the beach.

'Next day a powerful red-bearded Norwegian, whom I called the Viking, had taken to heart *Mischief*'s plight and was as anxious as myself to save her. He suggested that she should be hauled right out so that in the winter he could repair her. I doubted the feasibility because it meant hauling her at least 50 yards over very soft sand sloping up at about 15°. Clutching at straws, I agreed. Once more we took out the ballast and that evening the Viking and a bulldozer moved her about two yards. She still lay among the breakers, the wind continued blowing, and the swell rolling in lifted and dropped her heavily on the sand. A big float with an outboard engine used for bringing ashore stores, on which we had deposited the ballast, lay hard by on the beach; and the next night *Mischief*, driven ever higher by the seas, had her bowsprit broken on the float.

'The idea of hauling her right out seemed to be tacitly abandoned. Instead, on 30 July, we put a big patch over the hole, having arranged with *Brandal*, then about to leave, to tow us to Bodo. She was also to bring out a small motor pump to cope with the leaks, which by now were well beyond our two hand pumps. With another gale on 1 August the breakers tore off *Mischief*'s rudder, but *Brandal*, with whom the base spoke by radio telephone, reckoned they could still tow. *Brandal* arrived on 2 August, fetching up north of the island, in spite of radio beacons, radar and Loran, and that morning the big patch we had put on was torn off by the seas.

'Upon this the Viking and I reverted to the idea of leaving her there hauled out for the winter, but the Commandant thought little of it and said she must be towed. So on 3 August the Viking and I again put on a patch, a wet job since waves were sweeping the stage we had slung overside to work from. That evening I went on board *Brandal*. They agreed to lend us a small electric pump to reinforce the petrol pump they had brought, which we had already installed in the cockpit. I had to sign a guarantee against the loss of this pump. The Commandant also arranged for a walkie-talkie set and a field telephone to keep *Brandal* and *Mischief* in touch.

'Overnight we rove a 3-inch wire through a big block slung on the nearby rocks and passed a length of 6-inch nylon rope twice round *Mischief*'s hull. At 0700 on Sunday 4 August, a fortnight to the day since we first limped in, the Norwegians rallied in force to get us off.

Although the ballast was out it took some doing. Either the sand had piled up or she had dug herself in, so the biggest bulldozer, a real monster, dropped its scoop into the sand and, using the sand as a cushion advanced on *Mischief* and pushed her bodily sideways. The two bulldozers in tandem then coupled on to the wire, a big dory with an engine pulled from seawards, and *Mischief* slid slowly into deep water. Simon and I were on board with the pump going. It needed to be, for she leaked like a basket.

'Having secured astern of *Brandal*, lying half a mile out, we remained there, tossed about in a rough sea until late afternoon. Meantime, the float made two or three trips out to *Brandal*, the last with seven men from the base and the remaining three of our crew. Charles was to travel in her while the other two helped in *Mischief*. Since we were to be closely attended, Ian had consented to come. Our only contact with *Brandal* was by the float, and in the evening it came alongside with three of her crew to arrange the tow line, the electric pump, field telephone, walkie-talkie set, and a liferaft. Our own had no gas cylinder, that having been expended when Ian prematurely pulled the string a fortnight before. He and Ken now joined us, and were promptly seasick.

'For the tow they used a nylon warp shackled to 10 fathoms of our anchor chain on which they hung three big tyres to act as a spring. The remaining 35 fathoms of our chain, with the 1 cwt anchor attached, we led to *Mischief*'s stern to drop over when the tow started. This served in place of a rudder and kept her from yawing. The heavy electric cable to supply current from *Brandal* to the pump then merely dropped loose into the sea. Its own weight imposed a heavy strain, no current ever passed, and immediately the tow began *Brandal* told us it had broken. Had it been hitched to the tow line or to another line *Mischief* might have survived. This meant that the little petrol pump must function for three days without fail. I did not think it would. Since early morning Simon and I had been running it for five minutes in every 10 to keep the water at bay.

'At about 2000 in a rough sea the tow began. At 2100 Simon and I lay down, leaving Ken and Ian to carry on until 0100. With the water sloshing about inside, sleep was hardly possible and for food we made do with hard tack and a cup of tea. Just before midnight I learnt that the pump had given up; the engine ran but was not pumping. Three of us were ready enough to quit and I confess that the skipper and owner, who had so much more at stake, had no longer the will to persevere, a fortnight of trouble, toil, and anxiety having worn me down.

'*Brandal* had already been told. She lay to about a cable away and told us to bring off only personal gear. So we collected our gear, launched the liferaft, and abandoned *Mischief.* She had then about three feet of water inside her. Paddling over to *Brandal,* we climbed on board while three of her crew returned in the raft to salvage the two pumps and the telephone. The electric pump, which weighed a lot, we had already hoisted on deck through the skylight. The pumps met with scant ceremony, being thrown overboard on the end of a line to be hauled through the sea to *Brandal.* While *Brandal* got under way I remained on deck watching *Mischief,* still floating defiantly, until she was out of sight. We were then 30 miles east of Jan Mayen.

'As I have said, ice conditions in 1968 were unusually bad; in a normal year Jan Mayen is clear of ice by the end of May. And, apart from human failings, ice was the principal cause of the loss of *Mischief.* For me it meant the loss of more than a yacht. I felt like one who had betrayed and then deserted a stricken friend, a friend with whom for the last 14 years I had probably spent more time at sea than on land, and who, when not at sea, had seldom been out of my thoughts. Moreover, I could not help feeling that by my mistakes and by the failure of one of those who were there to safeguard her, we had broken faith; that the disaster or sequence of disasters need not have happened; and that more might have been done to save her. I shall never forget her.'

■ LESSONS LEARNED

Not many. *Mischief's* problems began with the unusually bad ice conditions of that year. Perhaps Tilman regretted his too kind considerations towards his relief watch in the 'miserably cold and damp' conditions that fateful night. Visibility was less than a quarter mile and having told Ian that he need not remain on deck all the time, it seems he 'interpreted this liberally and remained below most of his watch'. Less than two hours later 'a terrible crash' roused Tilman. Despite valiant efforts to save the vessel over the following days, even the redoubtable Tilman confessed he was worn down by toil and anxiety. The eloquence and depth of his regrets will strike a chord with any skipper.

INDEX